ELEPHANTS

Living Large

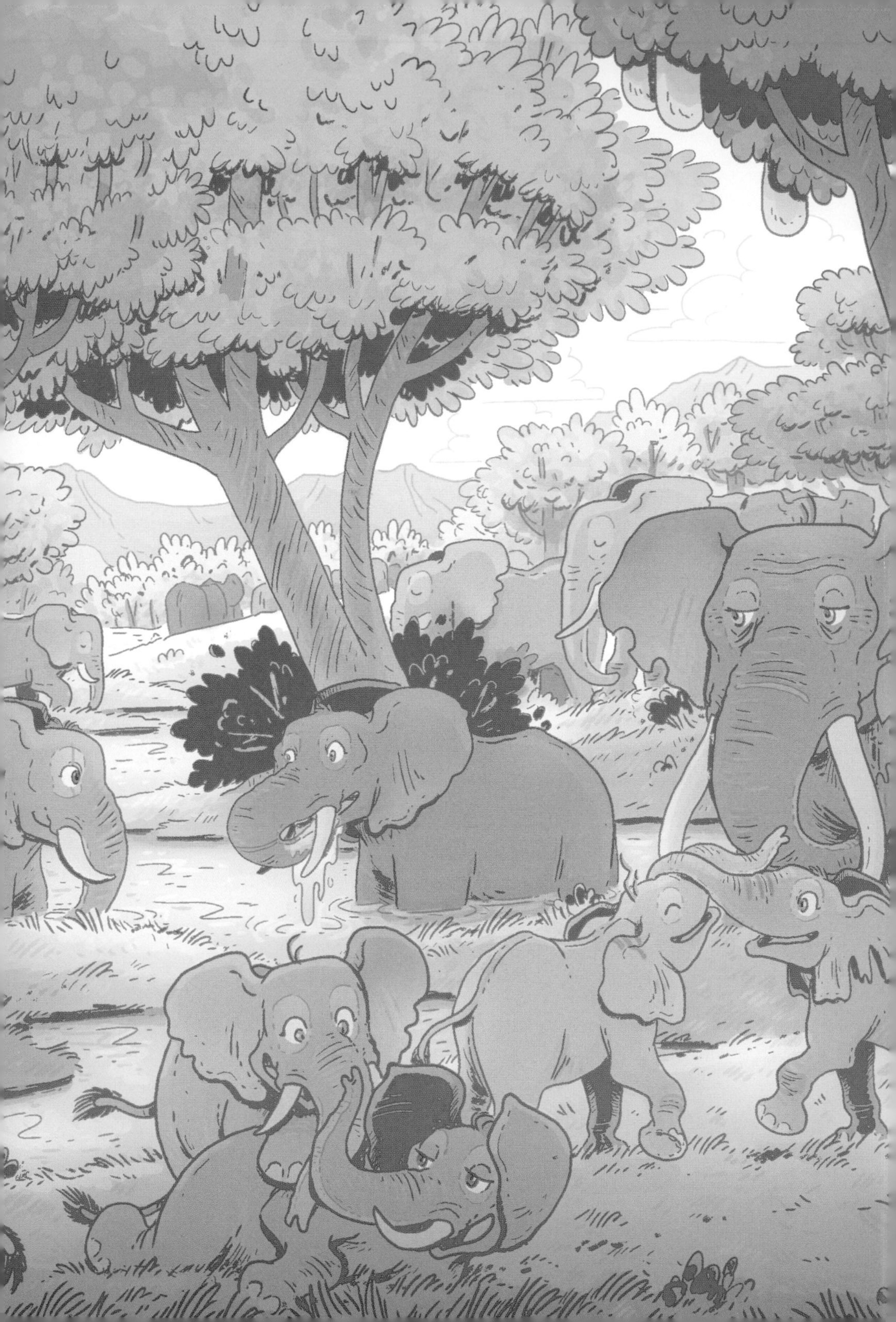

ELEPHANTS

Living Large

written by Jason Viola
illustrated by Falynn Koch

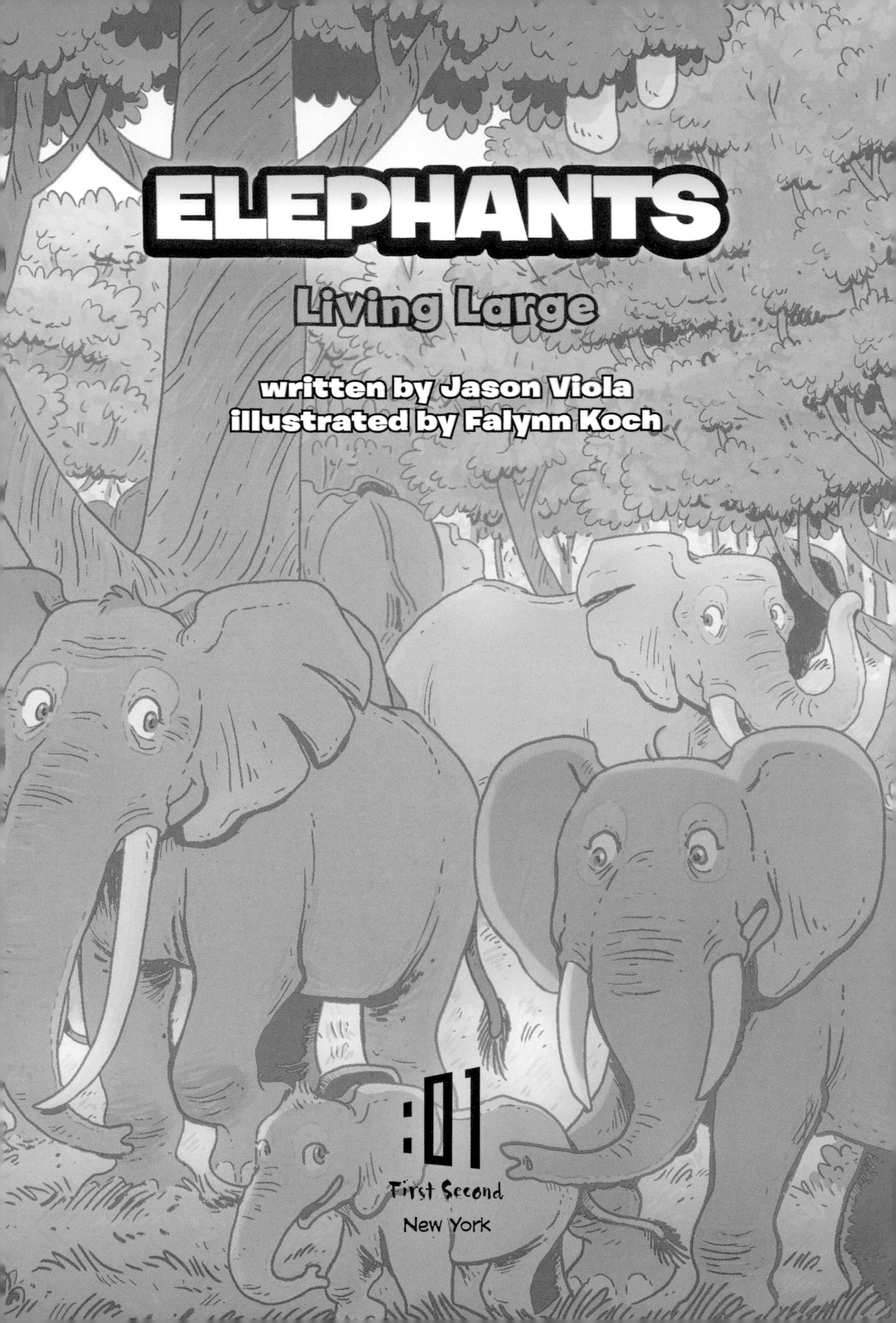

:01
First Second
New York

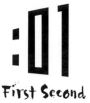

:01 First Second

Published by First Second
First Second is an imprint of Roaring Brook Press, a division of Holtzbrinck Publishing Holdings Limited Partnership
120 Broadway, New York, NY 10271
firstsecondbooks.com
mackids.com

Library of Congress Control Number: 2023937860

Our books may be purchased in bulk for promotional, educational, or business use. Please contact your local bookseller or the Macmillan Corporate and Premium Sales Department at (800) 221-7945 ext. 5442 or by email at MacmillanSpecialMarkets@macmillan.com.

FIRST EDITION

First edition, 2024
Edited by Dave Roman and Tim Stout
Cover and interior book design by Sunny Lee and Casper Manning
Production editing by Avia Perez
Elephants consultants: Caitlin O'Connell and Dr. Jenna Parker

Drawn digitally in Photoshop with the help of various brush collections by Kyle Webster. Penciled and inked with the Inkbox collection of brushes and colored with the Special Effects and Manga collections. Lettered with the Comicrazy font from Comicraft.

Printed in China by Toppan Leefung Printing Ltd., Dongguan City, Guangdong Province

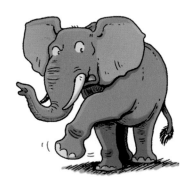

ISBN 978-1-250-26591-3 (paperback)
10 9 8 7 6 5 4 3 2 1

ISBN 978-1-250-26590-6 (hardcover)
10 9 8 7 6 5 4 3 2 1

Don't miss your next favorite book from First Second!
For the latest updates go to firstsecondnewsletter.com and sign up for our enewsletter.

BY ART WE LIVE

For an animal that looks as different from us as an elephant does, we are surprisingly similar in many ways, both socially and psychologically. Yes, there are some notable developmental differences, such as an elephant pregnancy lasting more than twice as long as a human's—twenty-two months in total! One of the advantages of such a long pregnancy is that elephants are born with the ability to run just a few hours after birth in order to survive in the wild, while it takes humans a year or more to learn how to walk. We're born weighing eight or so pounds, while an elephant weighs a whopping two hundred and fifty!

Despite these differences, if you were to track an elephant's social experience throughout its life, you'd see that they contend with similar challenges to our own. Whether it be navigating the schoolyard bully, an overly cautious mom or aunt, or an aggressive neighbor that doesn't want to share, elephants and humans have a lot of common experiences. Even a coming-of-age male elephant struggles with the issues of craving independence but not quite wanting to leave the protection of family. And watching an elephant family rally around a calf to rescue it from trouble is truly heartwarming, as is the joy of witnessing an extended family reunion.

Like some human cultures, elephants live within matriarchal societies, where an elder female makes decisions about where and when it's safe to move, and others within the family acknowledge and follow her lead. They have important rituals, such as greeting ceremonies that are similar to our own family gatherings, replete with touching and embracing, accompanied by excited rumblings and chatter—only elephants have an additional expression of joy at seeing distant relatives, manifesting in a mass release of bladders and bowels.

Okay, so perhaps we aren't *exactly* the same in how we express ourselves, but I can tell you that after studying African elephants in Namibia for thirty years, rarely a day goes by where I am not conscious of the life lessons they have taught me. For example, an elephant family member or close friend never takes a greeting for granted, even after a very short separation. Similar to our handshake, elephants greet each other by placing their trunk in another's mouth as a way of acknowledging that individual. This acknowledgment can also serve as a salute to a higher-ranking individual. In the presence of the highest-ranking male, other males will line up and wait their turn to salute him with a ritualized trunk-to-mouth greeting akin to kissing the ring of a king or queen or other high-ranking members of society.

When male elephants come of age, they leave the family that they grew up in and join groups of males within tightly bonded units. Bonds within these groups are reinforced by ritualized affiliative gestures, not unlike those displayed by human males meeting in a bar for a drink—including the good-natured backslapping, fist-bumping, and sparring. Male elephants practice all these important gestures while playing with other males within the immediate and extended family as they grow up. Examples include testing their strength through play fighting, called sparring, which is very similar to arm wrestling or fencing. Sparring allows males to practice an important survival skill—mainly winning challenges and avoiding a life-threatening wound while competing for a mate as an adult. Play also helps both elephants and humans figure out boundaries, learn who they can trust, and deal with aggressors.

Coming-of-age males can form such tight bonds with their male elders that they will accompany them when the elder is injured—even though slowing down would mean not being able to spend as much time eating or interacting with contemporaries. When such an elder loses his last molar in old age, sometimes a younger male will follow him around and take the time to chew his food for him. The ways in which elephants place great value in respecting and taking care of their elders can be quite an inspiration to us humans!

In a sense, elephants offer us the opportunity to look at ourselves in the mirror. Watching how elephants treat each other serves as an important inspiration to reflect upon the consequences of our own actions as humans and how we treat others around us.

This entertaining comic is not only a fun romp through many different scientific facts but it's also an unexpectedly poignant portrayal of the emotional arc of a coming-of-age elephant on their quest to understand themselves and the world around them. I hope you enjoy this educational journey as much as I did.

—Caitlin O'Connell
author of *The Elephant Scientist* and *Elephant Don*

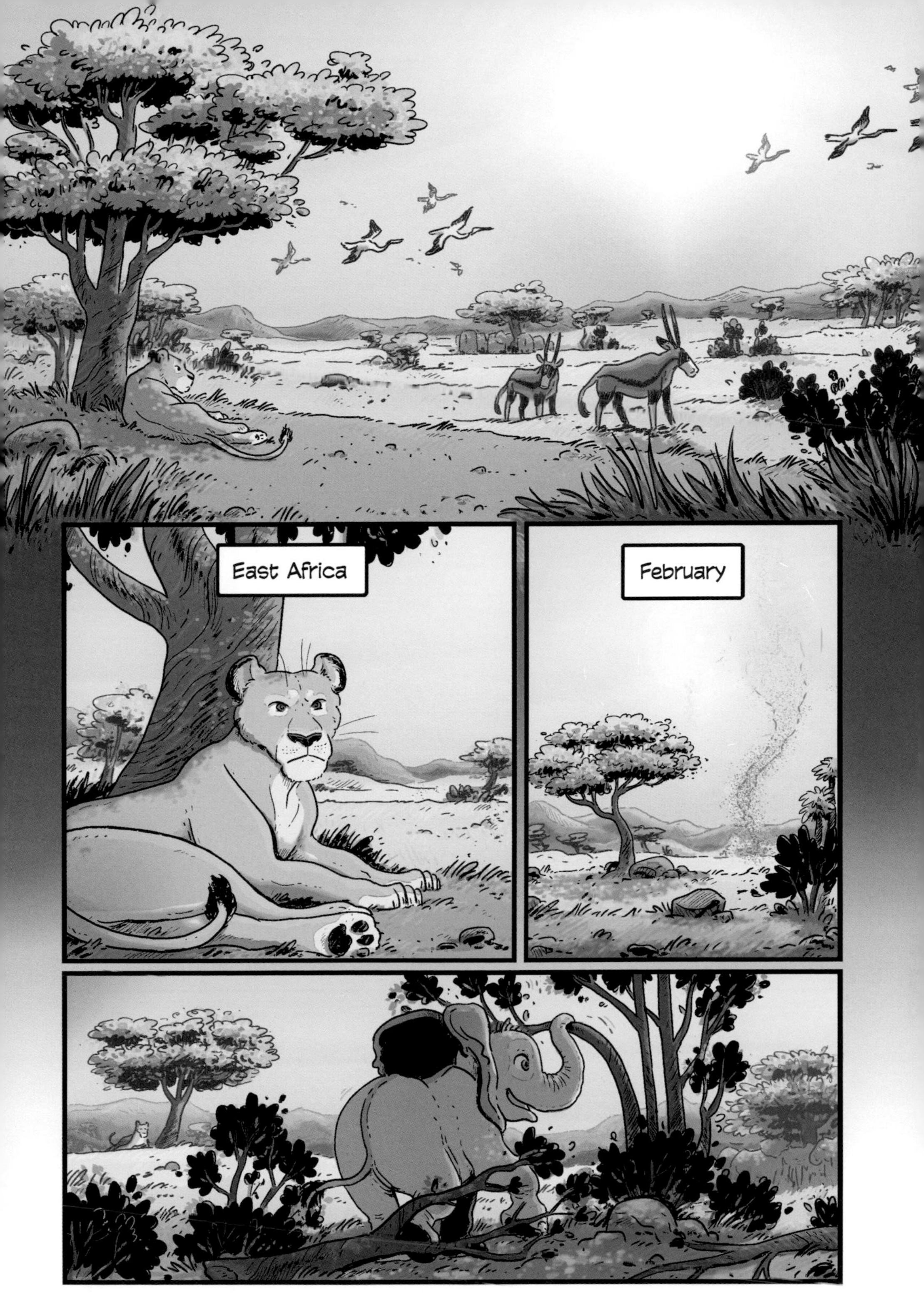
East Africa
February

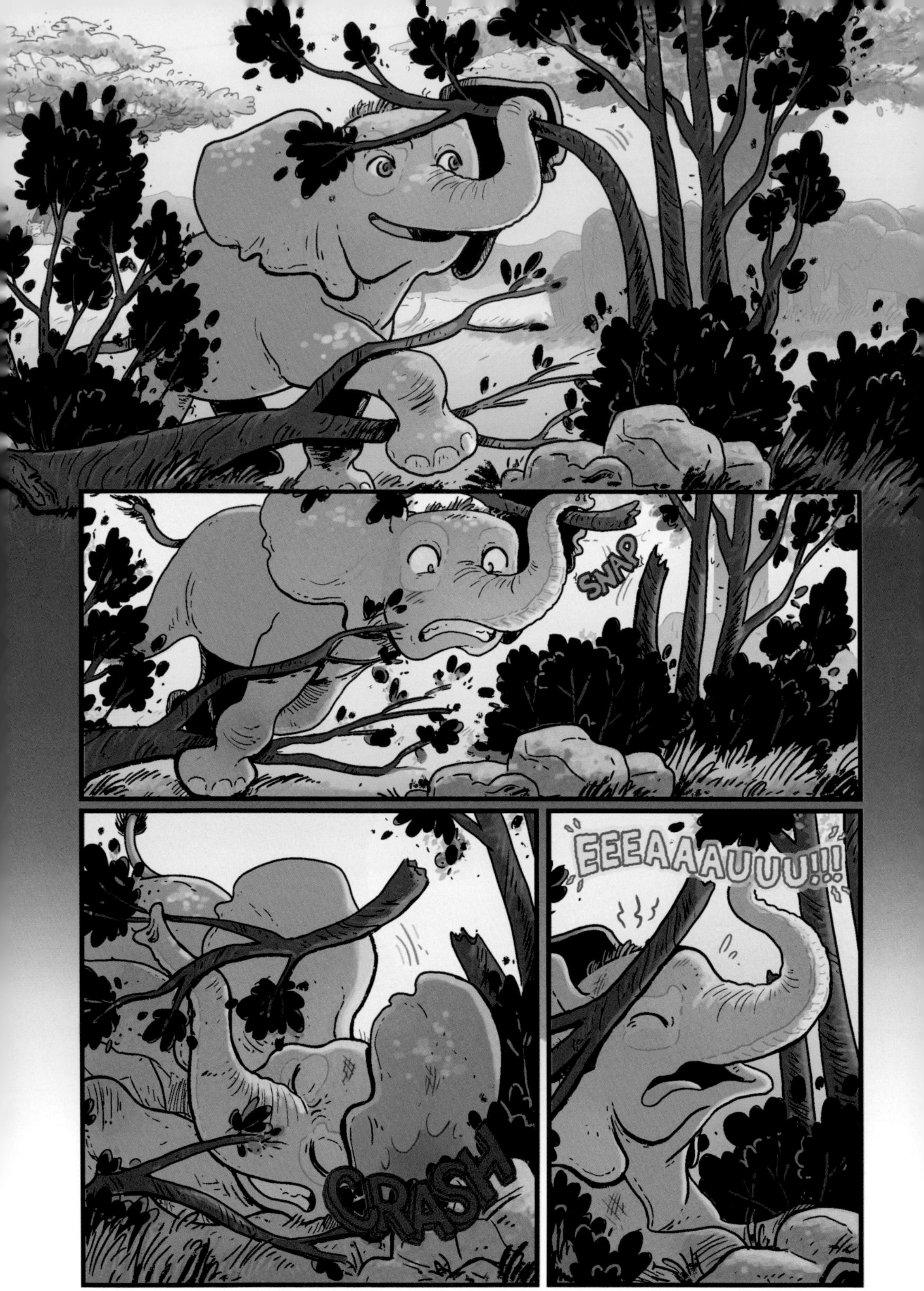
SNAP
CRASH
EEEAAAUUU!!!

Ẽeaauuu

Rummmble

My name is Duni. I'm eight years old. And trapped in this bush is my baby cousin Tamu.

We're *elephants*.

Looking out for one another is what being an elephant is all about.

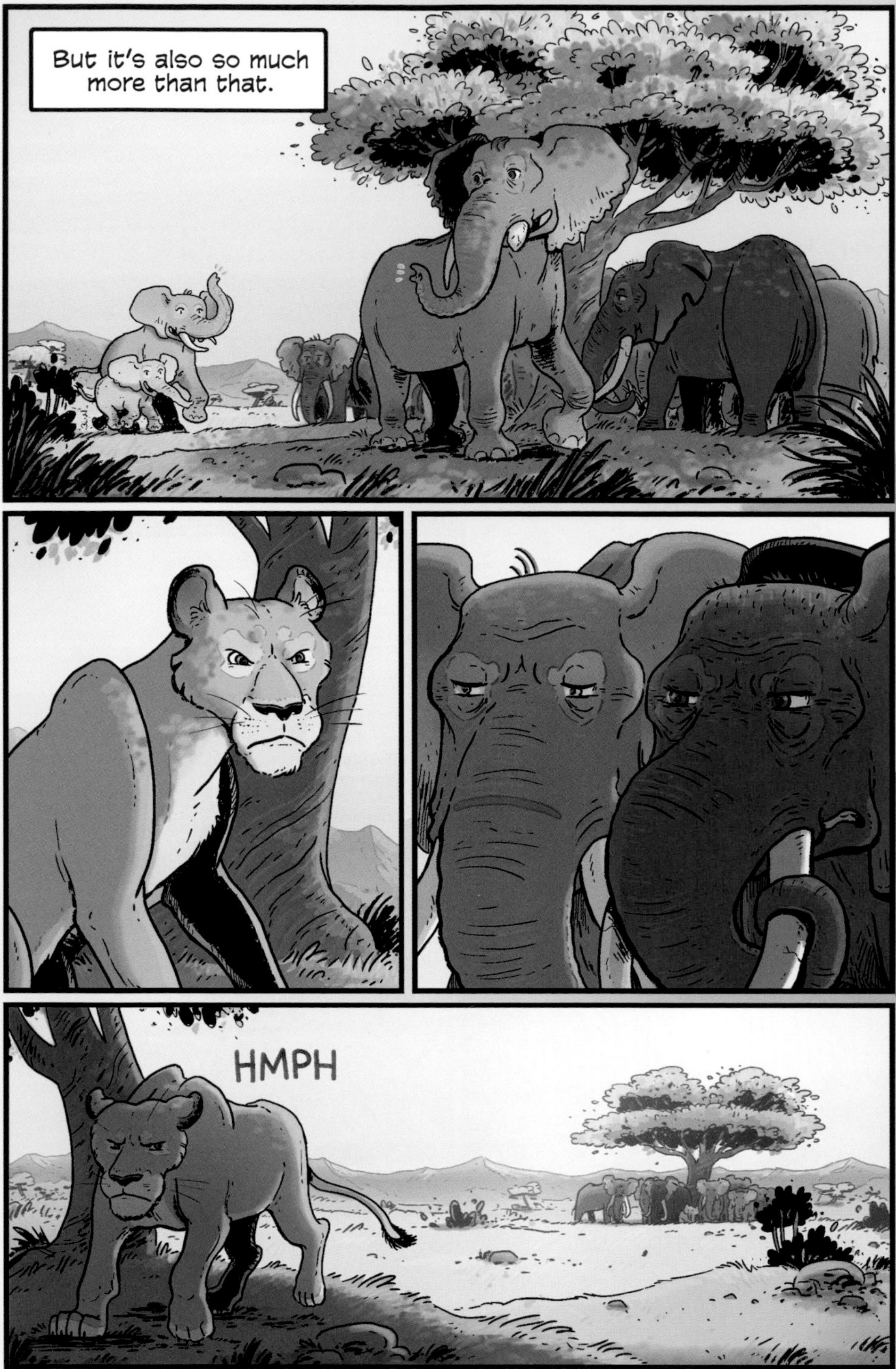
But it's also so much more than that.
HMPH

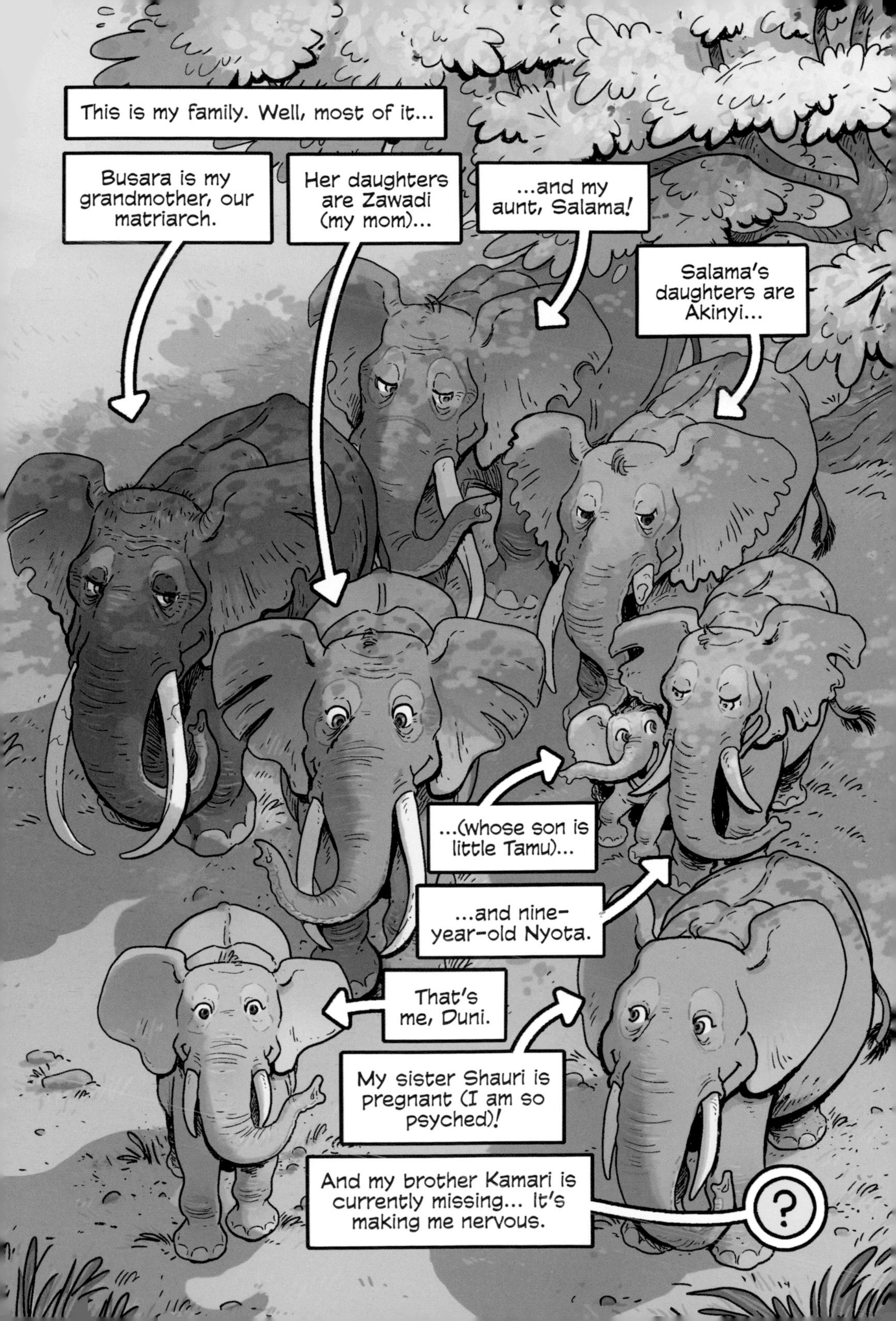
This is my family. Well, most of it...
Busara is my grandmother, our matriarch.
Her daughters are Zawadi (my mom)...
...and my aunt, Salama!
Salama's daughters are Akinyi...
...(whose son is little Tamu)...
...and nine-year-old Nyota.
That's me, Duni.
My sister Shauri is pregnant (I am so psyched)!
And my brother Kamari is currently missing... It's making me nervous.
?

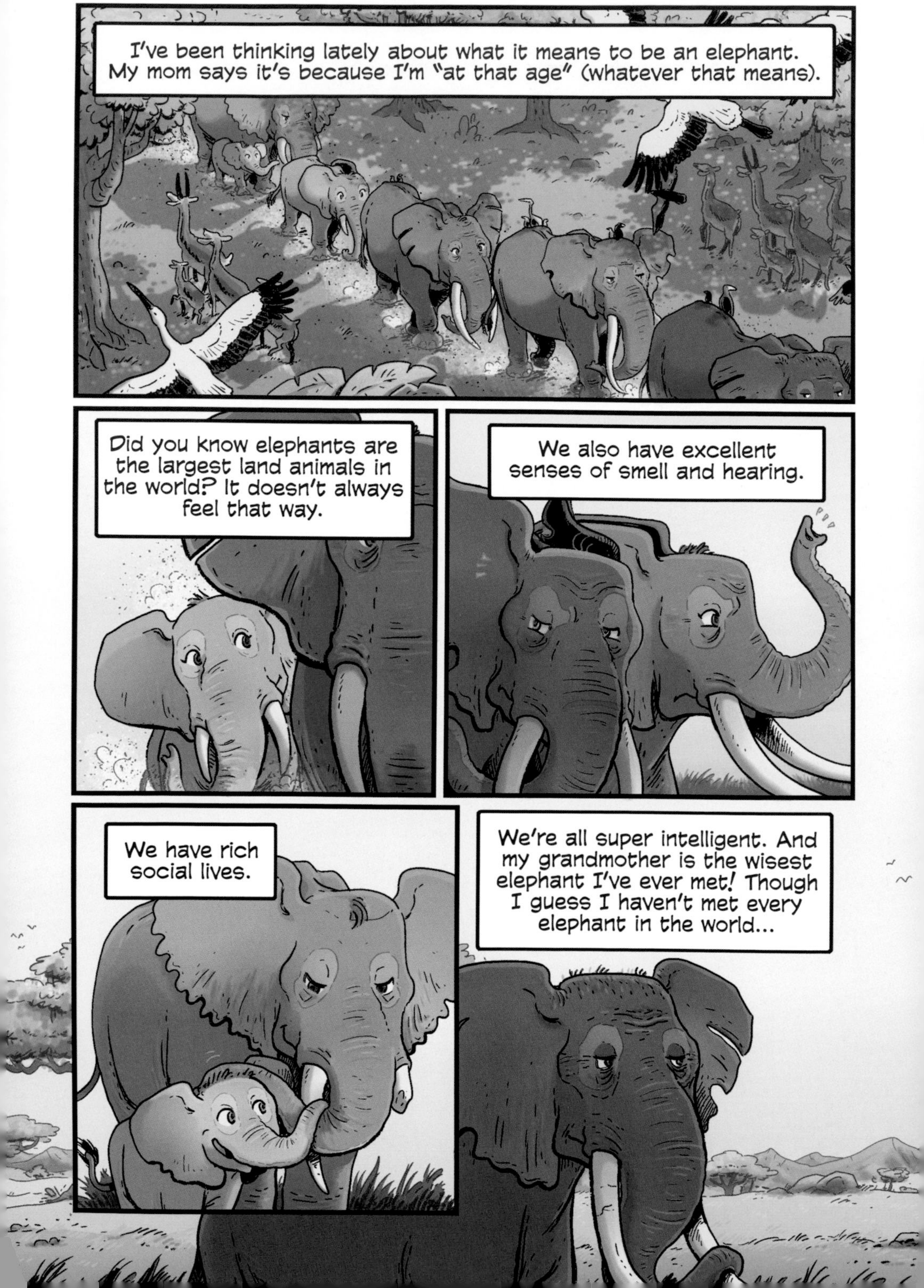

I've been thinking lately about what it means to be an elephant. My mom says it's because I'm "at that age" (whatever that means).
Did you know elephants are the largest land animals in the world? It doesn't always feel that way.
We also have excellent senses of smell and hearing.
We have rich social lives.
We're all super intelligent. And my grandmother is the wisest elephant I've ever met! Though I guess I haven't met every elephant in the world...

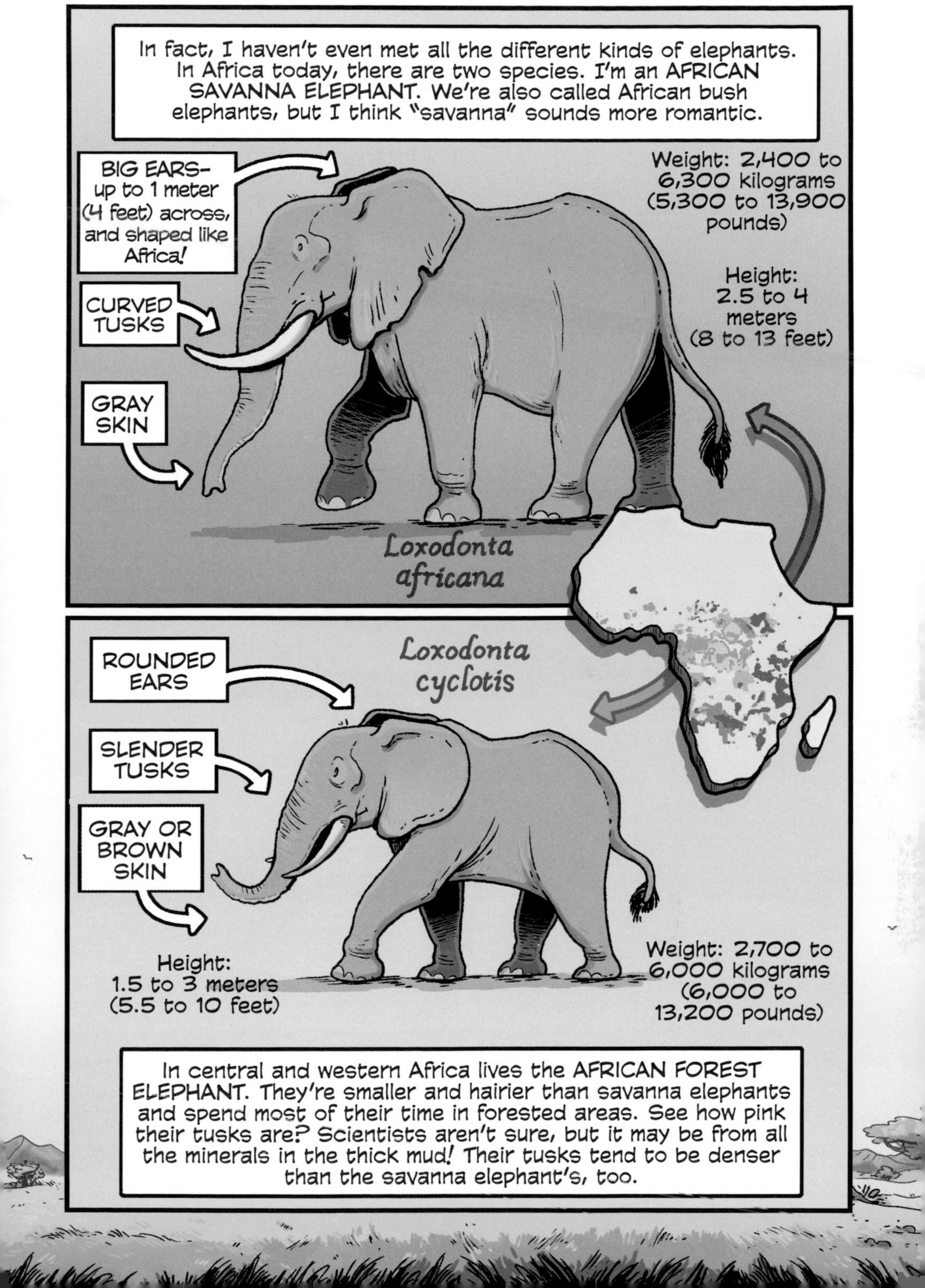

In fact, I haven't even met all the different kinds of elephants. In Africa today, there are two species. I'm an AFRICAN SAVANNA ELEPHANT. We're also called African bush elephants, but I think "savanna" sounds more romantic.
BIG EARS– up to 1 meter (4 feet) across, and shaped like Africa!
CURVED TUSKS
GRAY SKIN
Weight: 2,400 to 6,300 kilograms (5,300 to 13,900 pounds)
Height: 2.5 to 4 meters (8 to 13 feet)
Loxodonta africana
Loxodonta cyclotis
ROUNDED EARS
SLENDER TUSKS
GRAY OR BROWN SKIN
Height: 1.5 to 3 meters (5.5 to 10 feet)
Weight: 2,700 to 6,000 kilograms (6,000 to 13,200 pounds)
In central and western Africa lives the AFRICAN FOREST ELEPHANT. They're smaller and hairier than savanna elephants and spend most of their time in forested areas. See how pink their tusks are? Scientists aren't sure, but it may be from all the minerals in the thick mud! Their tusks tend to be denser than the savanna elephant's, too.

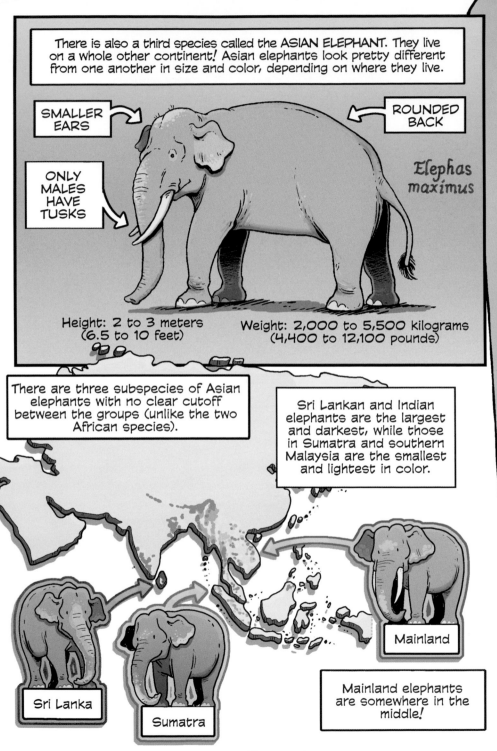

There is also a third species called the ASIAN ELEPHANT. They live on a whole other continent! Asian elephants look pretty different from one another in size and color, depending on where they live.

SMALLER EARS

ROUNDED BACK

ONLY MALES HAVE TUSKS

Elephas maximus

Height: 2 to 3 meters (6.5 to 10 feet)

Weight: 2,000 to 5,500 kilograms (4,400 to 12,100 pounds)

There are three subspecies of Asian elephants with no clear cutoff between the groups (unlike the two African species).

Sri Lankan and Indian elephants are the largest and darkest, while those in Sumatra and southern Malaysia are the smallest and lightest in color.

Sri Lanka

Sumatra

Mainland

Mainland elephants are somewhere in the middle!

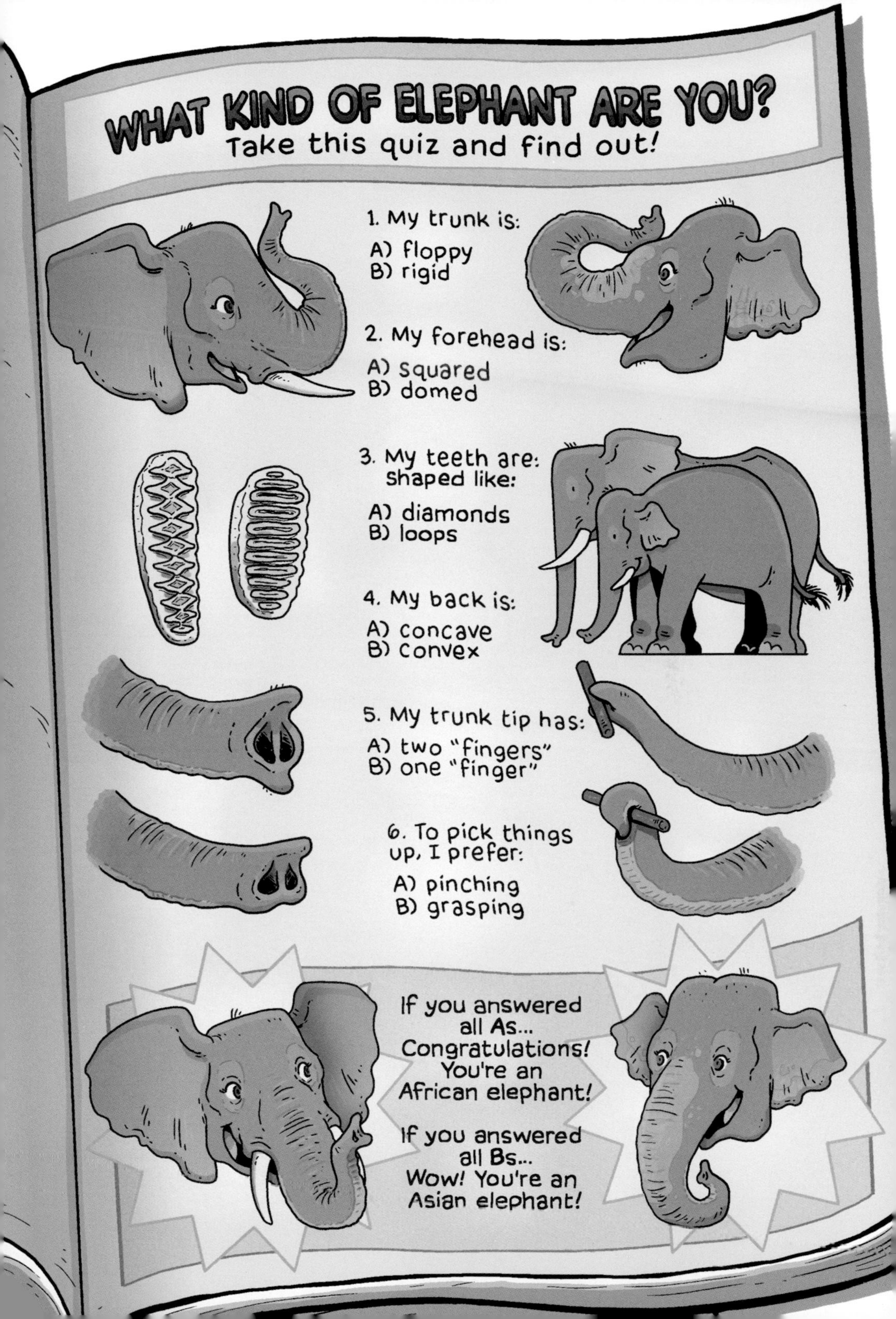

WHAT KIND OF ELEPHANT ARE YOU?
Take this quiz and find out!

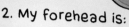

1. My trunk is:
   A) floppy
   B) rigid

2. My forehead is:
   A) squared
   B) domed

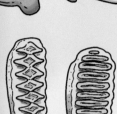

3. My teeth are: shaped like:
   A) diamonds
   B) loops

4. My back is:
   A) concave
   B) convex

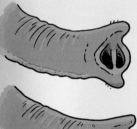
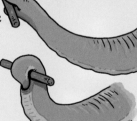
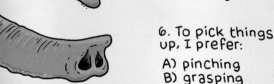

5. My trunk tip has:
   A) two "fingers"
   B) one "finger"

6. To pick things up, I prefer:
   A) pinching
   B) grasping

If you answered all As... Congratulations! You're an African elephant!

If you answered all Bs... Wow! You're an Asian elephant!

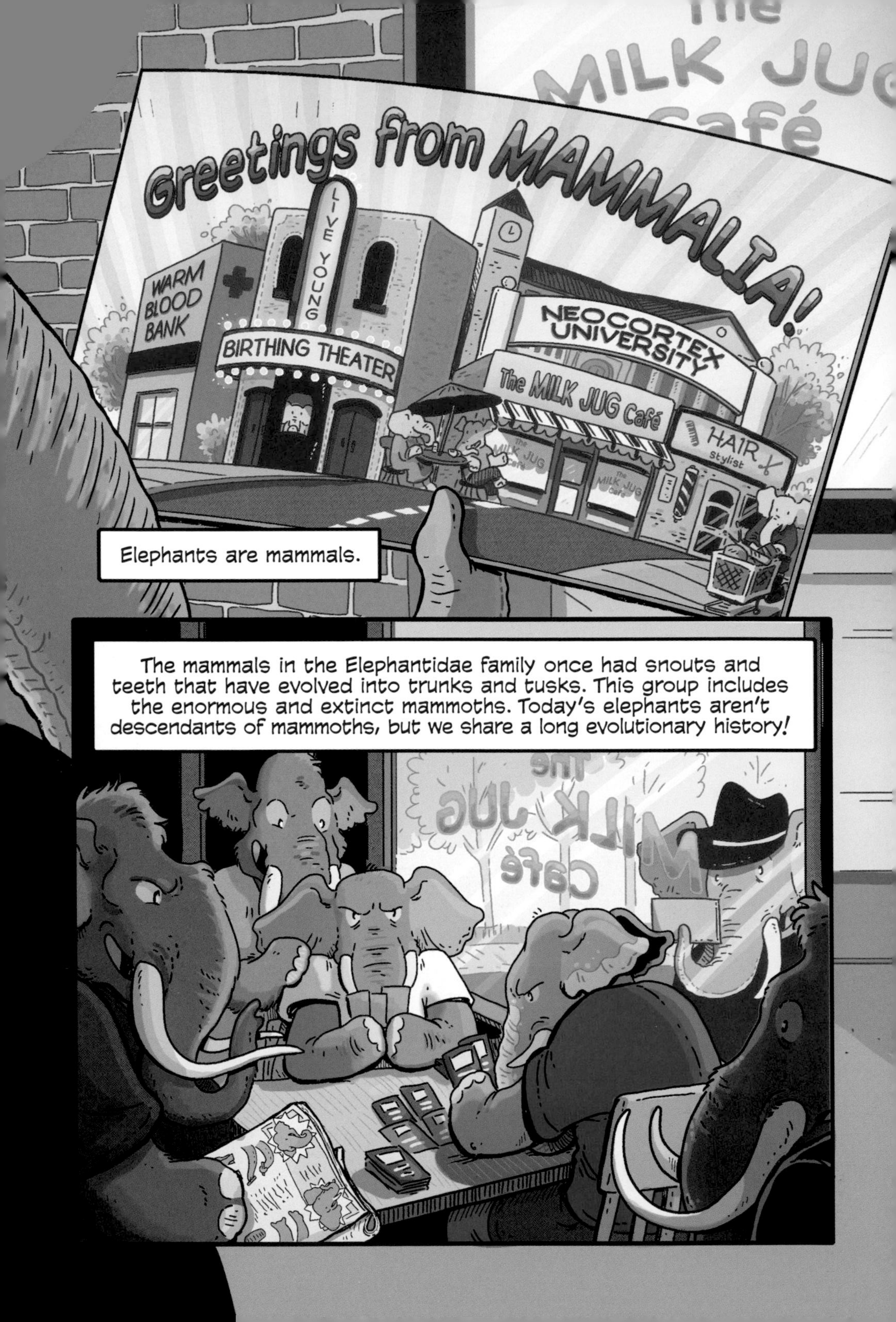
The MILK JUG Café
Greetings from MAMMALIA!
WARM BLOOD BANK
LIVE YOUNG
BIRTHING THEATER
NEOCORTEX UNIVERSITY
The MILK JUG Café
HAIR Stylist
Elephants are mammals.
The mammals in the Elephantidae family once had snouts and teeth that have evolved into trunks and tusks. This group includes the enormous and extinct mammoths. Today's elephants aren't descendants of mammoths, but we share a long evolutionary history!

Elephantidae is the only living family in the Proboscidea order, members of which first appeared in Africa about 60 million years ago.

Proboscideans were much smaller back then, about the size of a fox or a pig.

Many species of Proboscideans formed.

As they grew in size, they migrated into Europe and Asia 20 to 25 million years ago, and into North America around 16 million years ago.

Eritherium

Phosphatherium

Daoui

1st RADIATION

1st RADIATION

1st RADIATION

1st F

Platybelodon

Gomphothere

2nd

Fun
An an
mot
har

Stegotetrabelodon

Primelephas

TION #

3rd RADIATION #

3rd RADIATION

Fun fact:
Inspiration for
Middle-earth's
"Oliphaunts"

Fun fact:
Common ancesto
of mammoths
and elephants

Mammuthus

ON #

The Elephantidae family arose 7 to 8 million years ago, producing Loxodonta (African elephants), Elephas (Asian elephants), and Mammuthus (mammoths).

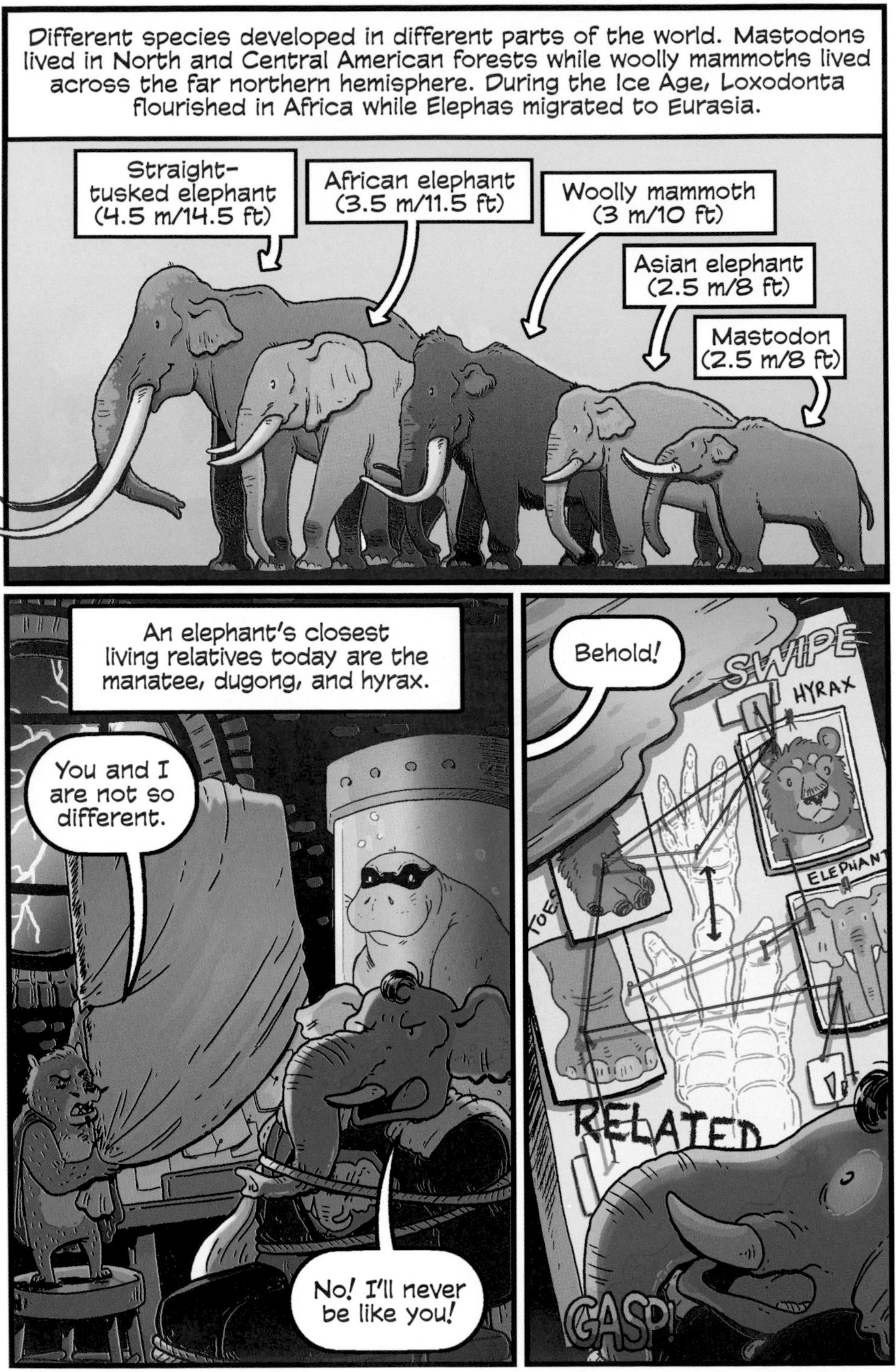
Different species developed in different parts of the world. Mastodons lived in North and Central American forests while woolly mammoths lived across the far northern hemisphere. During the Ice Age, Loxodonta flourished in Africa while Elephas migrated to Eurasia.
Straight-tusked elephant (4.5 m/14.5 ft)
African elephant (3.5 m/11.5 ft)
Woolly mammoth (3 m/10 ft)
Asian elephant (2.5 m/8 ft)
Mastodon (2.5 m/8 ft)
An elephant's closest living relatives today are the manatee, dugong, and hyrax.
You and I are not so different.
No! I'll never be like you!
Behold!
SWIPE
HYRAX
ELEPHANT
TOES
RELATED
GASP!

It's easy to forget that elephants today live in all different kinds of environments. What would life be like in the mountains? I'm just used to the seasons of the savanna in East Africa.

We go through four seasons here: two wet and two dry. During the short dry season, we spend our days searching for water, looking for food, and waiting for rain.

Salama stops us... There's something ahead.

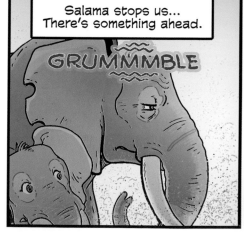

GRUMMMBLE

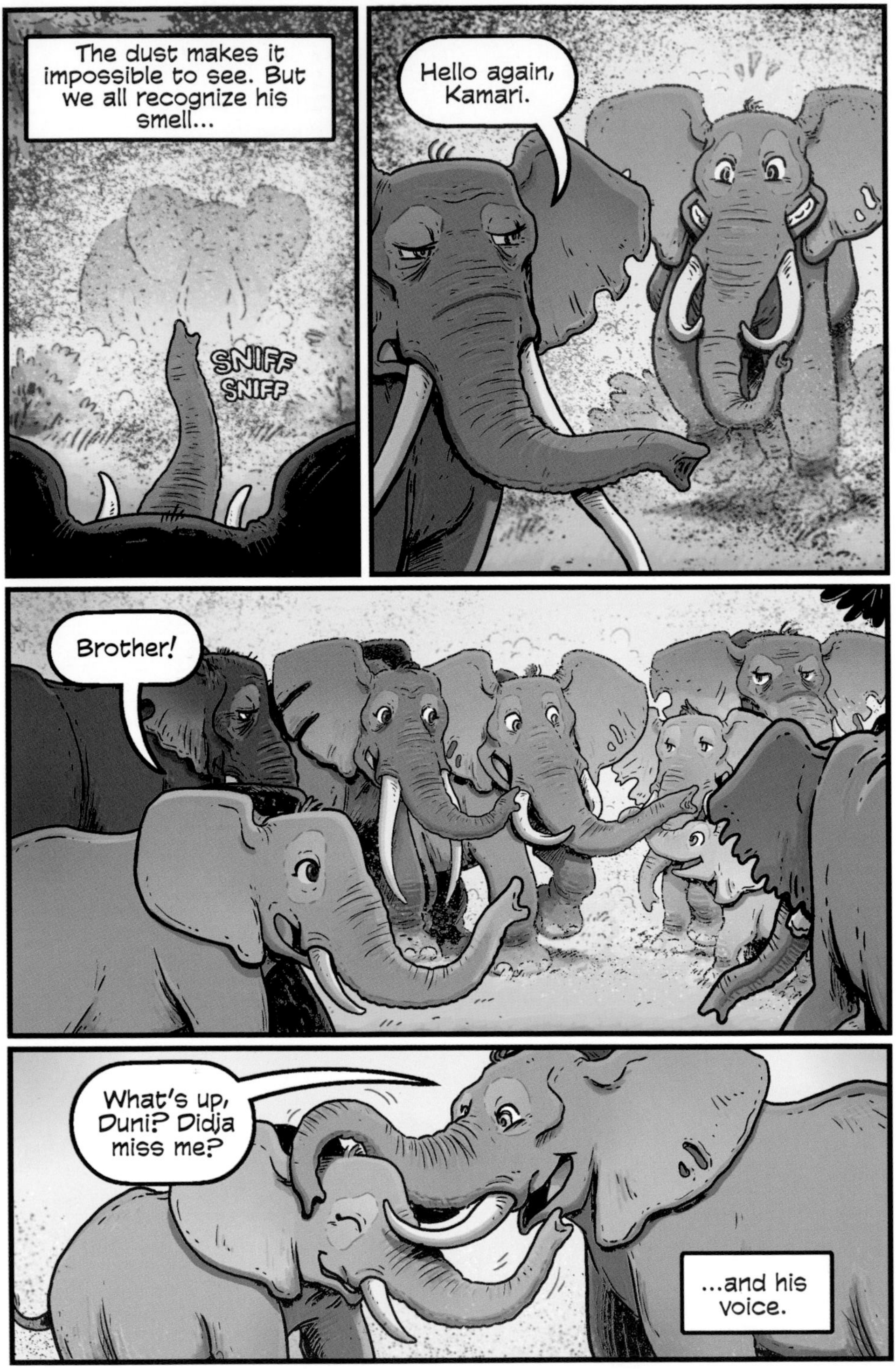

The dust makes it impossible to see. But we all recognize his smell...
SNIFF SNIFF
Hello again, Kamari.
Brother!
What's up, Duni? Didja miss me?
...and his voice.

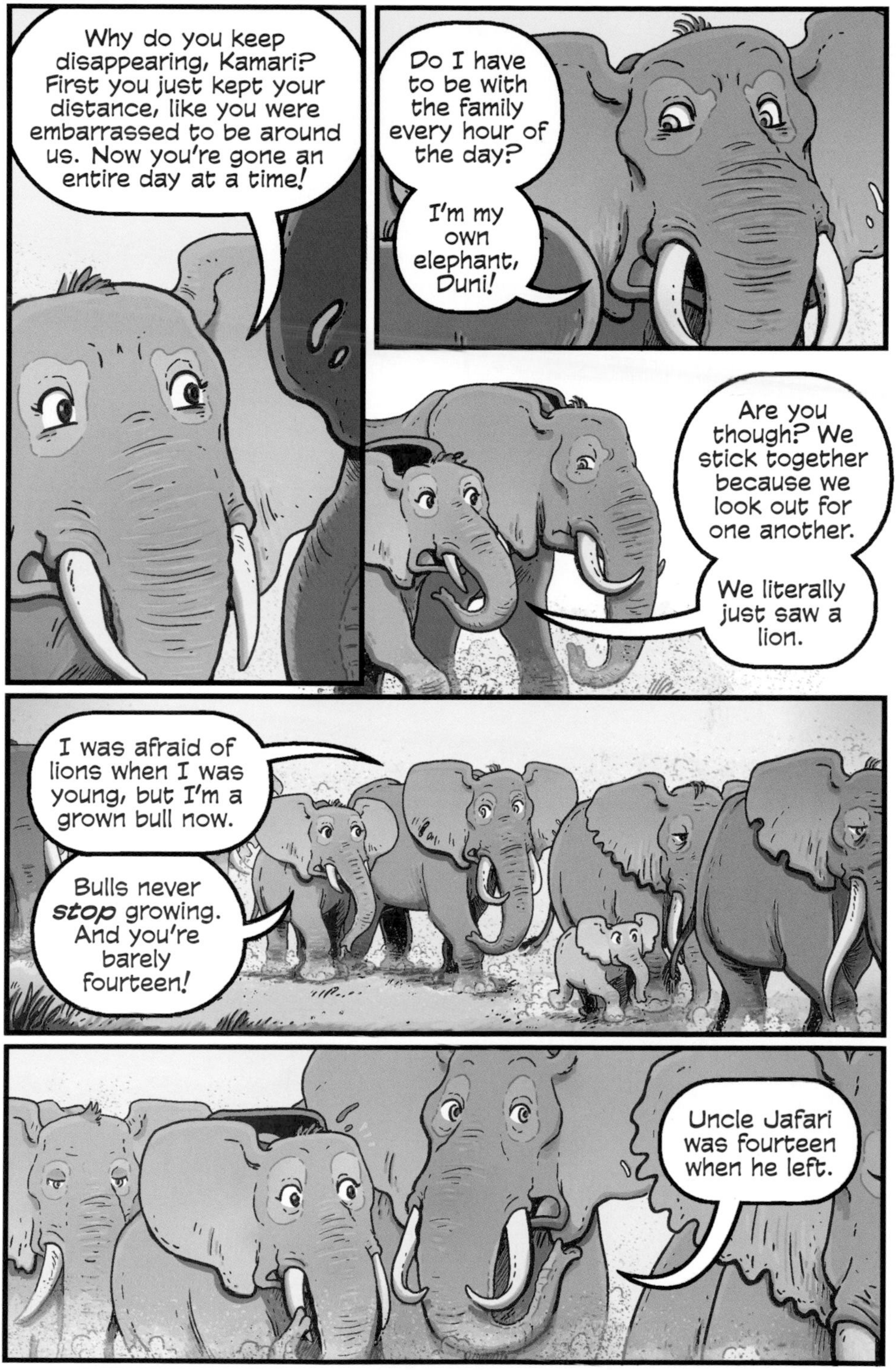

Why do you keep disappearing, Kamari? First you just kept your distance, like you were embarrassed to be around us. Now you're gone an entire day at a time!
Do I have to be with the family every hour of the day?
I'm my own elephant, Duni!
Are you though? We stick together because we look out for one another.
We literally just saw a lion.
I was afraid of lions when I was young, but I'm a grown bull now.
Bulls never *stop* growing. And you're barely fourteen!
Uncle Jafari was fourteen when he left.

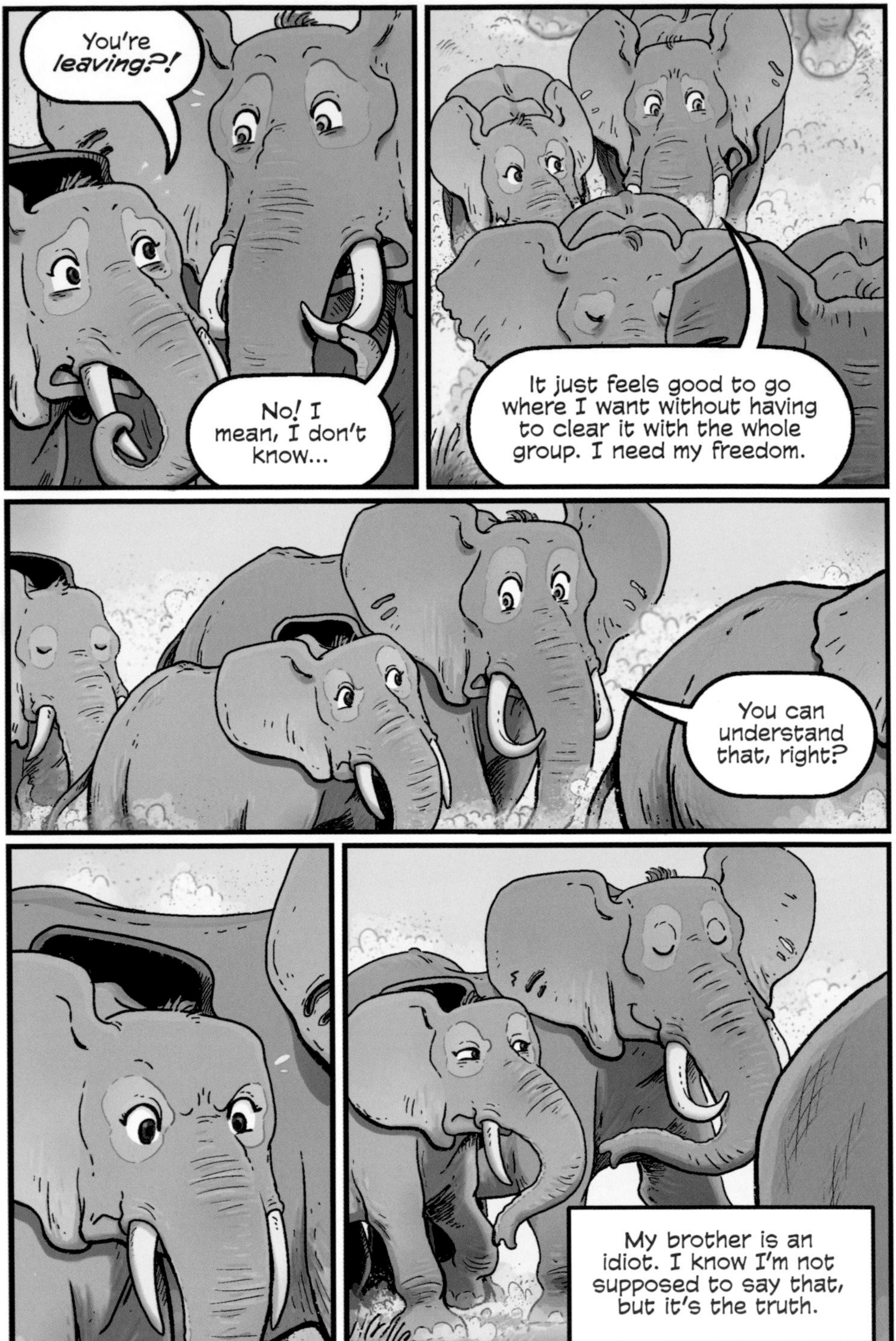
You're *leaving?!*
No! I mean, I don't know...
It just feels good to go where I want without having to clear it with the whole group. I need my freedom.
You can understand that, right?
My brother is an idiot. I know I'm not supposed to say that, but it's the truth.

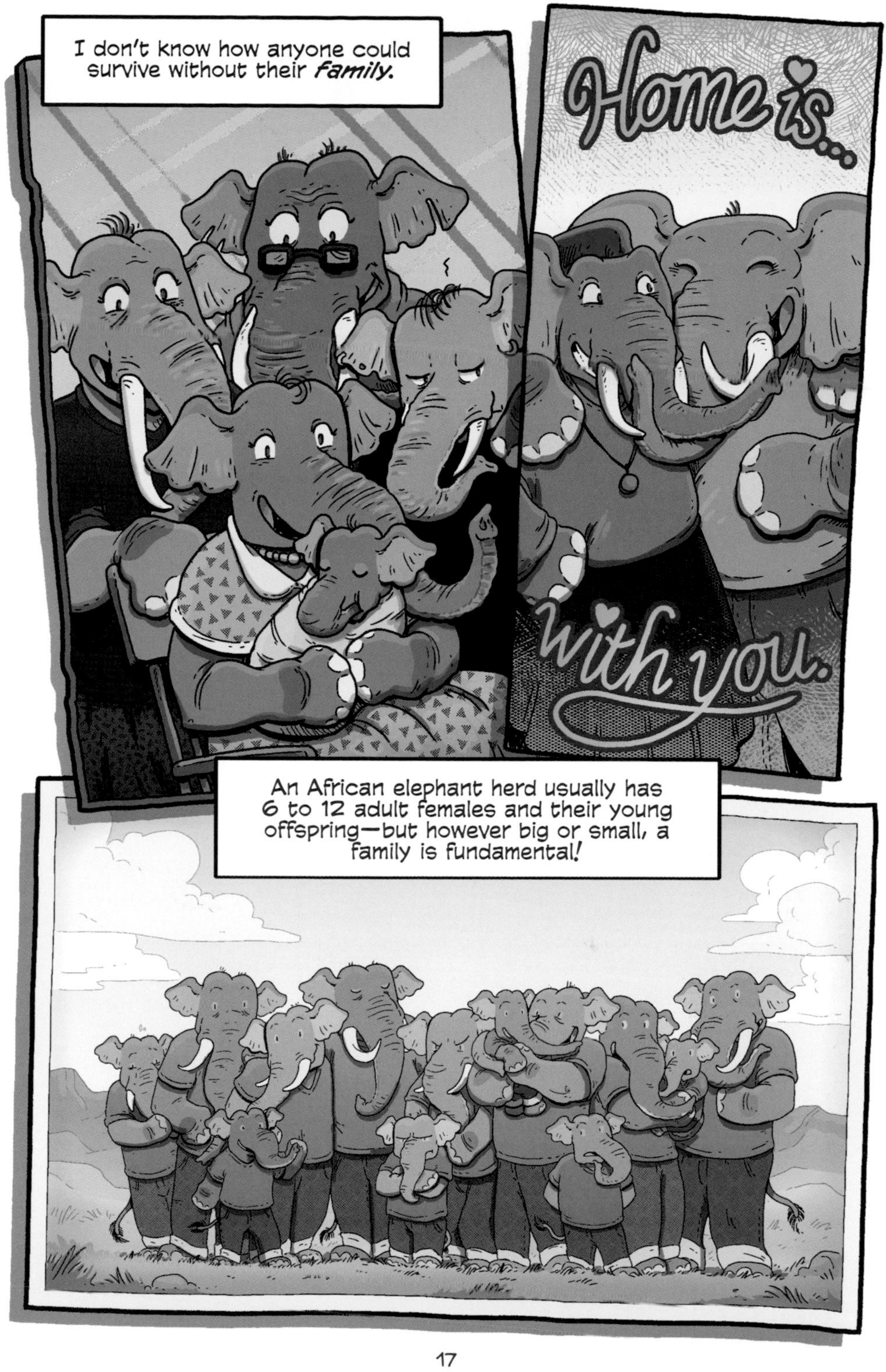

I don't know how anyone could survive without their *family.*
Home is...
with you.
An African elephant herd usually has 6 to 12 adult females and their young offspring—but however big or small, a family is fundamental!

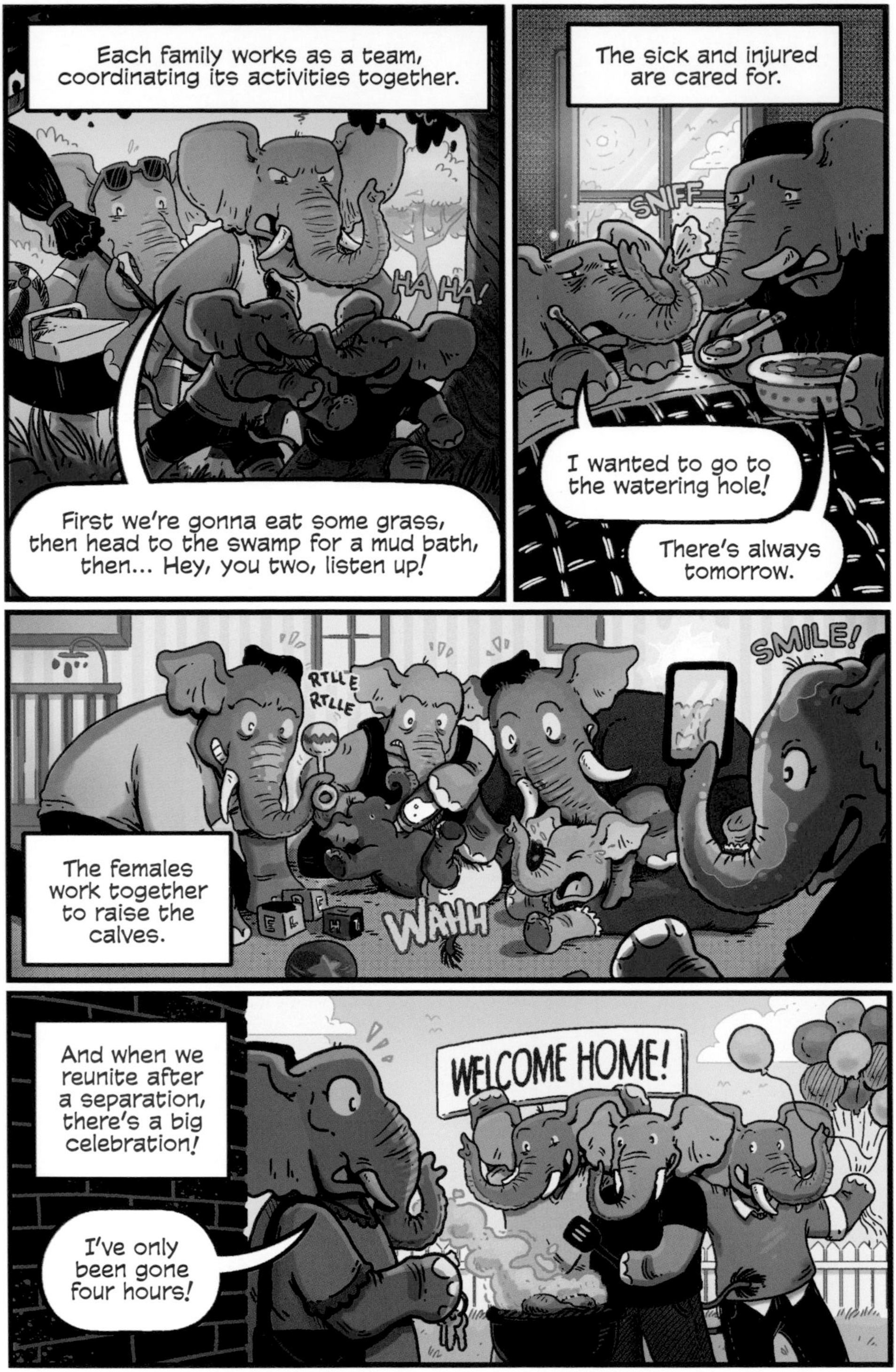
Each family works as a team, coordinating its activities together.
HA HA!
First we're gonna eat some grass, then head to the swamp for a mud bath, then... Hey, you two, listen up!
The sick and injured are cared for.
SNIFF
I wanted to go to the watering hole!
There's always tomorrow.
RTLLE RTLLE
SMILE!
The females work together to raise the calves.
WAHH
And when we reunite after a separation, there's a big celebration!
WELCOME HOME!
I've only been gone four hours!

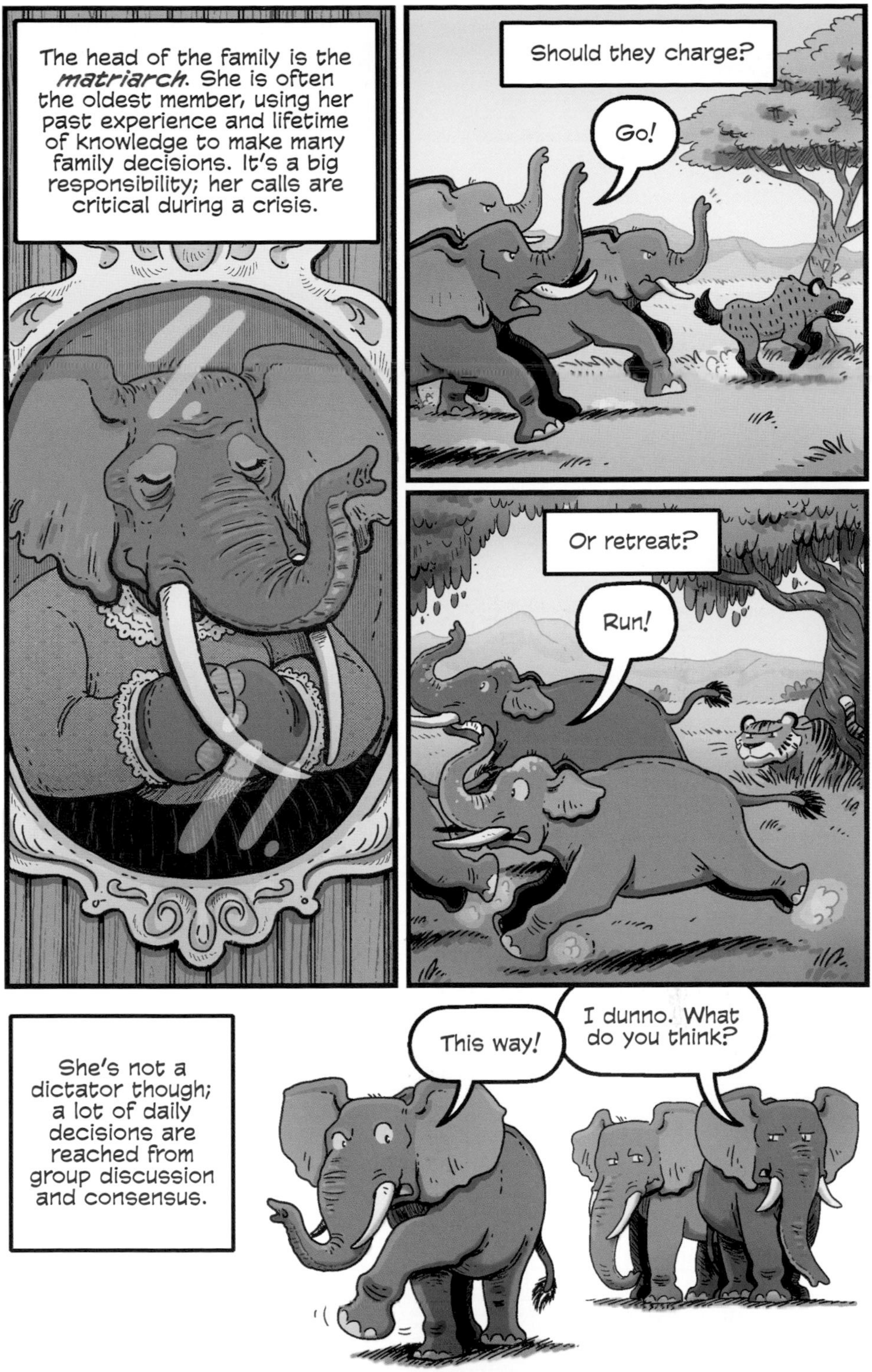
The head of the family is the *matriarch*. She is often the oldest member, using her past experience and lifetime of knowledge to make many family decisions. It's a big responsibility; her calls are critical during a crisis.
Should they charge?
Go!
Or retreat?
Run!
She's not a dictator though; a lot of daily decisions are reached from group discussion and consensus.
This way!
I dunno. What do you think?

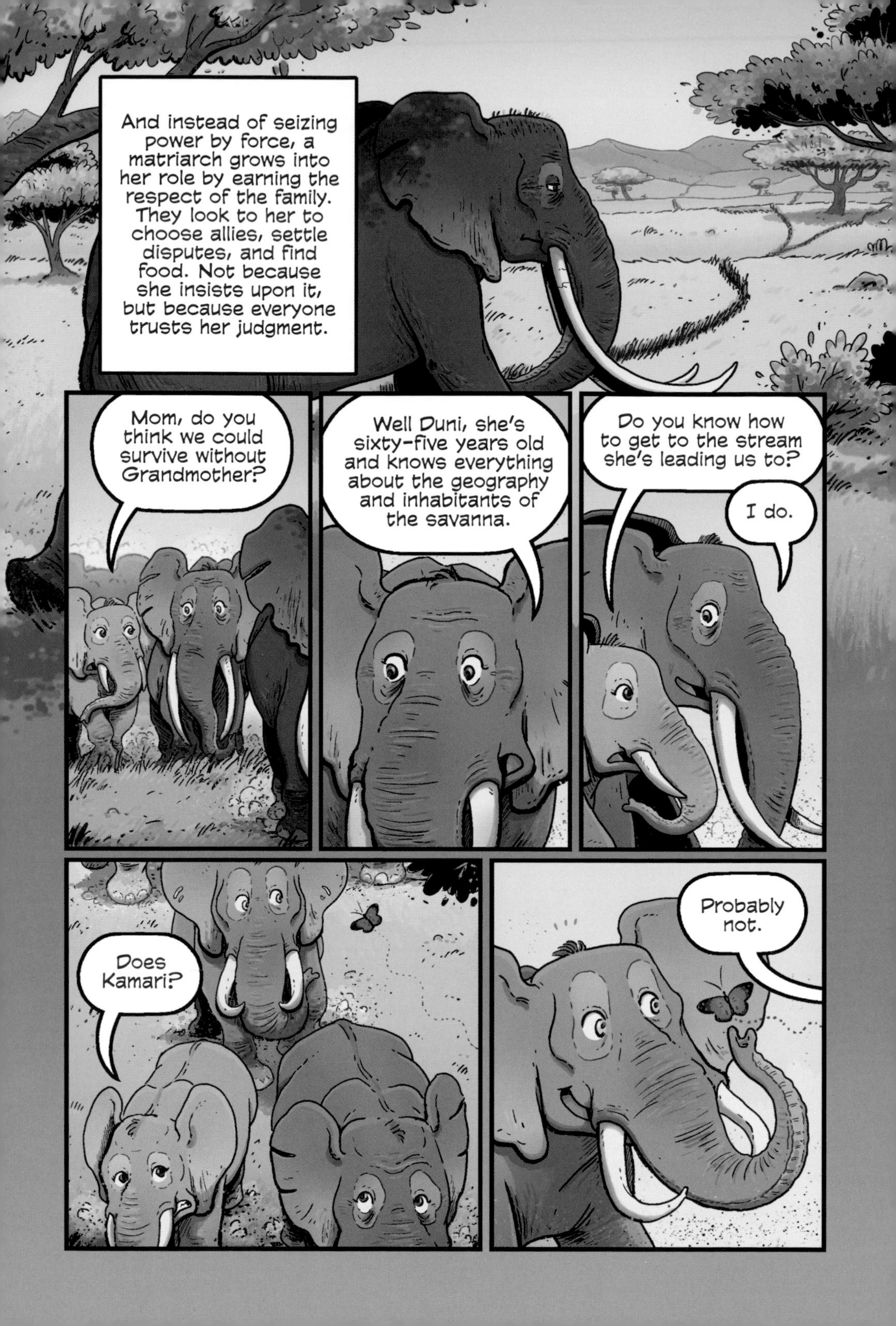
And instead of seizing power by force, a matriarch grows into her role by earning the respect of the family. They look to her to choose allies, settle disputes, and find food. Not because she insists upon it, but because everyone trusts her judgment.
Mom, do you think we could survive without Grandmother?
Well Duni, she's sixty-five years old and knows everything about the geography and inhabitants of the savanna.
Do you know how to get to the stream she's leading us to?
I do.
Does Kamari?
Probably not.

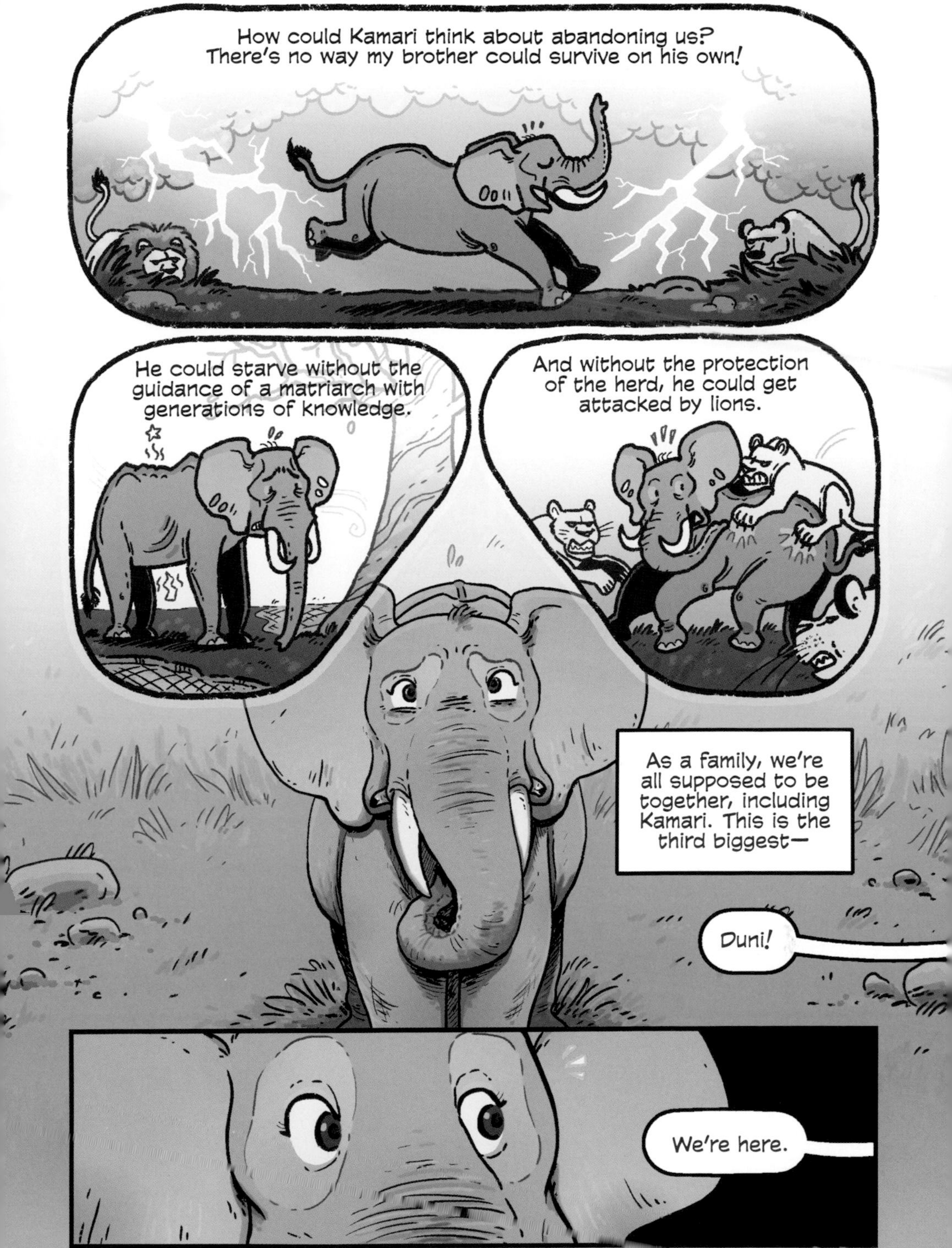

How could Kamari think about abandoning us? There's no way my brother could survive on his own!
He could starve without the guidance of a matriarch with generations of knowledge.
And without the protection of the herd, he could get attacked by lions.
As a family, we're all supposed to be together, including Kamari. This is the third biggest—
Duni!
We're here.

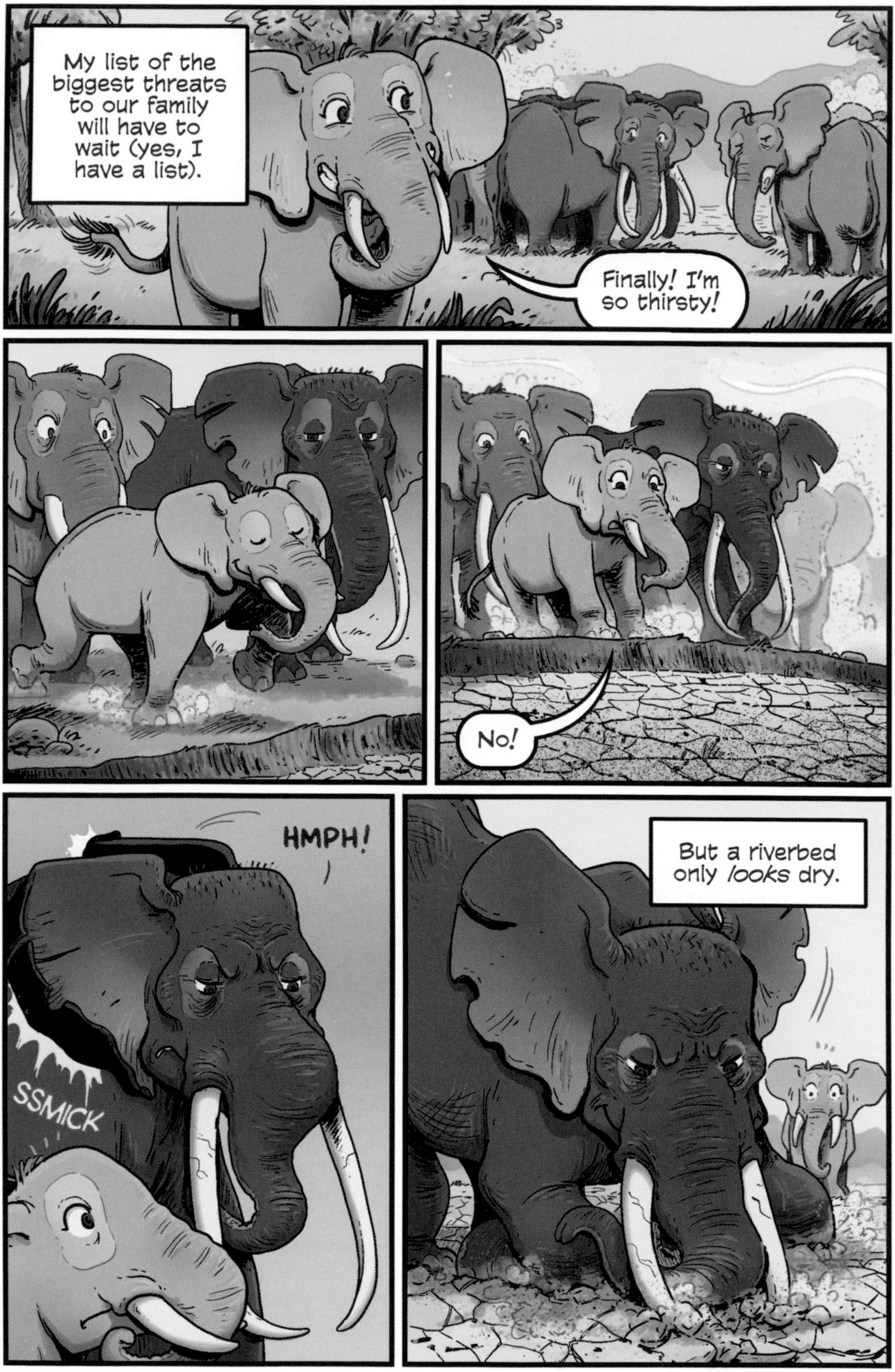

My list of the biggest threats to our family will have to wait (yes, I have a list).
Finally! I'm so thirsty!
No!
HMPH!
SSMICK
But a riverbed only *looks* dry.

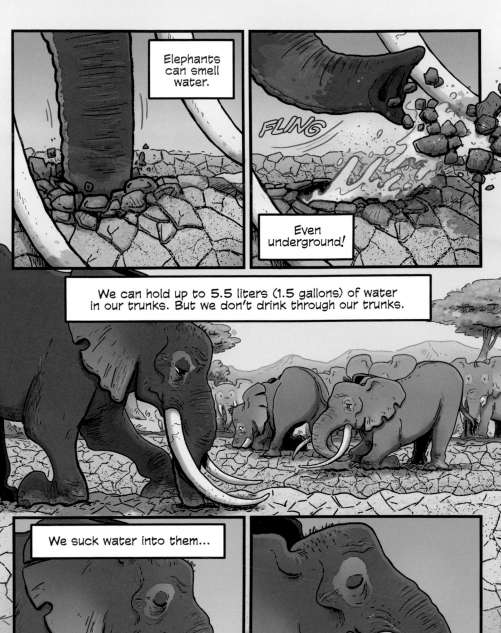

Elephants can smell water.

Even underground!

FLING

We can hold up to 5.5 liters (1.5 gallons) of water in our trunks. But we don't drink through our trunks.

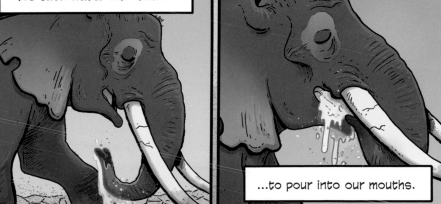

We suck water into them...

...to pour into our mouths.

An elephant *trunk* contains about 40,000 muscle bundles that contract and expand with a variable amount of force.

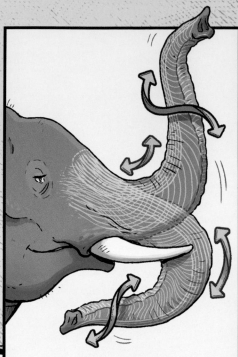

Similar to a tongue, a trunk has no skeleton and is made of tightly packed muscle fibers that work together and allow it to bend, lift, extend, shorten, and twist in all directions.

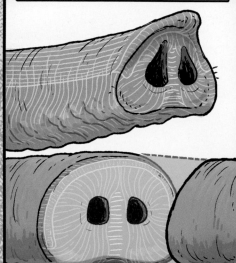

The trunk is a *prehensile* organ used to grasp, hold, and dig. It's as agile as a human hand...

PICK

...but much more powerful.

SNAP

In addition to drinking, we use it to eat...

...to cool off...

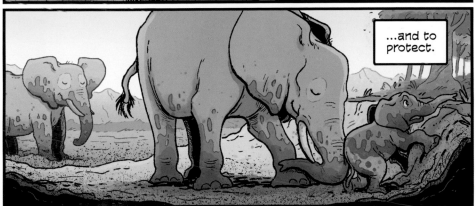

...and to protect.

Sensitive whiskers called *vibrissae* surround the tip, while many short *vellus vibrissae* lie beneath the skin's surface.

The tip is rich with sensory receptors called *Pacinian corpuscles* that detect pressure and vibration—even another elephant family's vocalizations or the tremors caused by their approach.

At the surface are *Meissner's corpuscles*—nerve endings like those found in your finger pads. They are super sensitive to texture and light touch.

This all helps with clearing away debris before drinking water...

...cleaning food...

...scratching an itch...

SKRITCH SKRATCH

...and comforting a loved one.

So sweet!

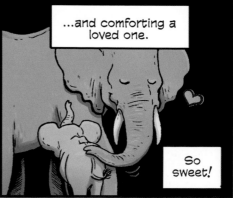

A trunk is also a sophisticated instrument for sniffing! We use it to detect predators, recognize relatives, and find water!

Up periscope!

Turbinates are bones inside the nasal cavity that hold millions of sensory cells. Elephants have more turbinates than any other animal!

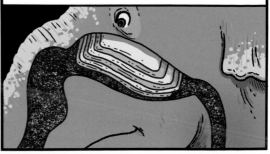

In the roof of the mouth are two pits that extend into tubes called the *vomeronasal organ*. The tubes are filled with sensory nerve endings.

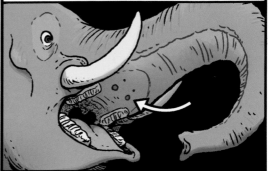

So we can carry smells to our mouth to see if another elephant is producing the right hormones for mating.

Ah, a sweet bouquet of depth and estrogen in this fine urine.

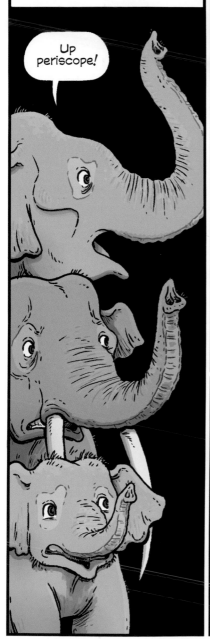

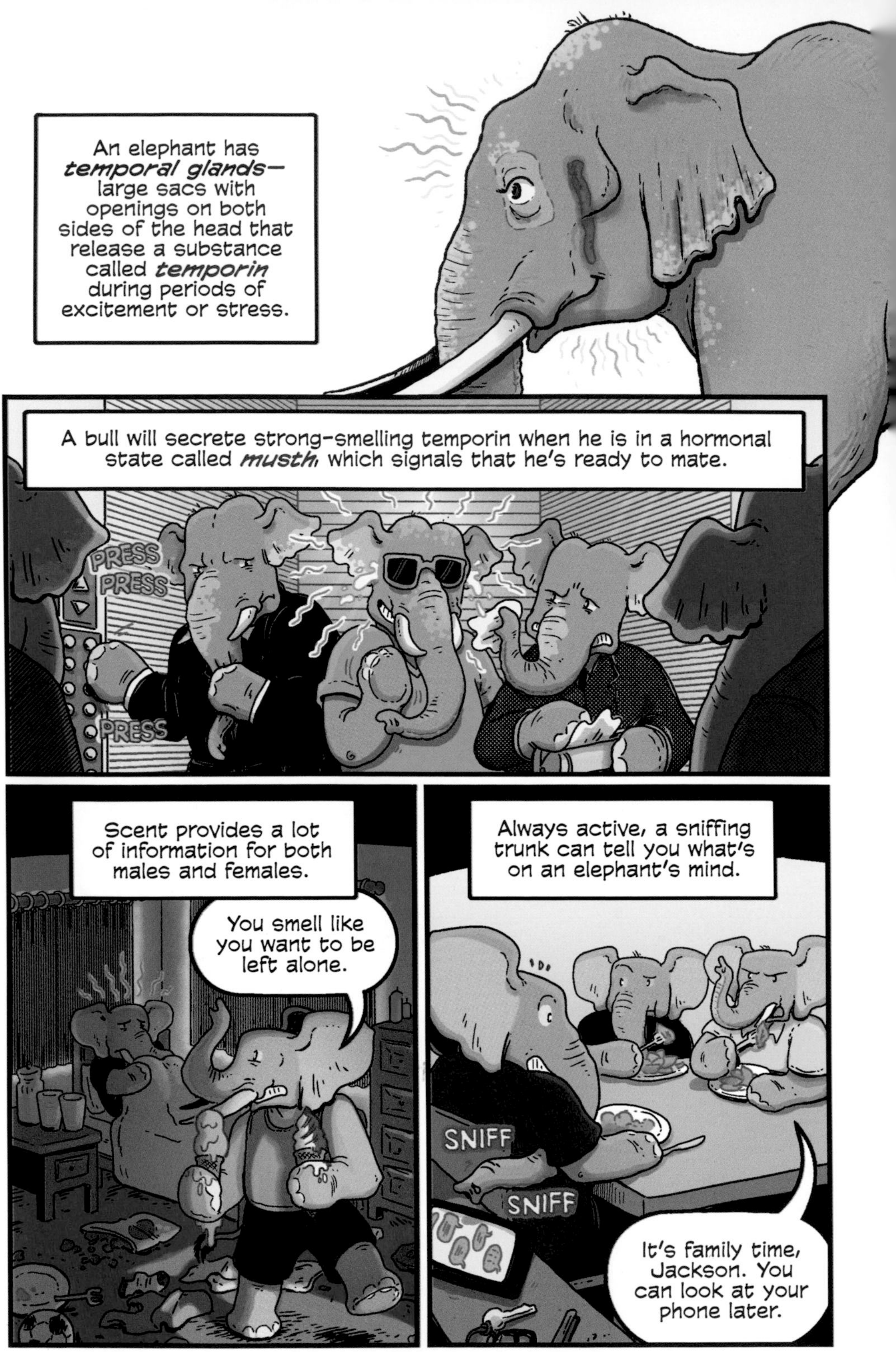
An elephant has *temporal glands*—large sacs with openings on both sides of the head that release a substance called *temporin* during periods of excitement or stress.
A bull will secrete strong-smelling temporin when he is in a hormonal state called *musth*, which signals that he's ready to mate.
PRESS
PRESS
PRESS
Scent provides a lot of information for both males and females.
You smell like you want to be left alone.
Always active, a sniffing trunk can tell you what's on an elephant's mind.
SNIFF
SNIFF
It's family time, Jackson. You can look at your phone later.

In addition to picking up expressive scents, the trunk itself is a communication tool, full of gestures...

GREETING

PLAYFULNESS

ASSERTION

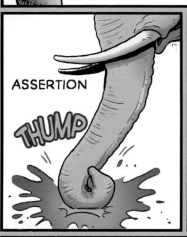

THUMP

DISCIPLINE

SWAT

AMBIVALENCE

...

COMFORT

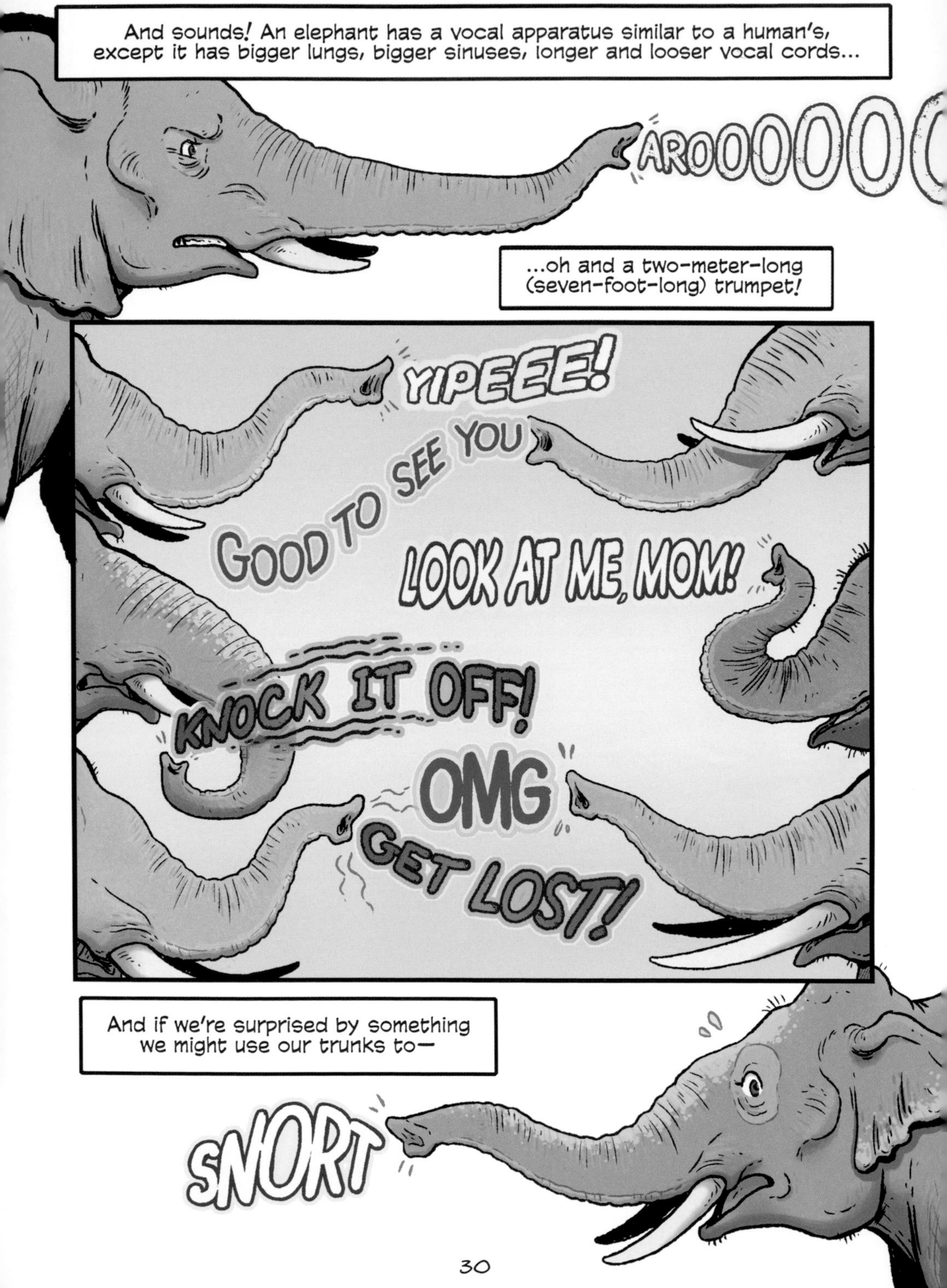

And sounds! An elephant has a vocal apparatus similar to a human's, except it has bigger lungs, bigger sinuses, longer and looser vocal cords...
AROOOOOOO
...oh and a two-meter-long (seven-foot-long) trumpet!
YIPEEE!
GOOD TO SEE YOU
LOOK AT ME, MOM!
KNOCK IT OFF!
OMG
GET LOST!
And if we're surprised by something we might use our trunks to—
SNORT

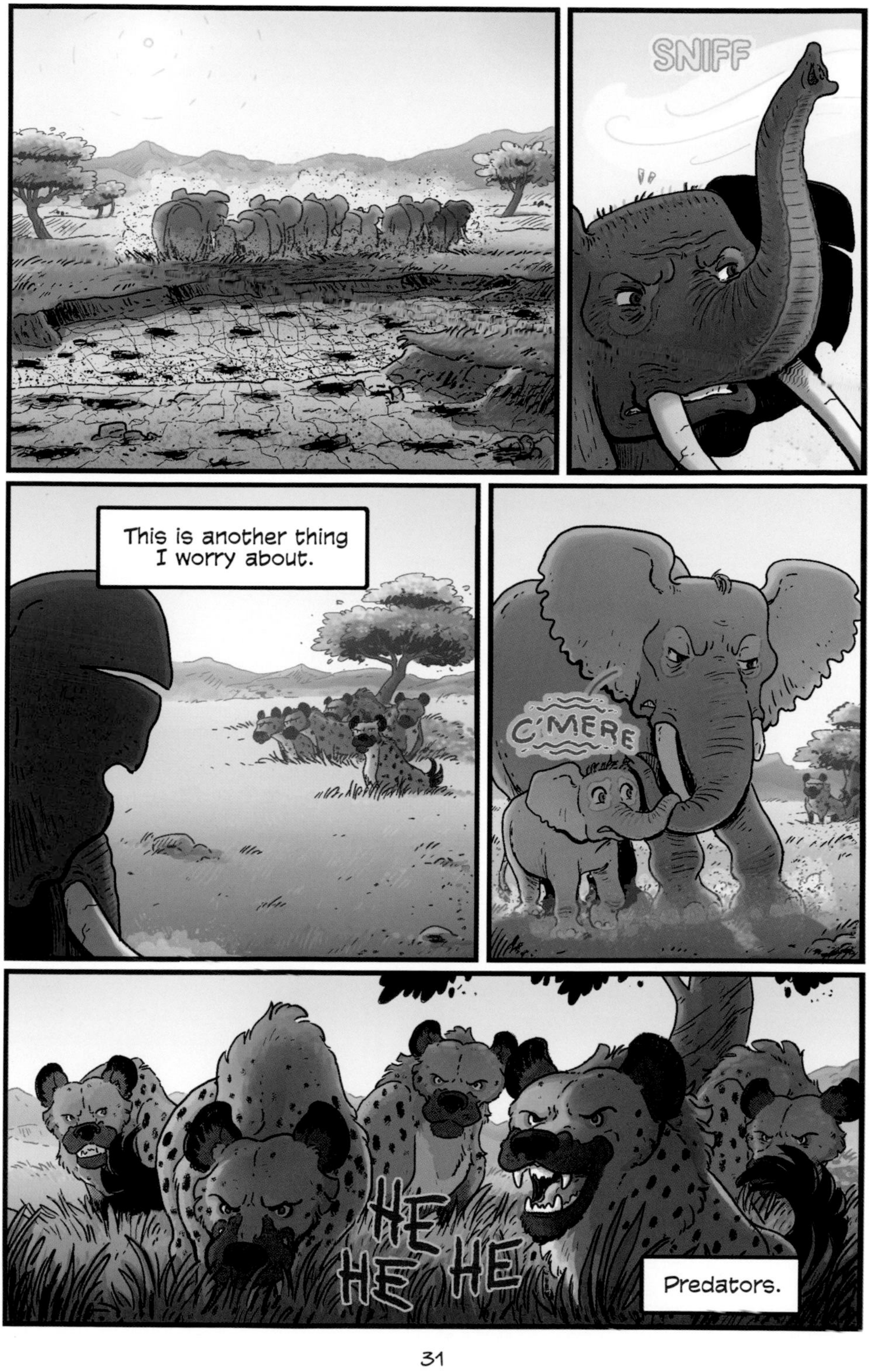
SNIFF
This is another thing I worry about.
C'MERE
HE HE HE HE
Predators.

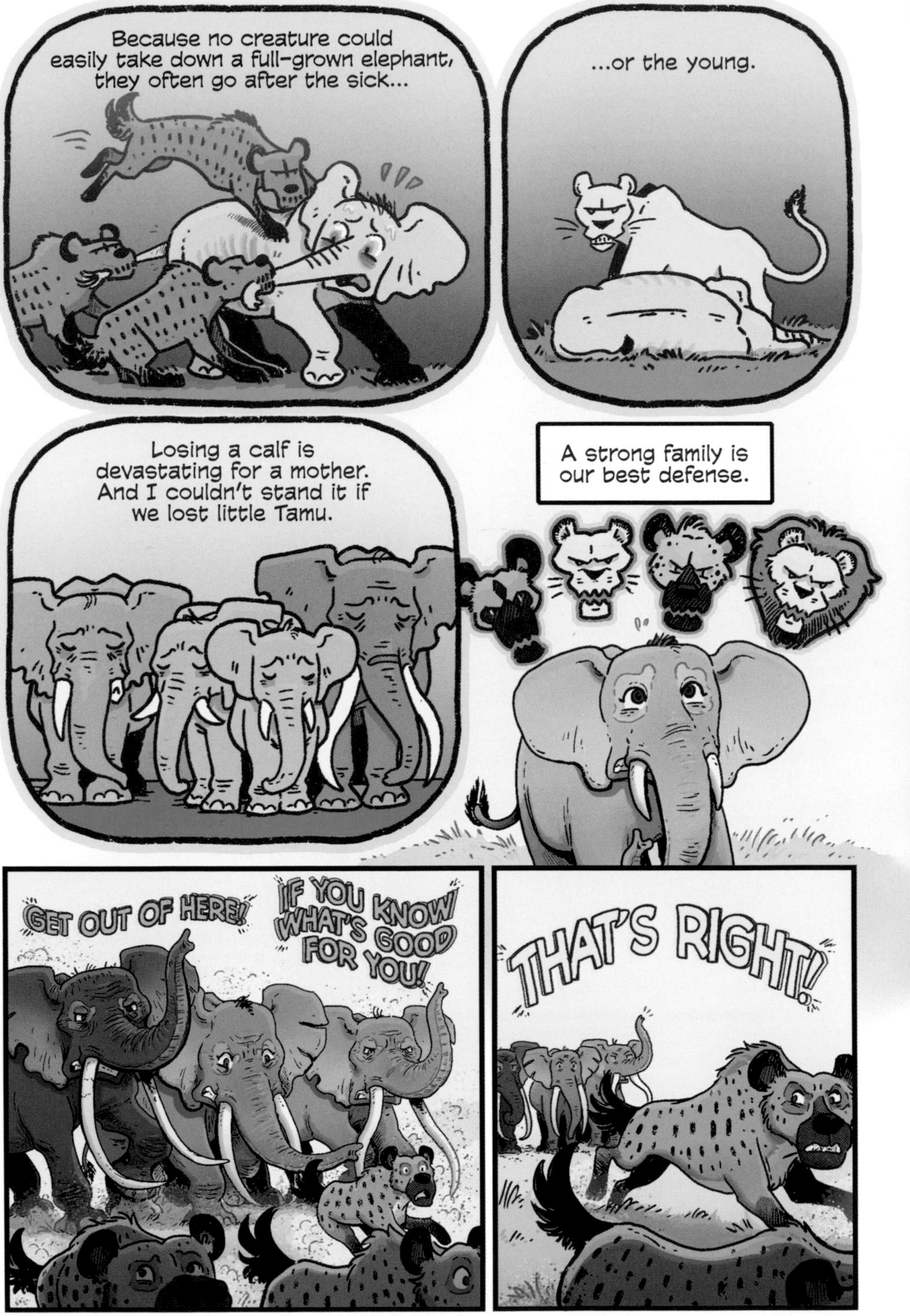
Because no creature could easily take down a full-grown elephant, they often go after the sick...
...or the young.
Losing a calf is devastating for a mother. And I couldn't stand it if we lost little Tamu.
A strong family is our best defense.
GET OUT OF HERE!
IF YOU KNOW WHAT'S GOOD FOR YOU!
THAT'S RIGHT!

Here are a few notable predators we need to keep an eye out for:

LION **Level 5**

TIGER **Level 4**

Location: African savanna and grasslands
Attack: Charges and leaps, pulling its prey down before biting the throat. Females hunt in groups and are joined by males when going after large prey.

♥♥♥ HP 🐰🐰🐰 Speed

Location: Asian forests
Attack: Hunts alone, ambushing elephant calves. It goes for the throat and uses its forelimbs to help wrestle its prey to the ground.

♥♥♥ HP 🐰🐰🐰 Speed

SPOTTED HYENA **Level 3**

WILD DOG **Level 1**

Location: African savanna and grasslands
Attack: Hunts in groups, usually targeting the old or sick. Sometimes scavenges prey that is already dead.

♥♥♥ HP 🐰🐰🐰 Speed

Location: African savannas and Asian mountains
Attack: Hunts in packs, taking turns biting and chasing young or sick elephants until they are completely exhausted.

♥♥♥ HP 🐰🐰🐰 Speed

NILE CROCODILE **Level 2**

Location: African rivers and lakes
Attack: Swims quietly underwater, waiting with patience before jumping up and biting down in an effort to drown a young elephant. Only the largest crocodiles will attempt it.

♥♥♥ HP 🐰🐰🐰 Speed

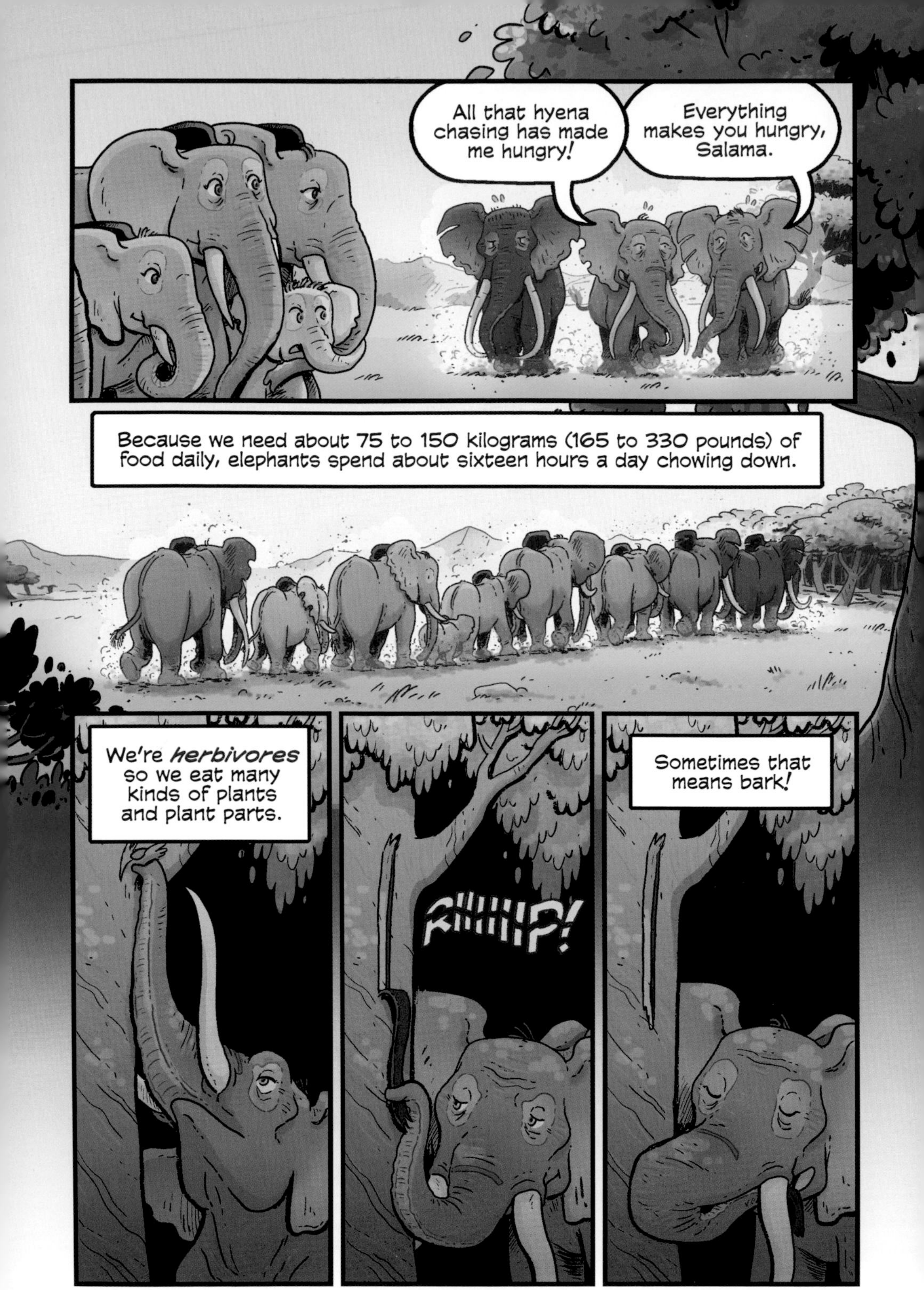

All that hyena chasing has made me hungry!
Everything makes you hungry, Salama.
Because we need about 75 to 150 kilograms (165 to 330 pounds) of food daily, elephants spend about sixteen hours a day chowing down.
We're *herbivores* so we eat many kinds of plants and plant parts.
RIIIIIIP!
Sometimes that means bark!

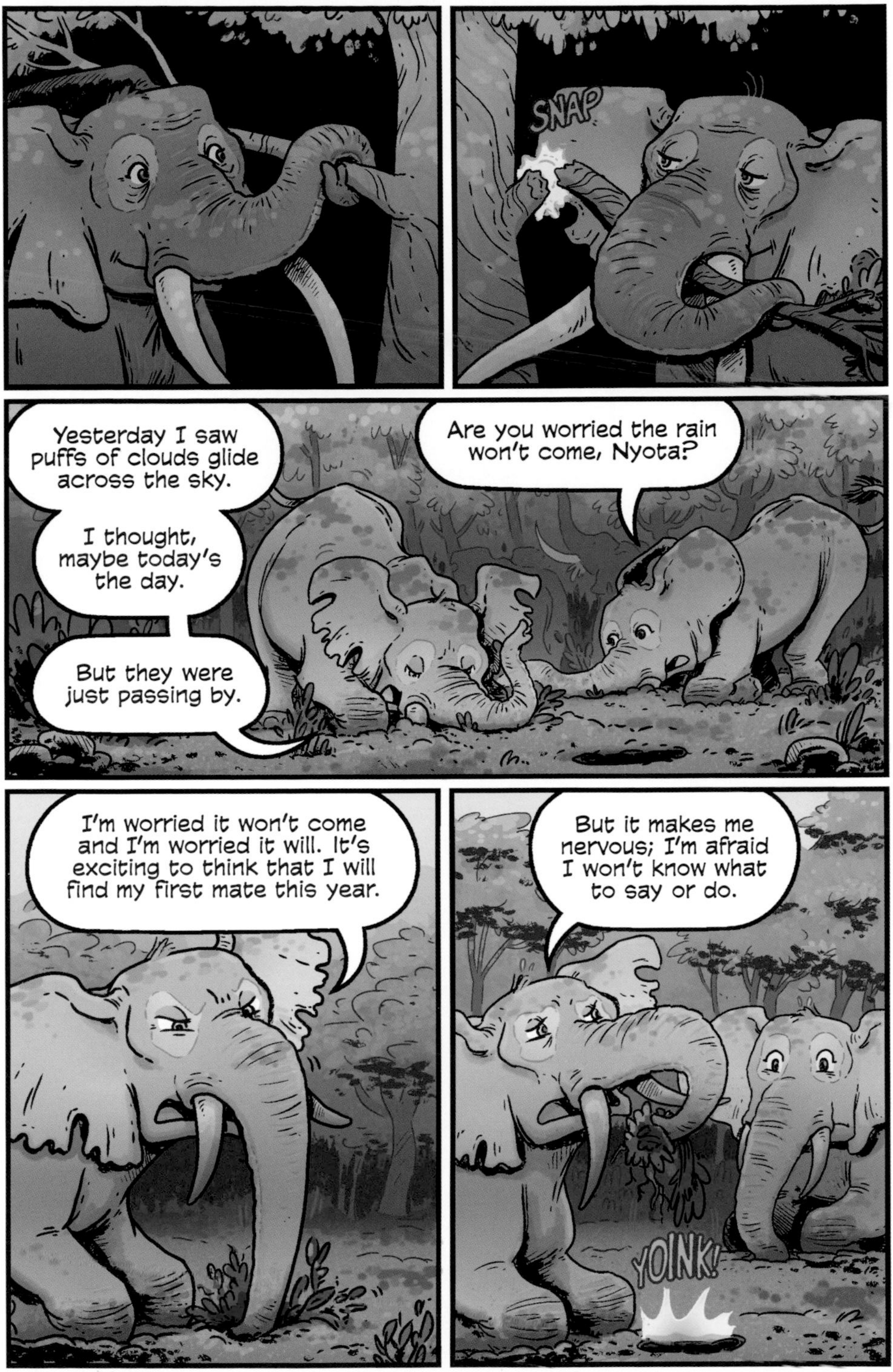

SNAP
Yesterday I saw puffs of clouds glide across the sky.
I thought, maybe today's the day.
But they were just passing by.
Are you worried the rain won't come, Nyota?
I'm worried it won't come and I'm worried it will. It's exciting to think that I will find my first mate this year.
But it makes me nervous; I'm afraid I won't know what to say or do.
YOINK!

You'll have help! The family will guide you every step of the way. Everyone's there for you.

That's true.

I don't blame her. I can't imagine having to mate with a huge and heavy bull. It sounds terrifying.

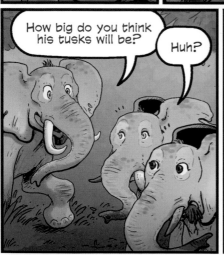

How big do you think his tusks will be?

Huh?

Some of the bulls I've seen have humongous tusks. Like a million times the size of the matriarch's. How big are your dream bull's tusks?

I don't know.

What's that got to do with anything?

I want to have the world's biggest tusks! Like ten feet long at least.

Go away, Kamari!

I don't get his obsession with tusk size. Bigger tusks don't make an elephant more attractive or successful.

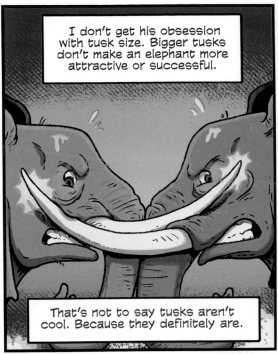

That's not to say tusks aren't cool. Because they definitely are.

Elephant tusks are made of a hard material called ivory, which is mostly *dentin*. Dentin is a calcified tissue that forms teeth! Tusks are our incisors (like your front teeth).

Like any tooth, there is a pulp cavity inside a tusk that contains tissues connected to nerves. This part of the tusk is embedded in the jaw.

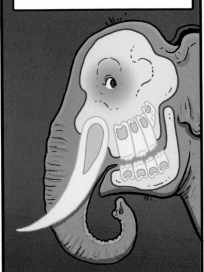

Calves are born with "milk tusks" that fall out around twelve months. Then permanent tusks start growing in—and they never stop! They can grow up to 17 cm (6.5 in) per year.

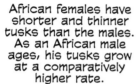

TUSKS!

African females have shorter and thinner tusks than the males. As an African male ages, his tusks grow at a comparatively higher rate.

Some elephants are tuskless, or at least appear tuskless. An Asian female's tusks are either completely missing or else not visible below her lip.

Who Wears Them Best?

CELEBRATE EVERY BODY

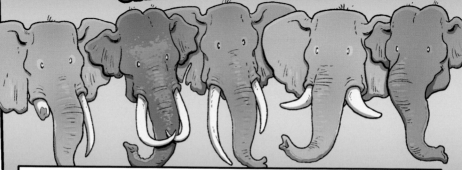

There's a wide variety of tusk size and symmetry. And just like humans have a dominant hand, elephants have a master tusk! My mother and sister are right-tusked but I'm left-tusked. I try not to be self-conscious about it; for me, left feels "right"!

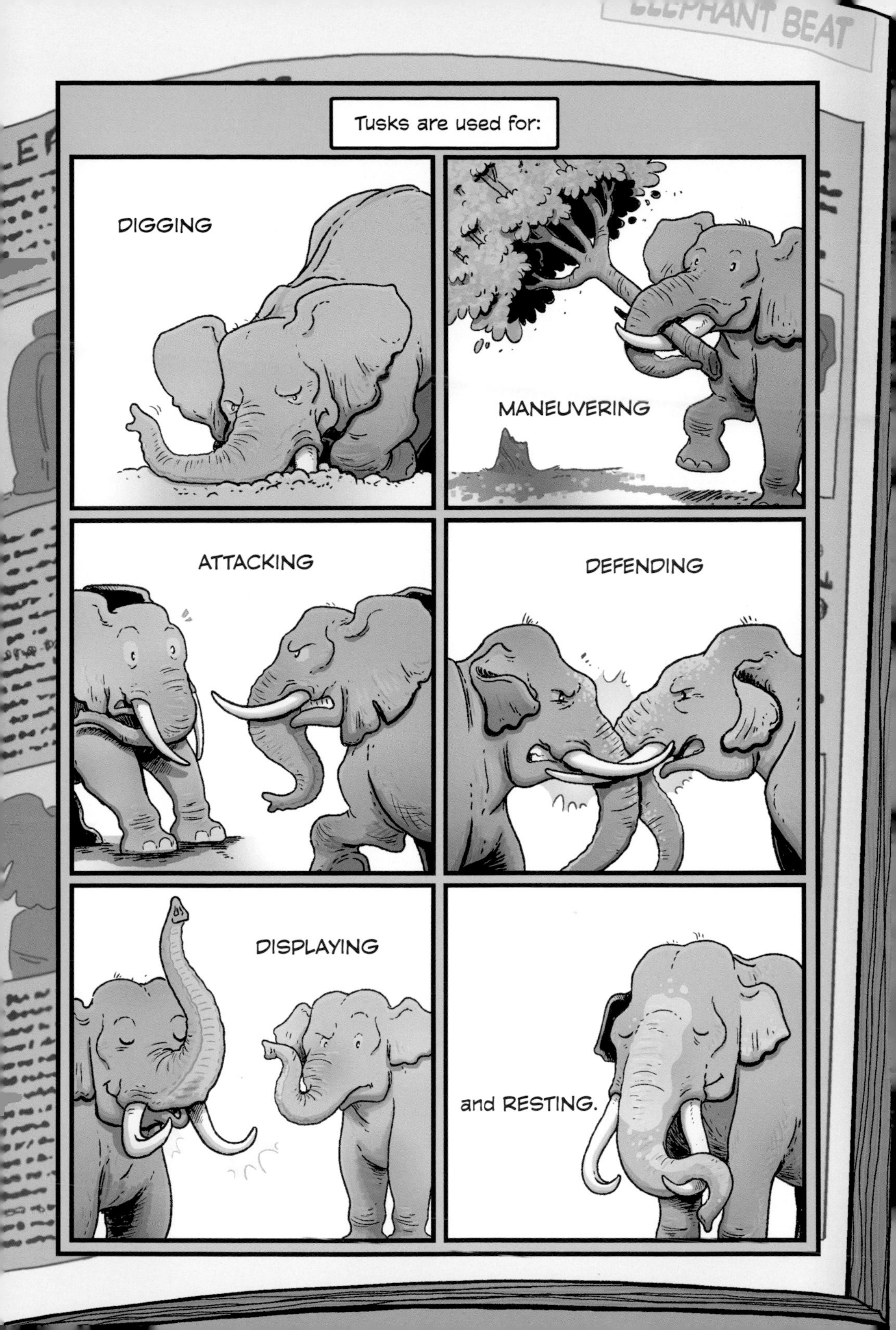
ELEPHANT BEAT
Tusks are used for:
DIGGING
MANEUVERING
ATTACKING
DEFENDING
DISPLAYING
and RESTING.

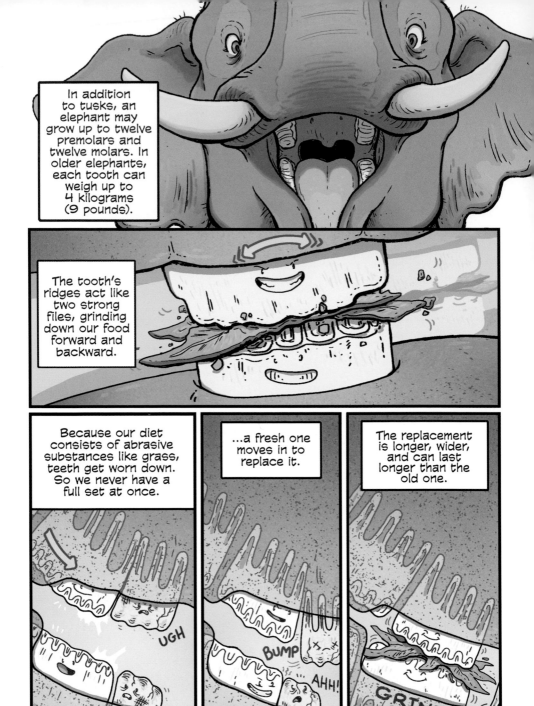

In addition to tusks, an elephant may grow up to twelve premolars and twelve molars. In older elephants, each tooth can weigh up to 4 kilograms (9 pounds).

The tooth's ridges act like two strong files, grinding down our food forward and backward.

Because our diet consists of abrasive substances like grass, teeth get worn down. So we never have a full set at once.

Instead, as one tooth starts to fall...

UGH

...a fresh one moves in to replace it.

BUMP

AHH!

The replacement is longer, wider, and can last longer than the old one.

GRIND

The worn-out tooth is pushed forward and wears down into a shelf in the front of the mouth. The tooth's roots are absorbed as the shelf breaks off.

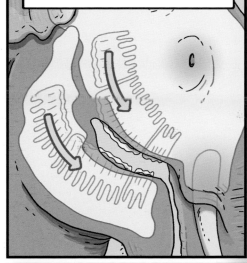

An elephant can go through six sets of teeth. At around age forty, only the final set is left.

These teeth need to last the rest of the elephant's life to allow proper chewing.

My sister says that Grandmother is on her last tooth.

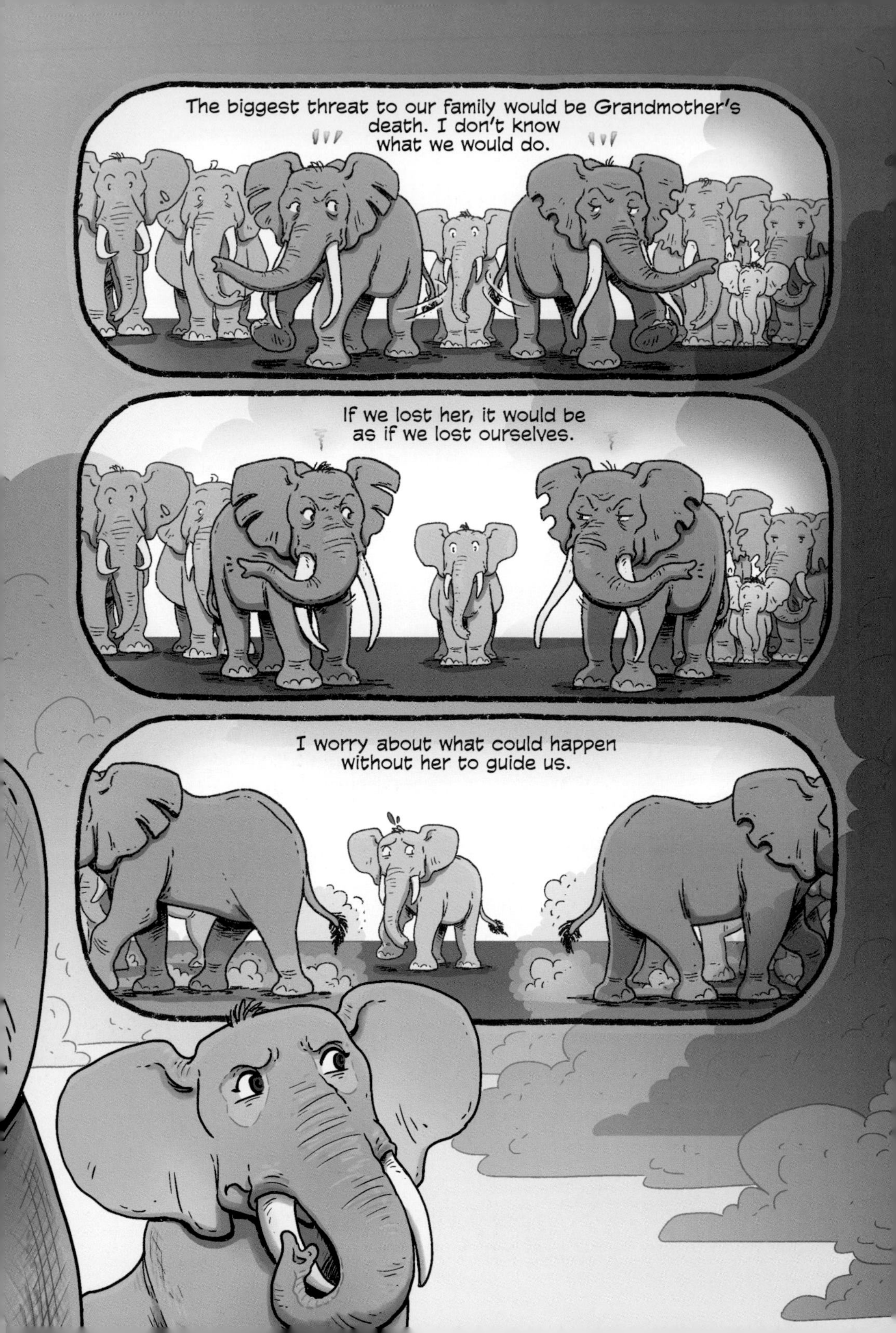
The biggest threat to our family would be Grandmother's death. I don't know what we would do.
If we lost her, it would be as if we lost ourselves.
I worry about what could happen without her to guide us.

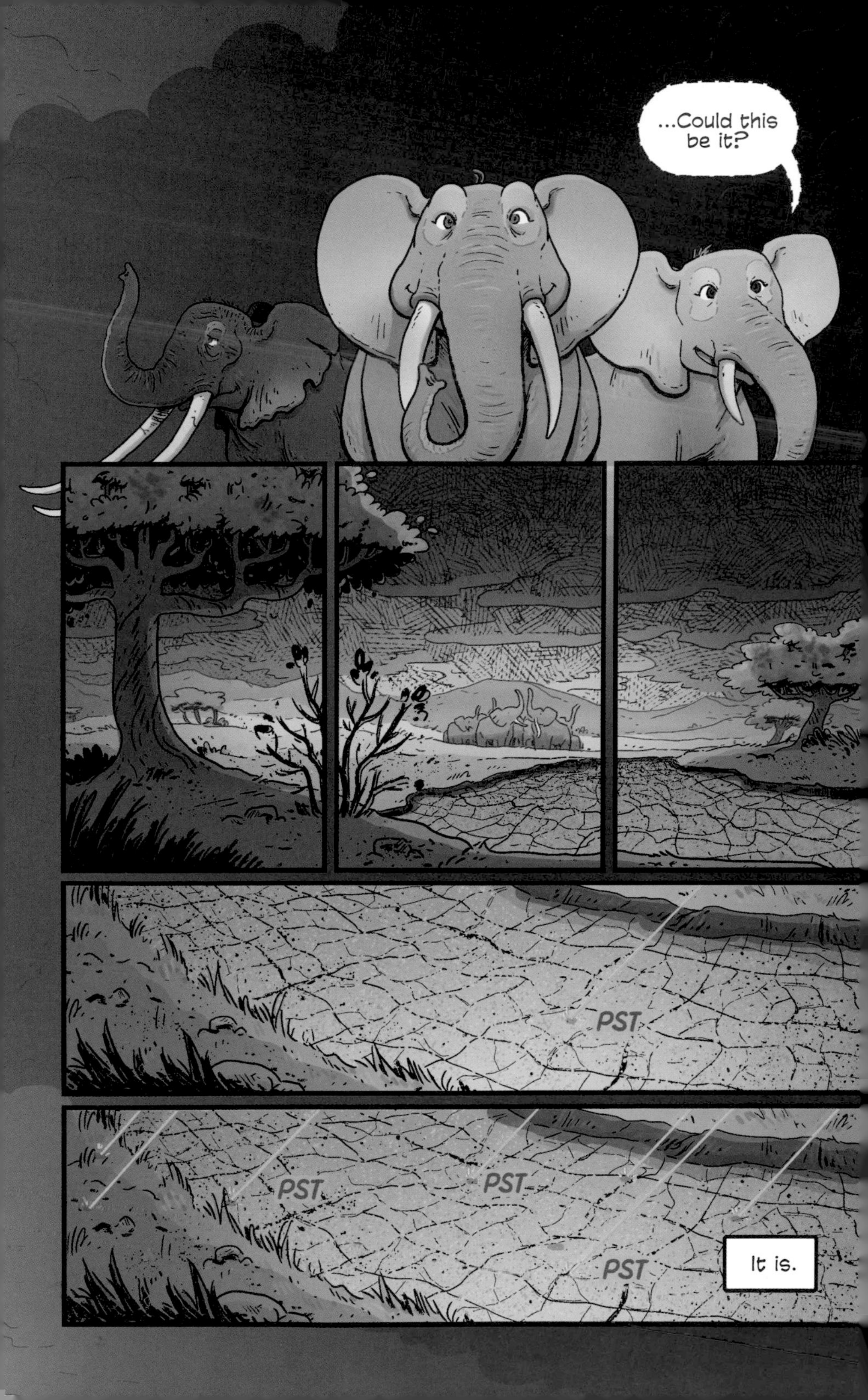
...Could this be it?
PST
PST
PST
PST
It is.

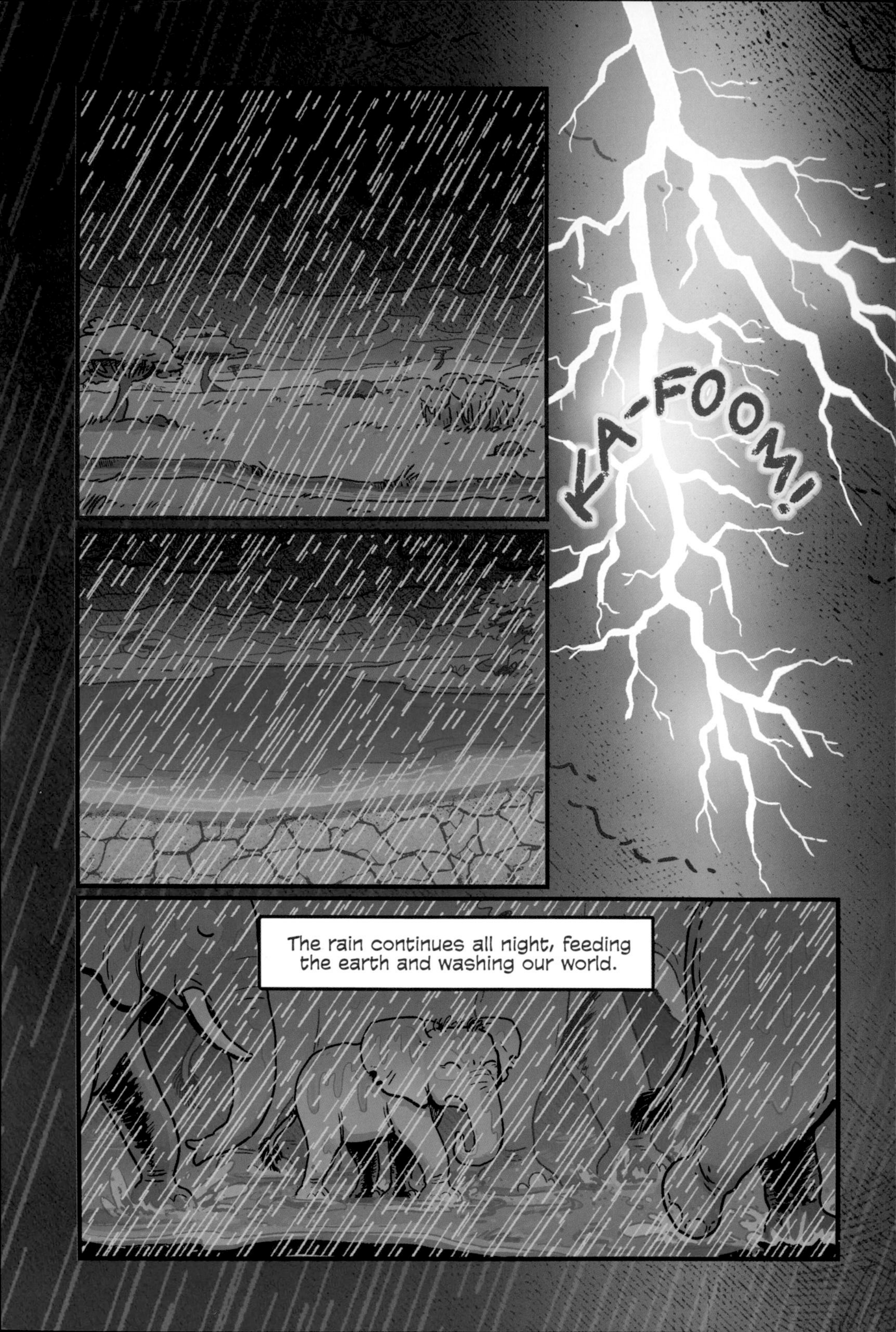
KA-FOOM!
The rain continues all night, feeding the earth and washing our world.

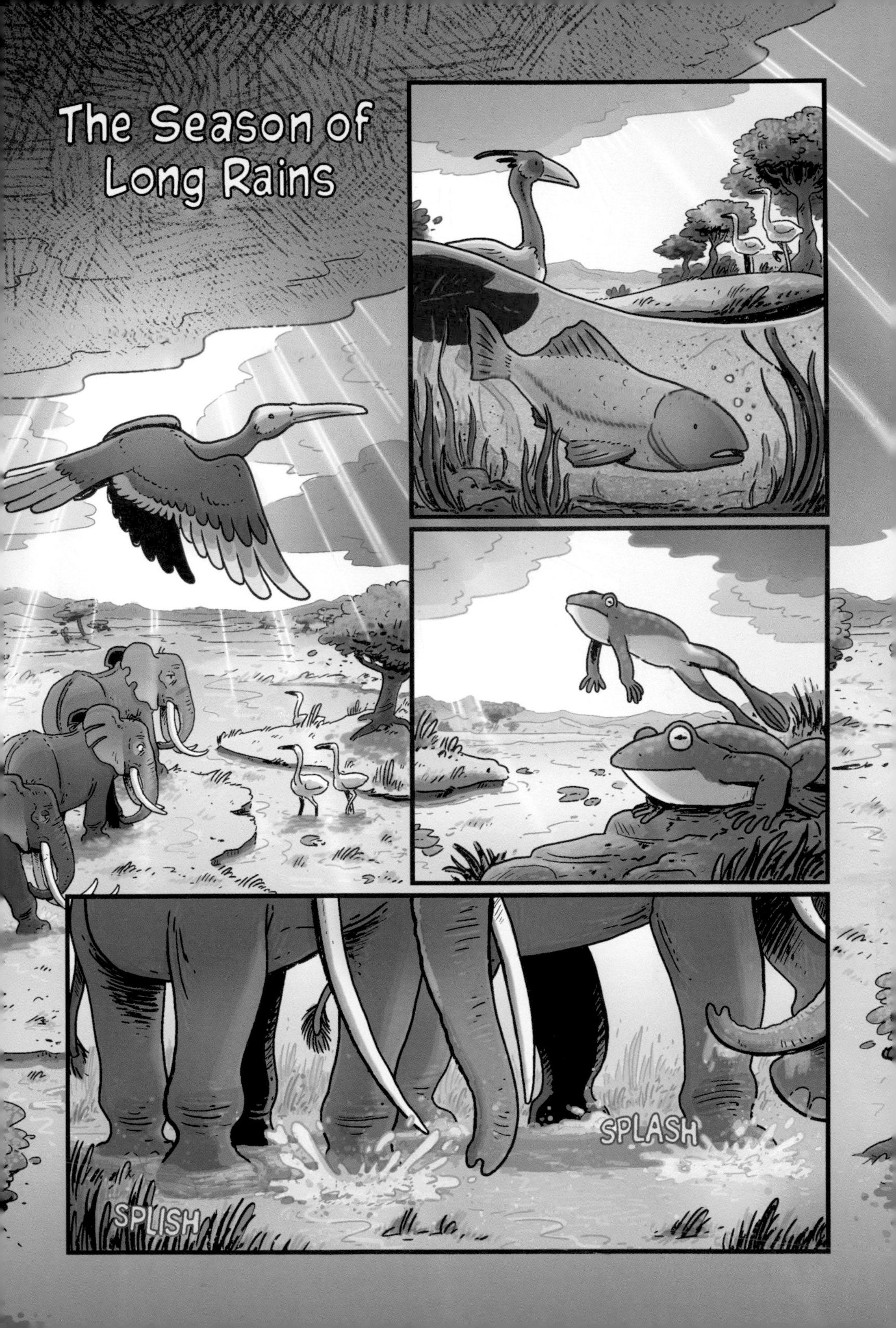
The Season of Long Rains
SPLASH
SPLISH

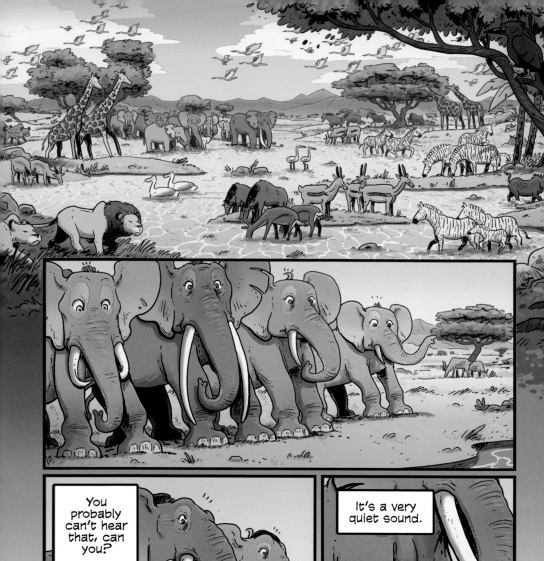

You probably can't hear that, can you?

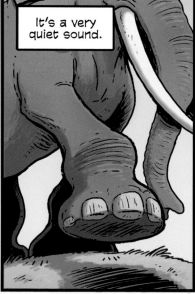

It's a very quiet sound.

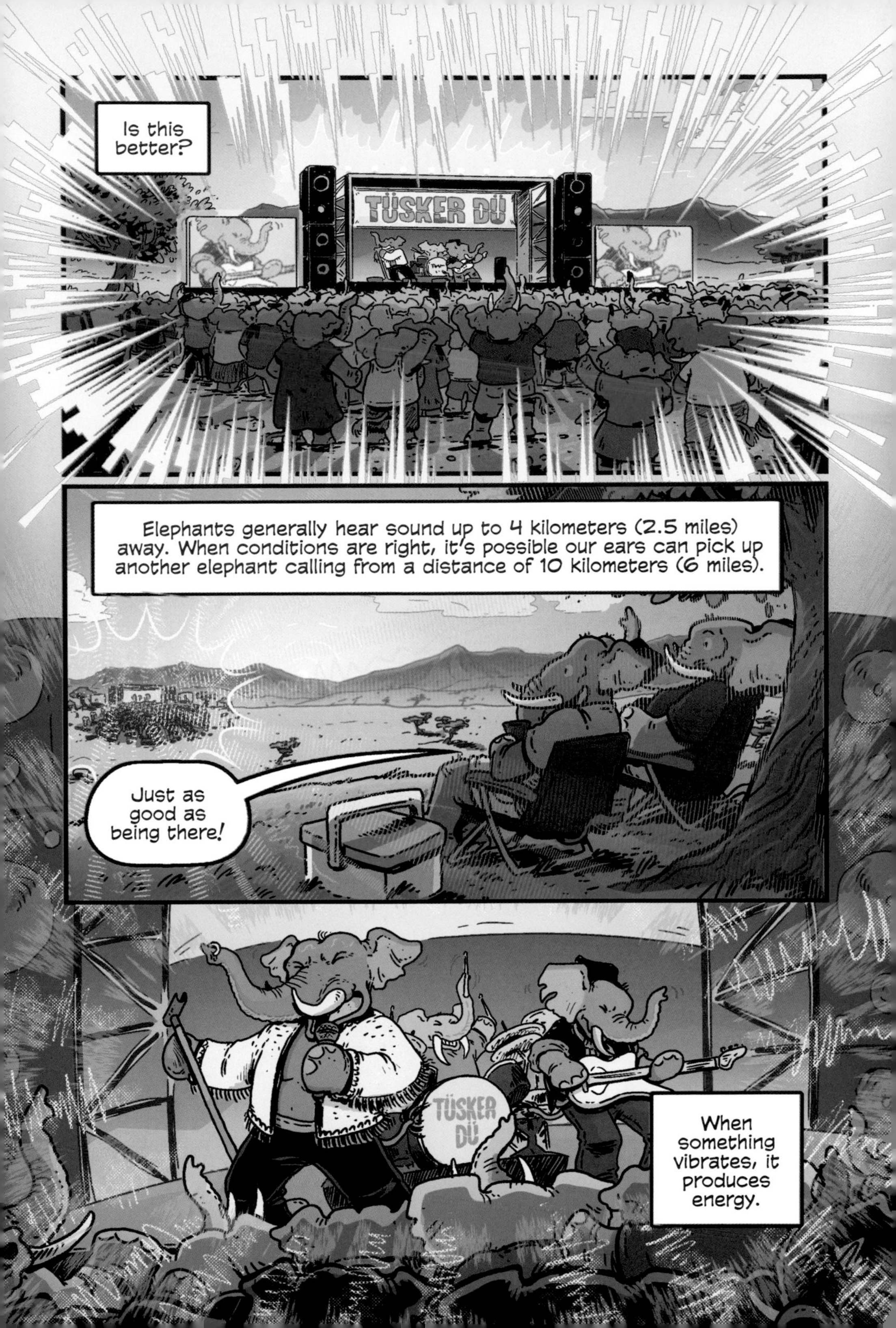

Is this better?
TÜSKER DÜ
Elephants generally hear sound up to 4 kilometers (2.5 miles) away. When conditions are right, it's possible our ears can pick up another elephant calling from a distance of 10 kilometers (6 miles).
Just as good as being there!
TÜSKER DÜ
When something vibrates, it produces energy.

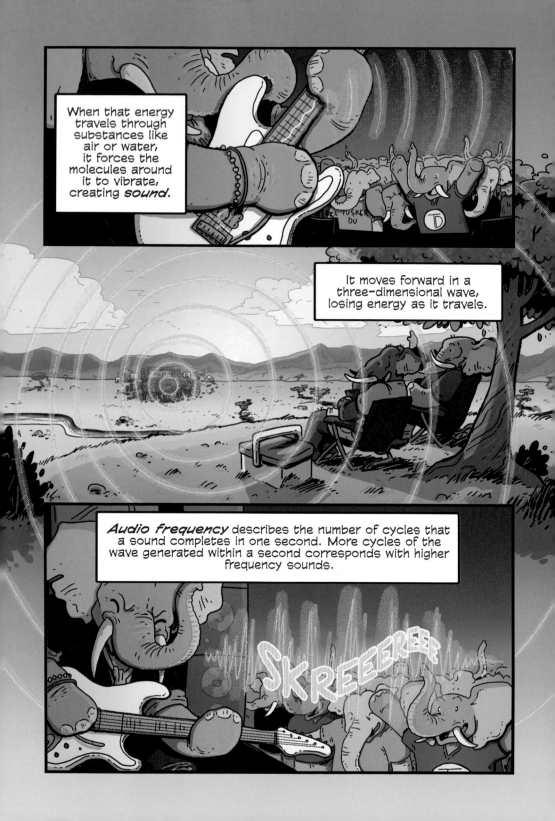

When that energy travels through substances like air or water, it forces the molecules around it to vibrate, creating *sound*.

It moves forward in a three-dimensional wave, losing energy as it travels.

Audio frequency describes the number of cycles that a sound completes in one second. More cycles of the wave generated within a second corresponds with higher frequency sounds.

SKREEEREE

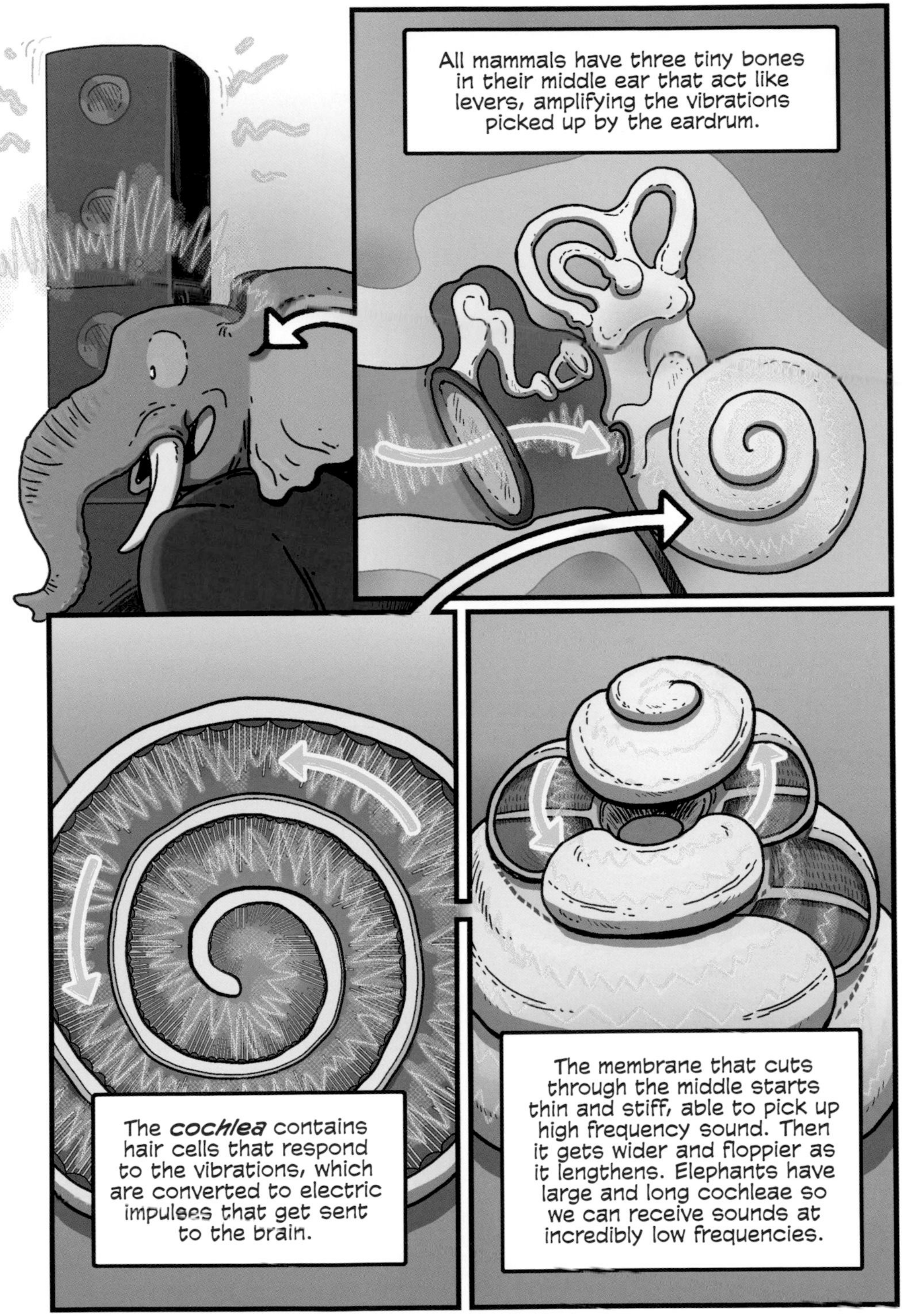
All mammals have three tiny bones in their middle ear that act like levers, amplifying the vibrations picked up by the eardrum.
The *cochlea* contains hair cells that respond to the vibrations, which are converted to electric impulses that get sent to the brain.
The membrane that cuts through the middle starts thin and stiff, able to pick up high frequency sound. Then it gets wider and floppier as it lengthens. Elephants have large and long cochleae so we can receive sounds at incredibly low frequencies.

But this sound is so quiet, even we can't hear it with our ears.

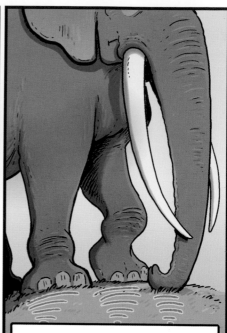

You might think of hearing and touch as two different senses. But it's not that simple.

Remember, sound comes from a vibration. Sometimes it travels through the air. But sometimes it's below our feet.

Oooooooh

Aeeeaiii

The speed at which sound travels depends partly on what it's traveling through. For example, sound travels faster in water than air.

And sometimes even faster in solid matter like the surface of the earth. Called *seismic communication*, this is how elephants send and receive sounds over long distances.

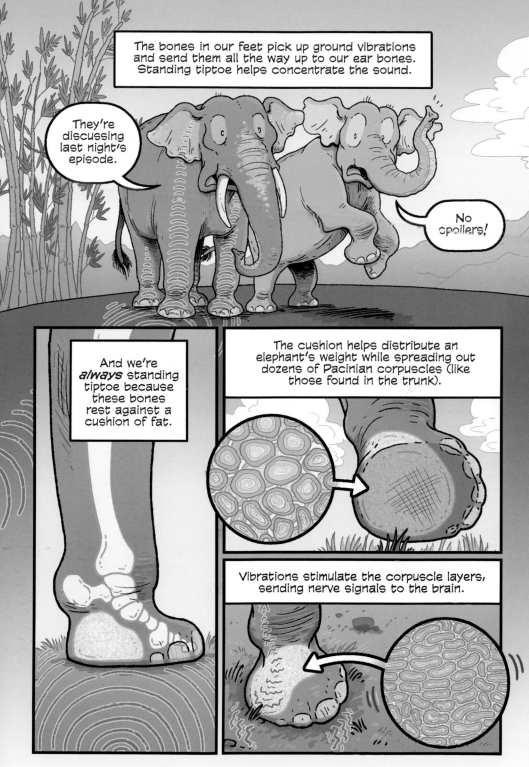

The bones in our feet pick up ground vibrations and send them all the way up to our ear bones. Standing tiptoe helps concentrate the sound.

They're discussing last night's episode.

No spoilers!

And we're *always* standing tiptoe because these bones rest against a cushion of fat.

The cushion helps distribute an elephant's weight while spreading out dozens of Pacinian corpuscles (like those found in the trunk).

Vibrations stimulate the corpuscle layers, sending nerve signals to the brain.

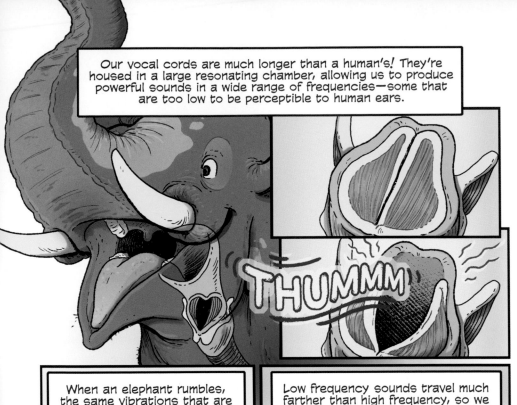

Our vocal cords are much longer than a human's! They're housed in a large resonating chamber, allowing us to produce powerful sounds in a wide range of frequencies—some that are too low to be perceptible to human ears.

THUMMM

When an elephant rumbles, the same vibrations that are sent through the air are also sent in the ground.

Can you believe that ending?

Low frequency sounds travel much farther than high frequency, so we can pick up these seismic signals a great distance away.

I really should start watching that show.

BUS STOP

Can you believe that ending?

Even through our feet, we can tell who's talking. Elephants respond more strongly to a rumble coming from a family member than one from another herd.

It's so good!

Darlene's never steered me wrong.

Start with the second season!

52

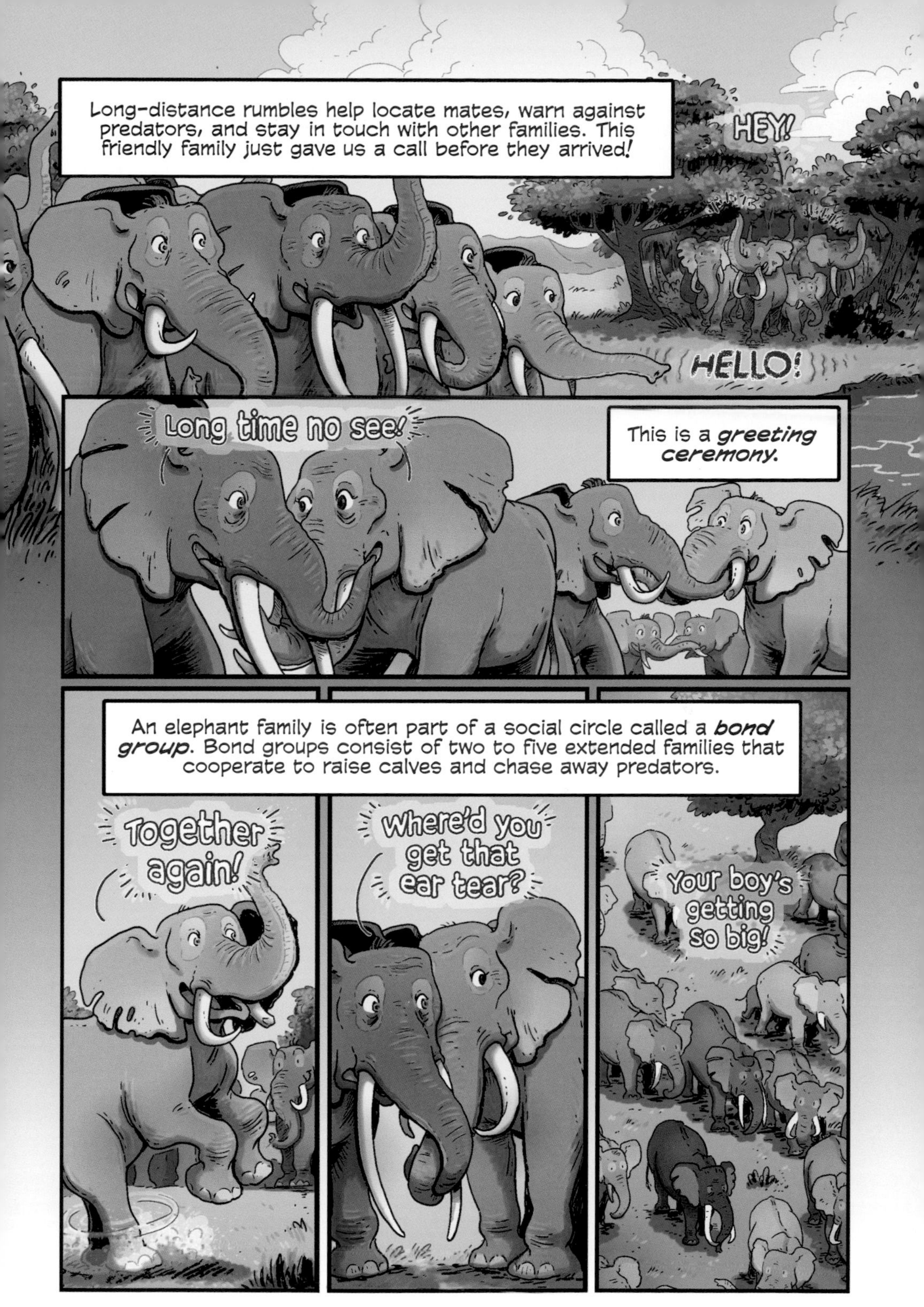

Long-distance rumbles help locate mates, warn against predators, and stay in touch with other families. This friendly family just gave us a call before they arrived!
HEY!
HELLO!
Long time no see!
This is a *greeting ceremony.*
An elephant family is often part of a social circle called a ***bond group***. Bond groups consist of two to five extended families that cooperate to raise calves and chase away predators.
Together again!
Where'd you get that ear tear?
Your boy's getting so big!

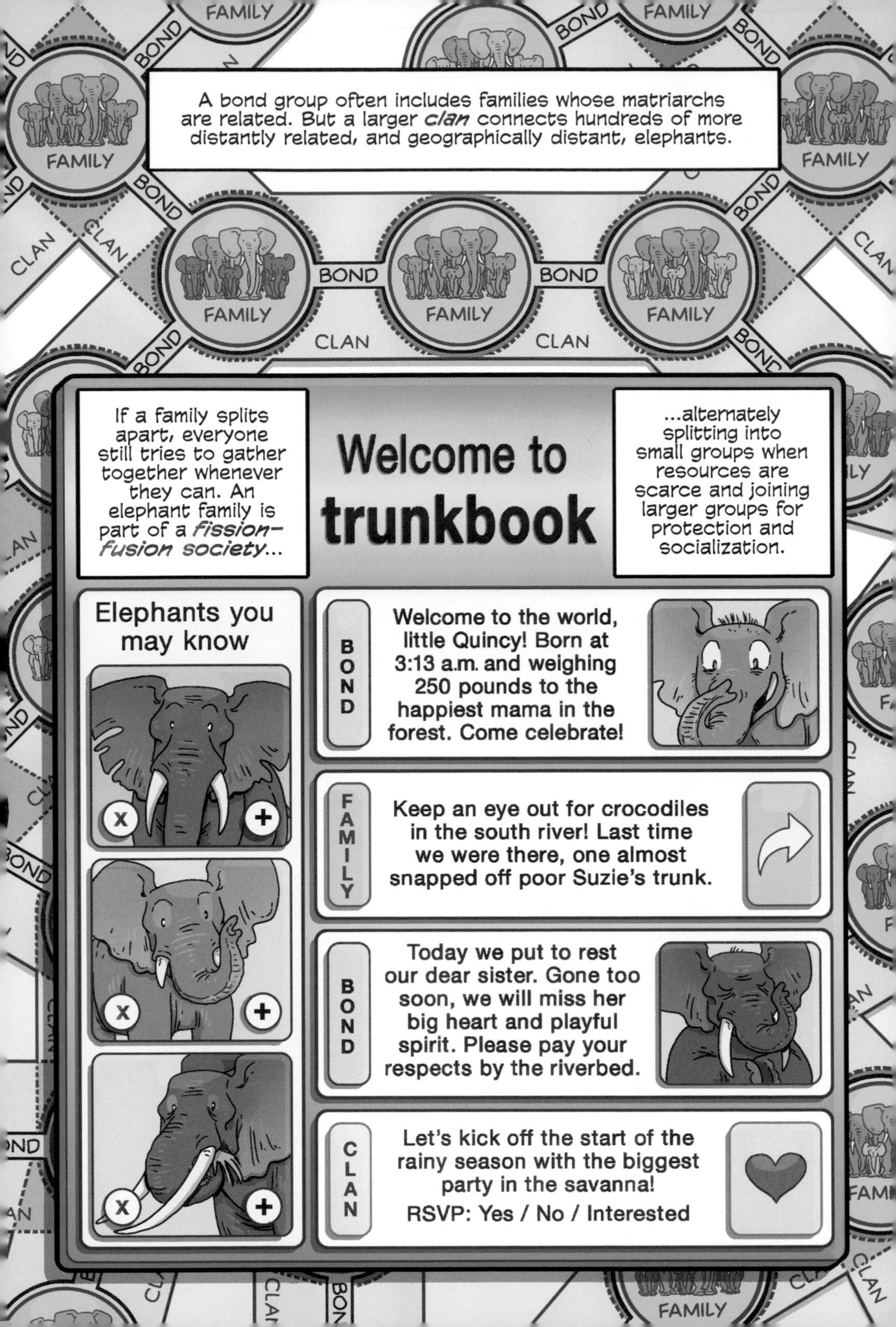

A bond group often includes families whose matriarchs are related. But a larger *clan* connects hundreds of more distantly related, and geographically distant, elephants.
FAMILY
BOND
CLAN
If a family splits apart, everyone still tries to gather together whenever they can. An elephant family is part of a *fission-fusion society*...
Welcome to trunkbook
...alternately splitting into small groups when resources are scarce and joining larger groups for protection and socialization.
Elephants you may know
BOND
Welcome to the world, little Quincy! Born at 3:13 a.m. and weighing 250 pounds to the happiest mama in the forest. Come celebrate!
FAMILY
Keep an eye out for crocodiles in the south river! Last time we were there, one almost snapped off poor Suzie's trunk.
BOND
Today we put to rest our dear sister. Gone too soon, we will miss her big heart and playful spirit. Please pay your respects by the riverbed.
CLAN
Let's kick off the start of the rainy season with the biggest party in the savanna!
RSVP: Yes / No / Interested

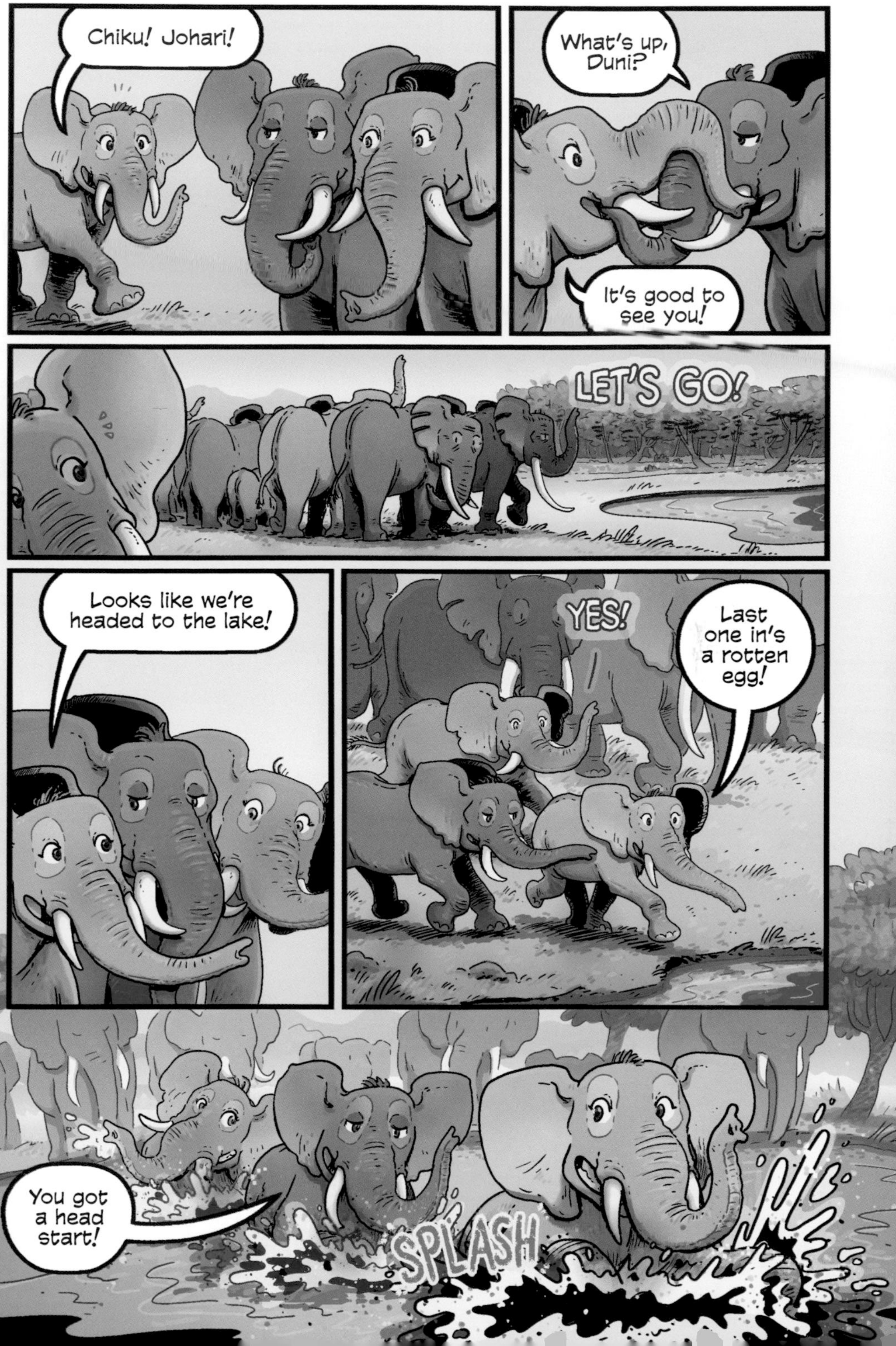
Chiku! Johari!
What's up, Duni?
It's good to see you!
LET'S GO!
Looks like we're headed to the lake!
YES!
Last one in's a rotten egg!
You got a head start!
SPLASH

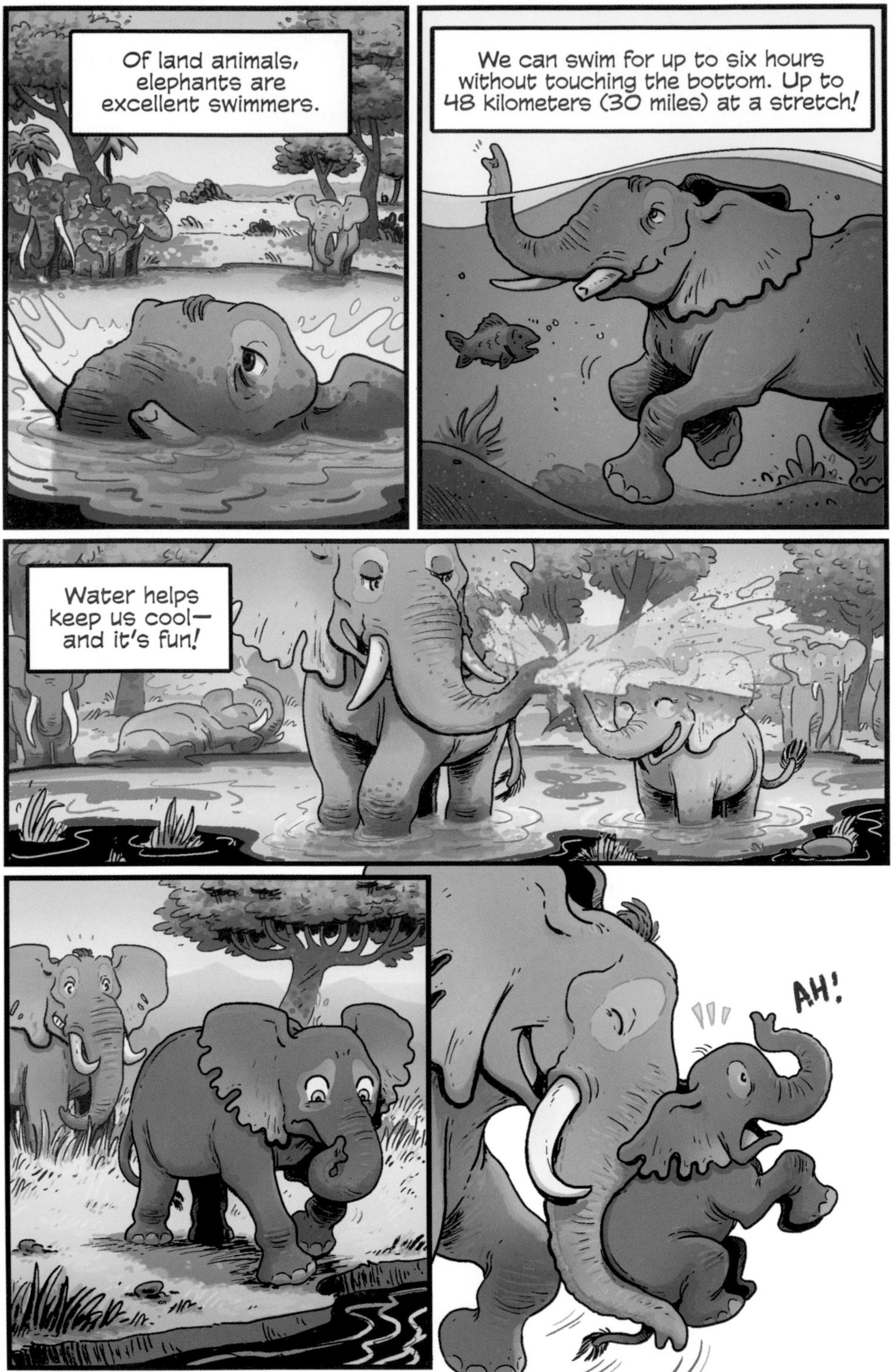
Of land animals, elephants are excellent swimmers.
We can swim for up to six hours without touching the bottom. Up to 48 kilometers (30 miles) at a stretch!
Water helps keep us cool—and it's fun!
AH!

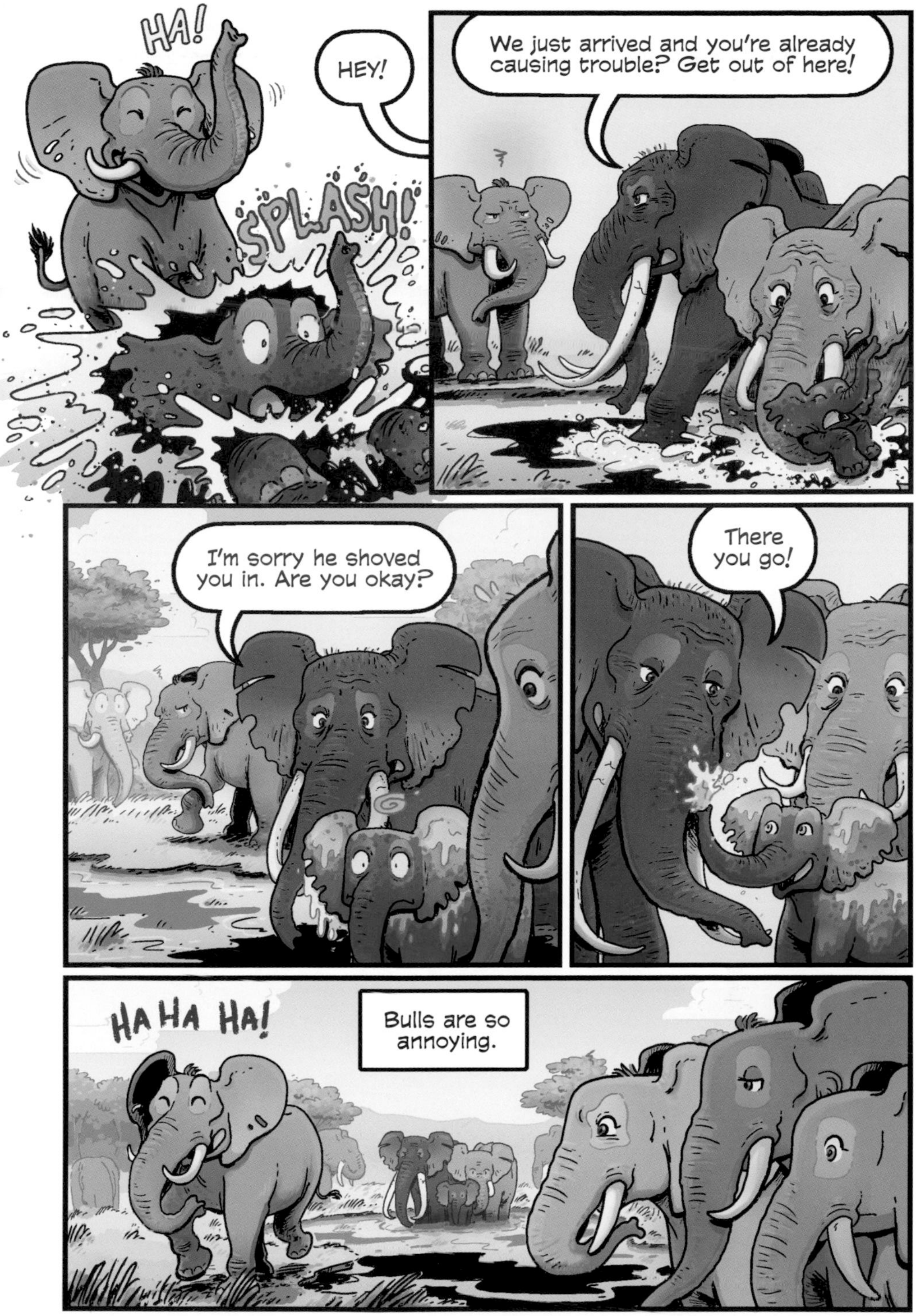
HA!
SPLASH!
HEY!
We just arrived and you're already causing trouble? Get out of here!
I'm sorry he shoved you in. Are you okay?
There you go!
HA HA HA!
Bulls are so annoying.

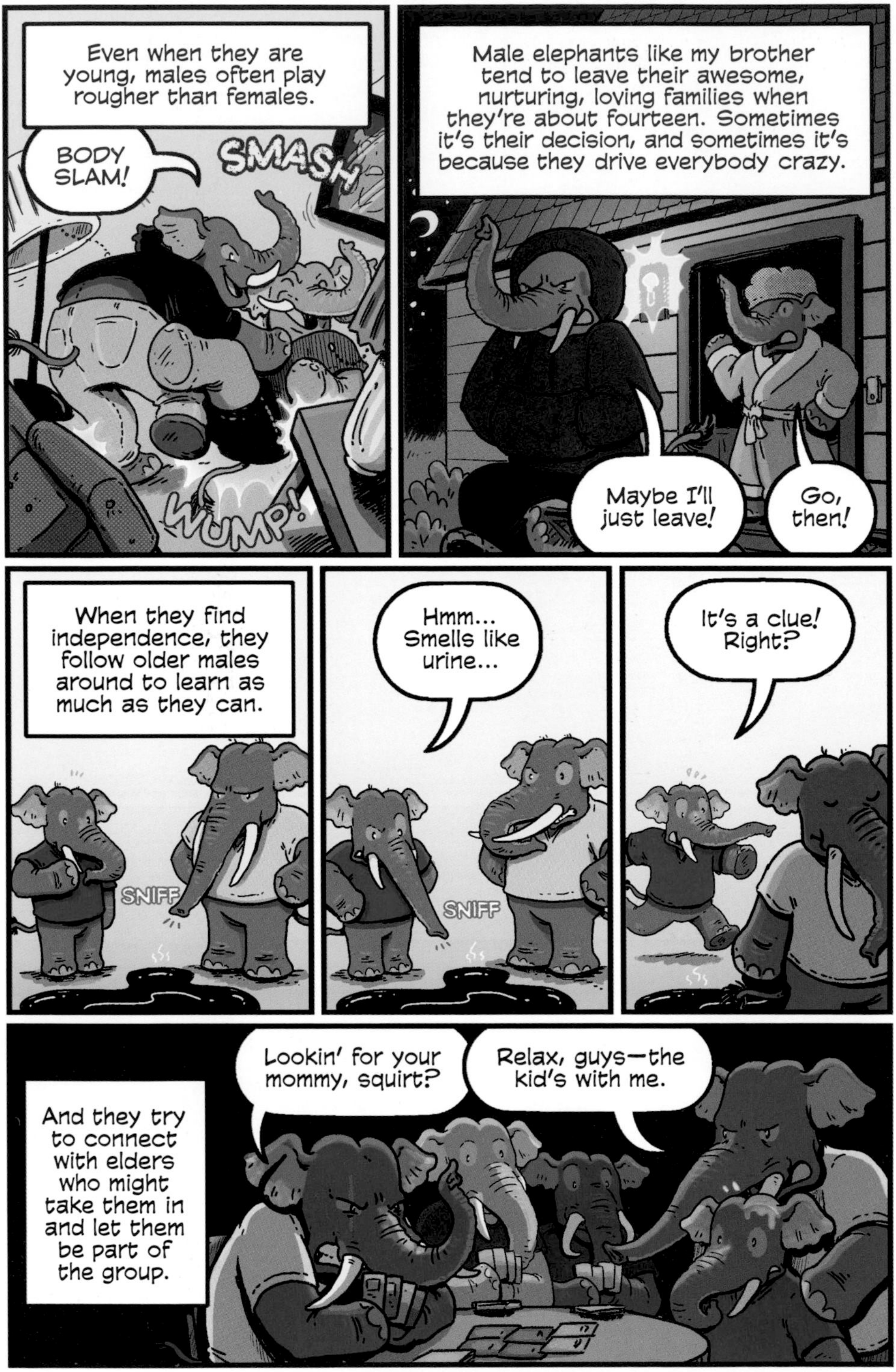
Even when they are young, males often play rougher than females.
BODY SLAM!
SMASH
WUMP!
Male elephants like my brother tend to leave their awesome, nurturing, loving families when they're about fourteen. Sometimes it's their decision, and sometimes it's because they drive everybody crazy.
Maybe I'll just leave!
Go, then!
When they find independence, they follow older males around to learn as much as they can.
SNIFF
Hmm... Smells like urine...
SNIFF
It's a clue! Right?
And they try to connect with elders who might take them in and let them be part of the group.
Lookin' for your mommy, squirt?
Relax, guys—the kid's with me.

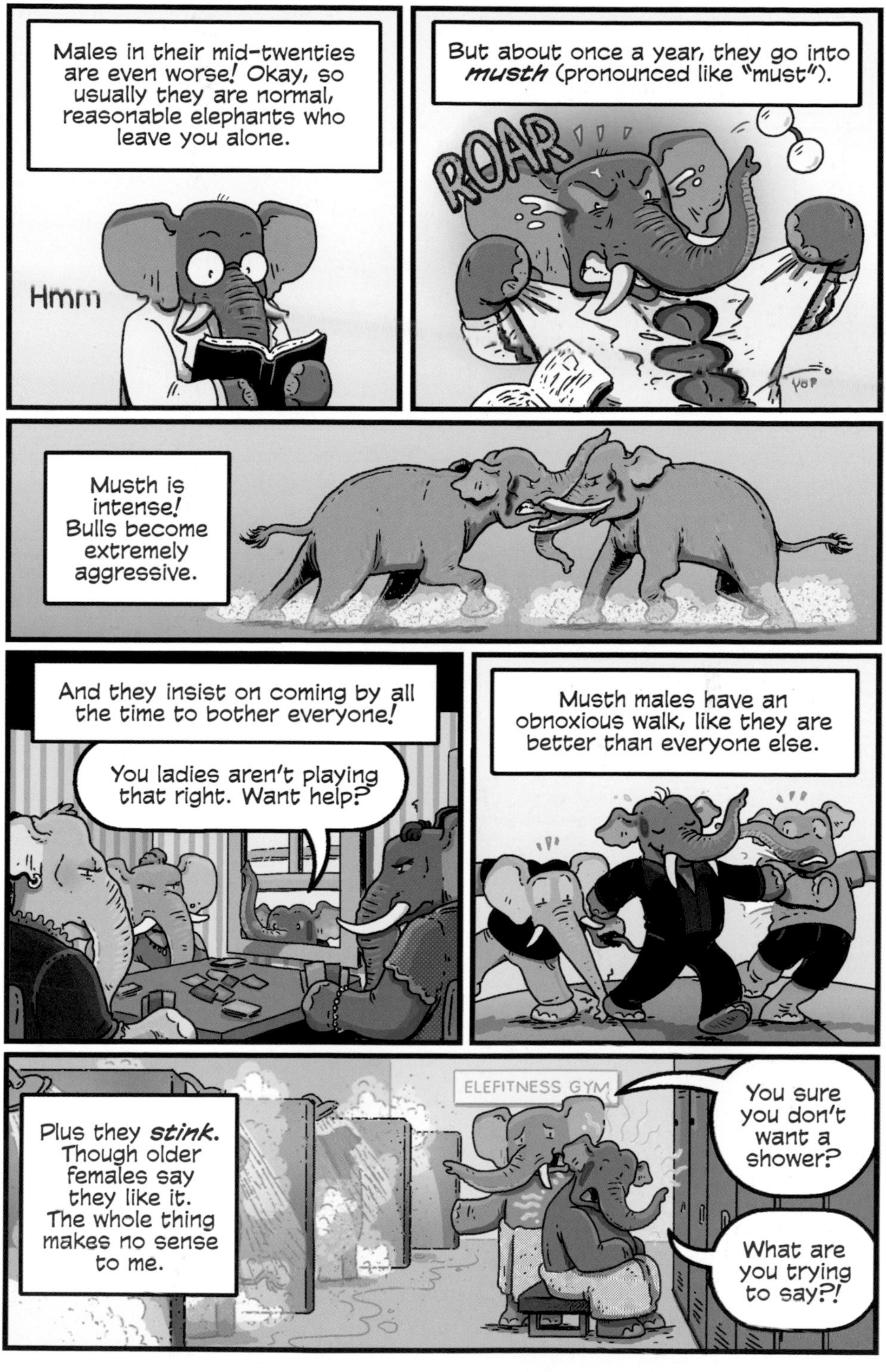
Males in their mid-twenties are even worse! Okay, so usually they are normal, reasonable elephants who leave you alone.
Hmm
But about once a year, they go into *musth* (pronounced like "must").
ROAR
Musth is intense! Bulls become extremely aggressive.
And they insist on coming by all the time to bother everyone!
You ladies aren't playing that right. Want help?
Musth males have an obnoxious walk, like they are better than everyone else.
ELEFITNESS GYM
Plus they *stink*. Though older females say they like it. The whole thing makes no sense to me.
You sure you don't want a shower?
What are you trying to say?!

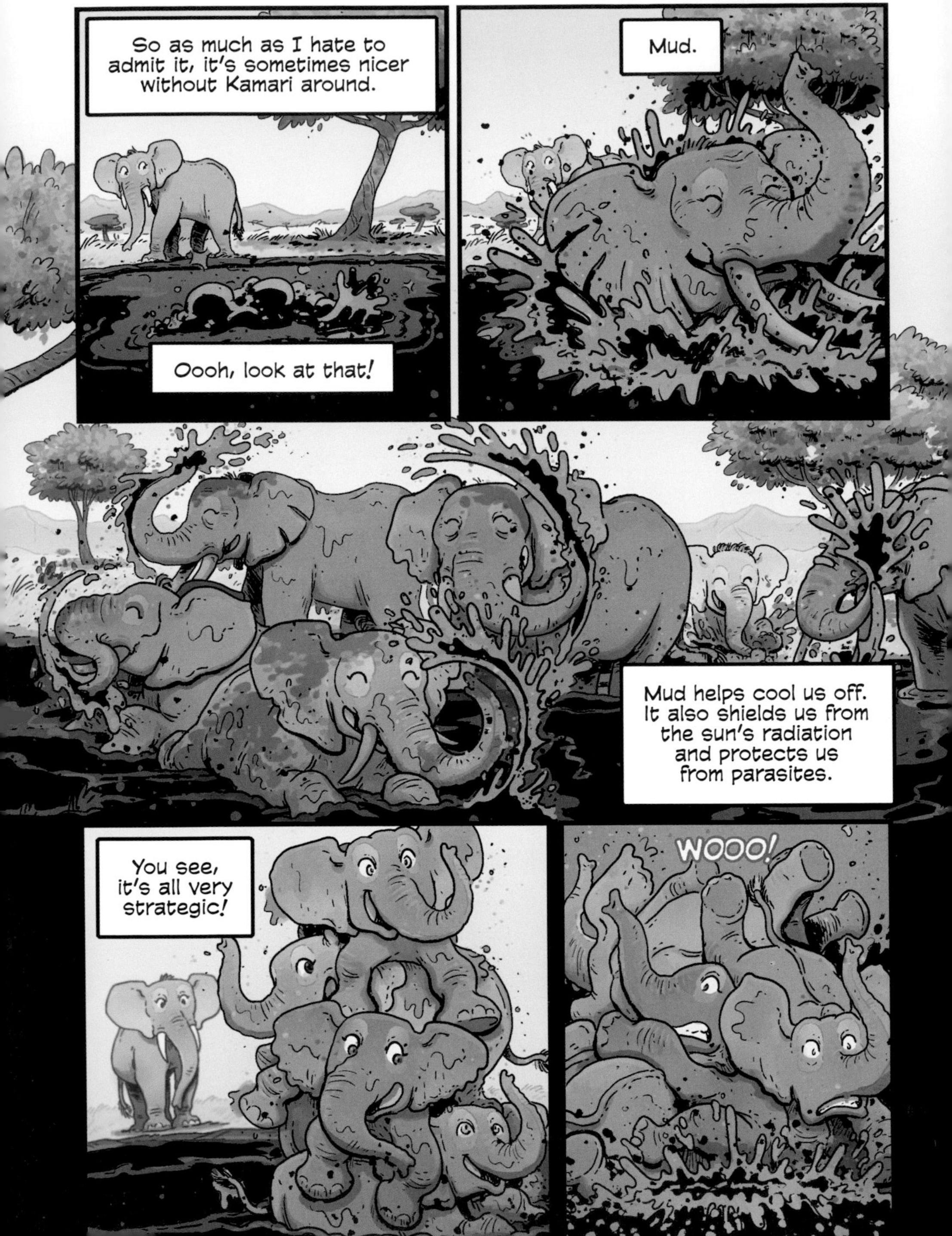

So as much as I hate to admit it, it's sometimes nicer without Kamari around.
Oooh, look at that!
Mud.
Mud helps cool us off. It also shields us from the sun's radiation and protects us from parasites.
You see, it's all very strategic!
WOOO!

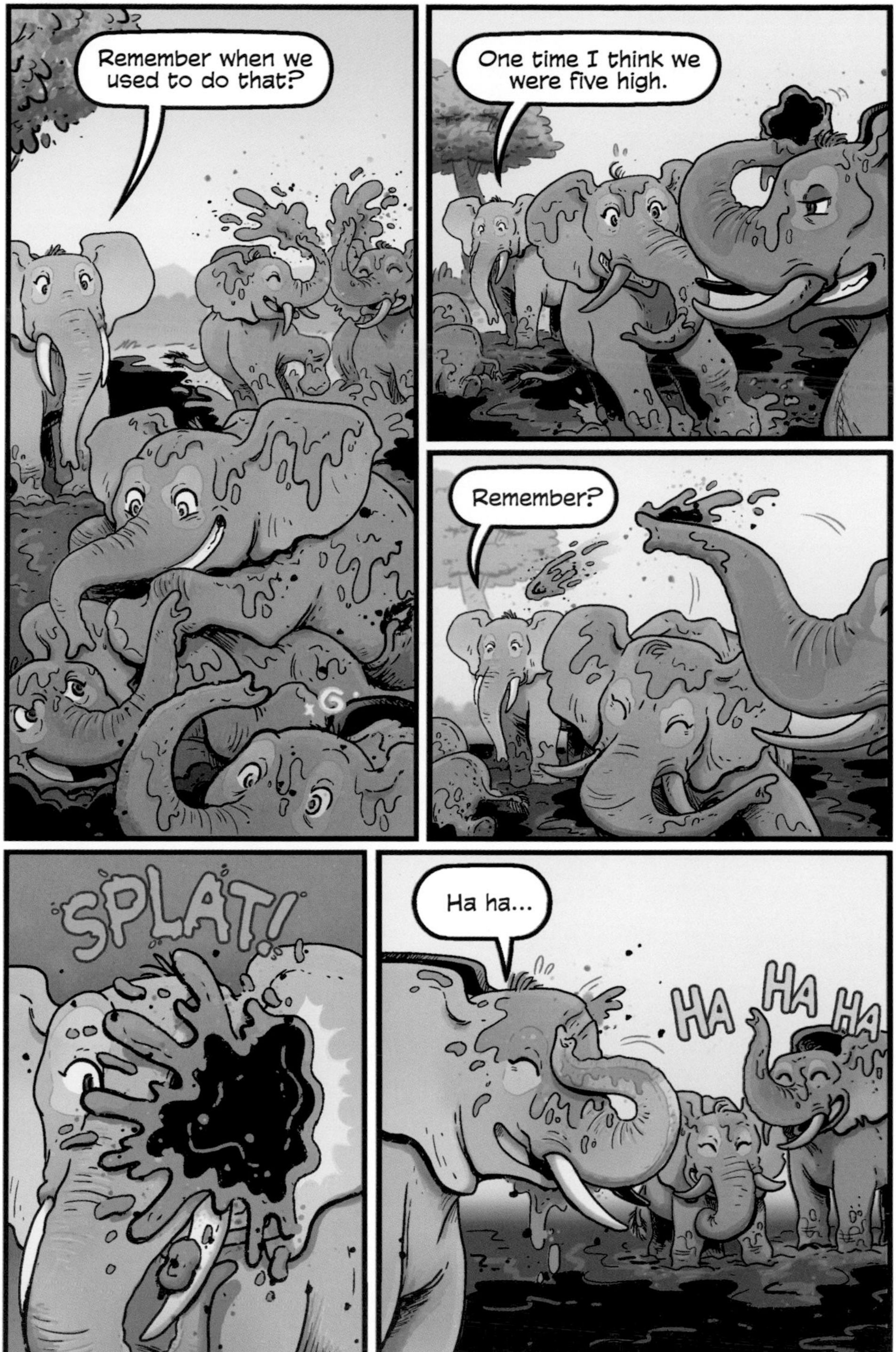
Remember when we used to do that?
One time I think we were five high.
Remember?
SPLAT!
Ha ha...
HA HA HA

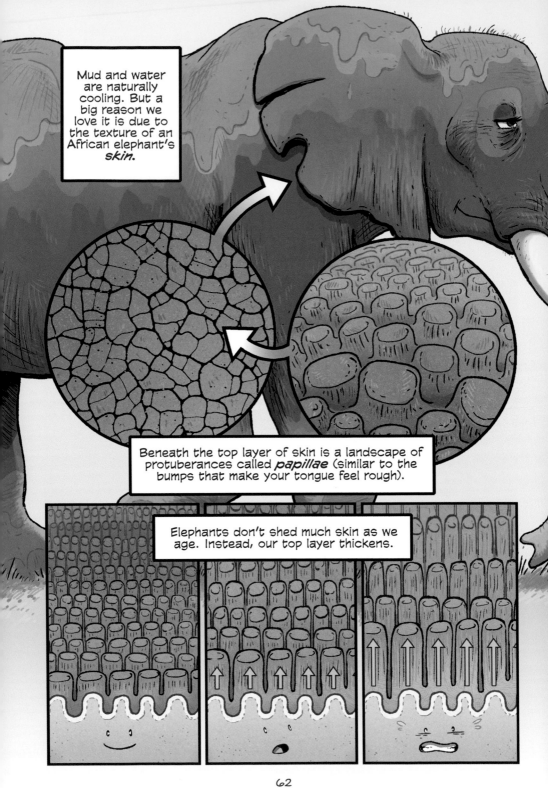

Mud and water are naturally cooling. But a big reason we love it is due to the texture of an African elephant's *skin*.

Beneath the top layer of skin is a landscape of protuberances called *papillae* (similar to the bumps that make your tongue feel rough).

Elephants don't shed much skin as we age. Instead, our top layer thickens.

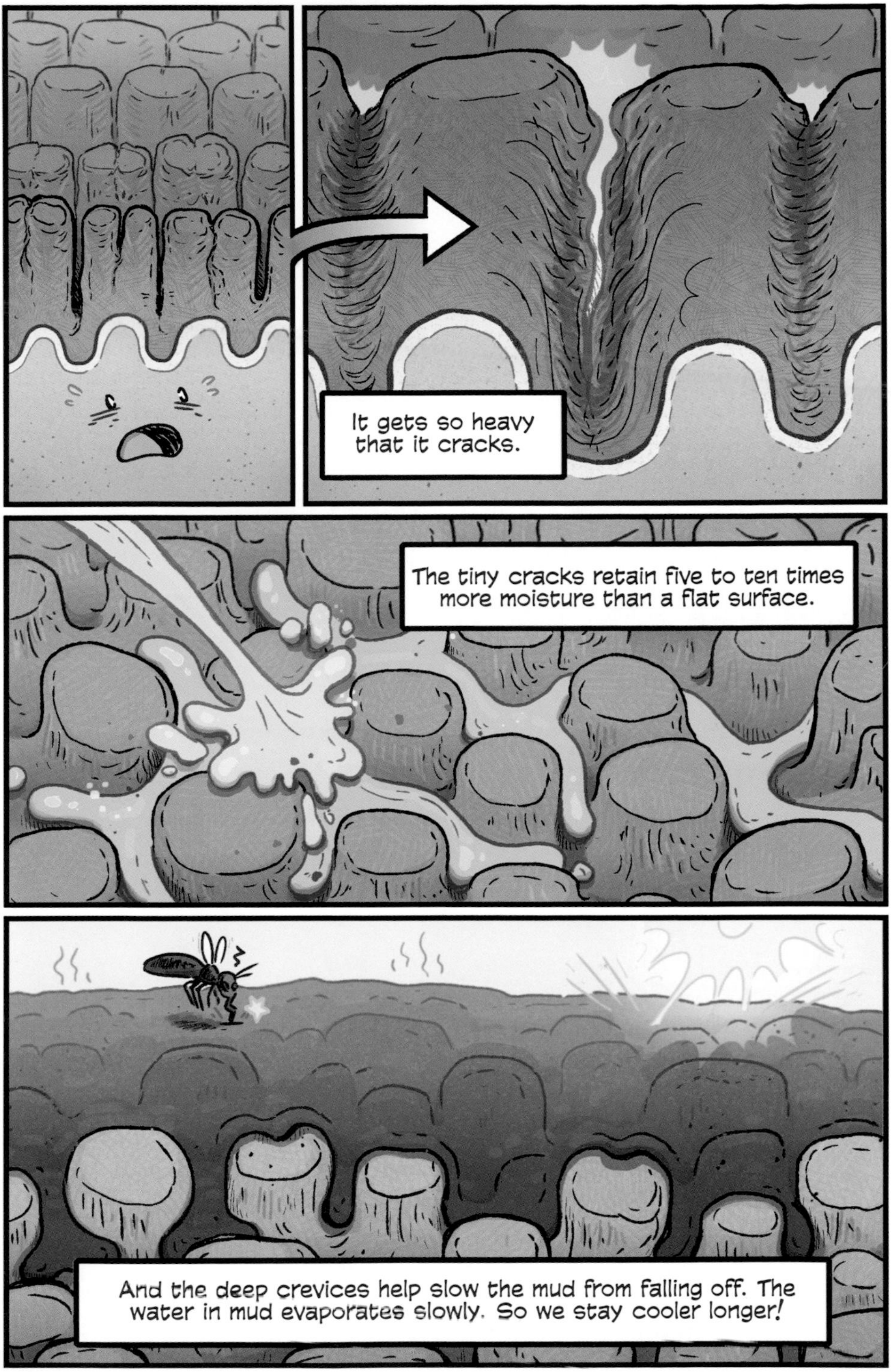
It gets so heavy that it cracks.
The tiny cracks retain five to ten times more moisture than a flat surface.
And the deep crevices help slow the mud from falling off. The water in mud evaporates slowly. So we stay cooler longer!

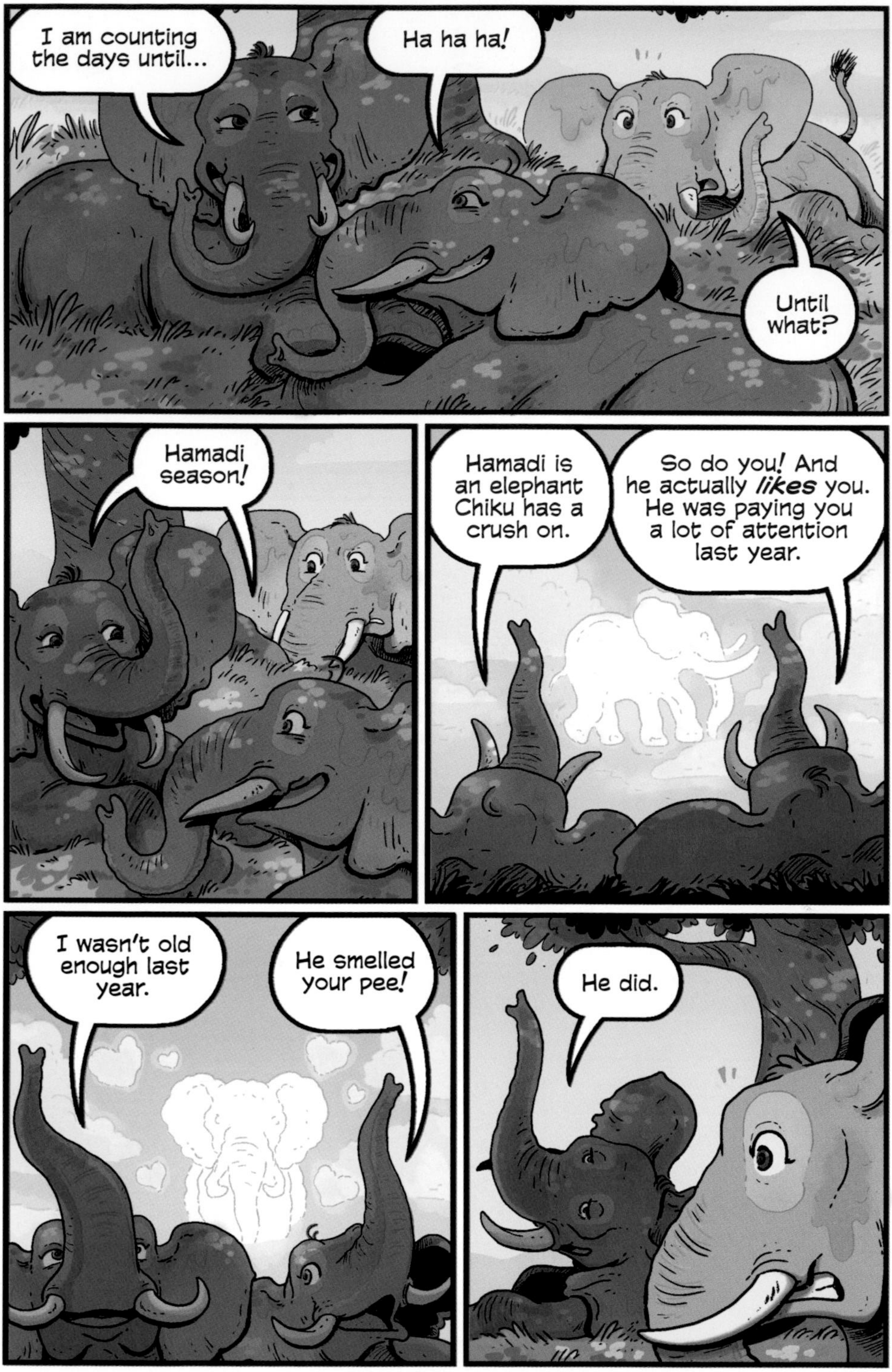
I am counting the days until...
Ha ha ha!
Until what?
Hamadi season!
Hamadi is an elephant Chiku has a crush on.
So do you! And he actually *likes* you. He was paying you a lot of attention last year.
I wasn't old enough last year.
He smelled your pee!
He did.

He was there when the whole clan got together last year, Duni.

You know who I'm talking about, right?

I guess I *must*...

If we're lucky he'll be *in* musth!

Ha!

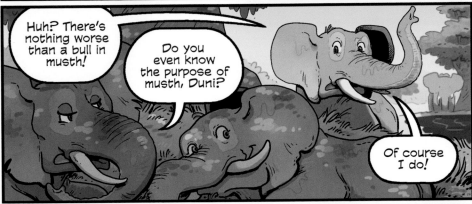

Huh? There's nothing worse than a bull in musth!

Do you even know the purpose of musth, Duni?

Of course I do!

...

Hamadi season!

Hee hee!

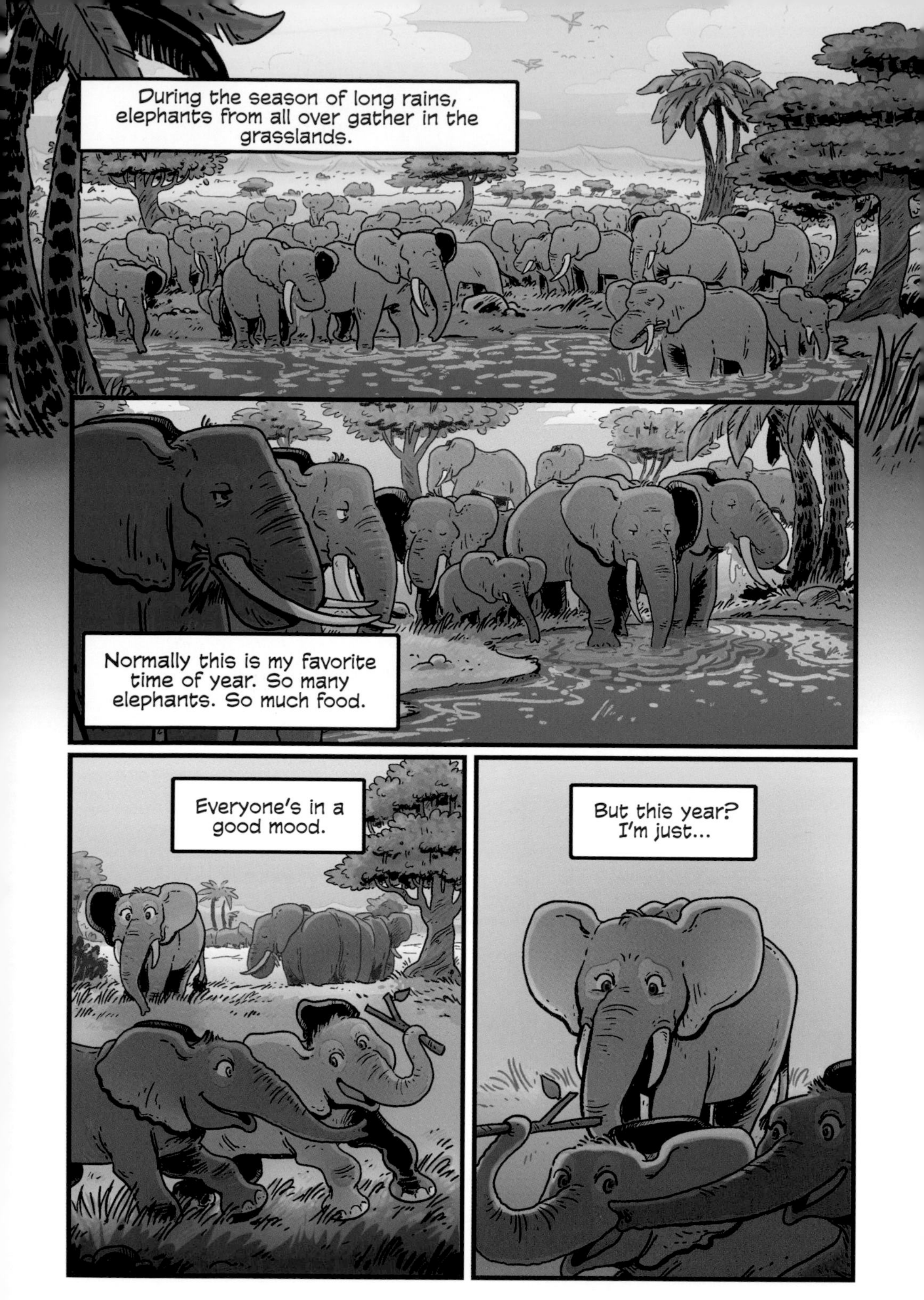
During the season of long rains, elephants from all over gather in the grasslands.
Normally this is my favorite time of year. So many elephants. So much food.
Everyone's in a good mood.
But this year? I'm just...

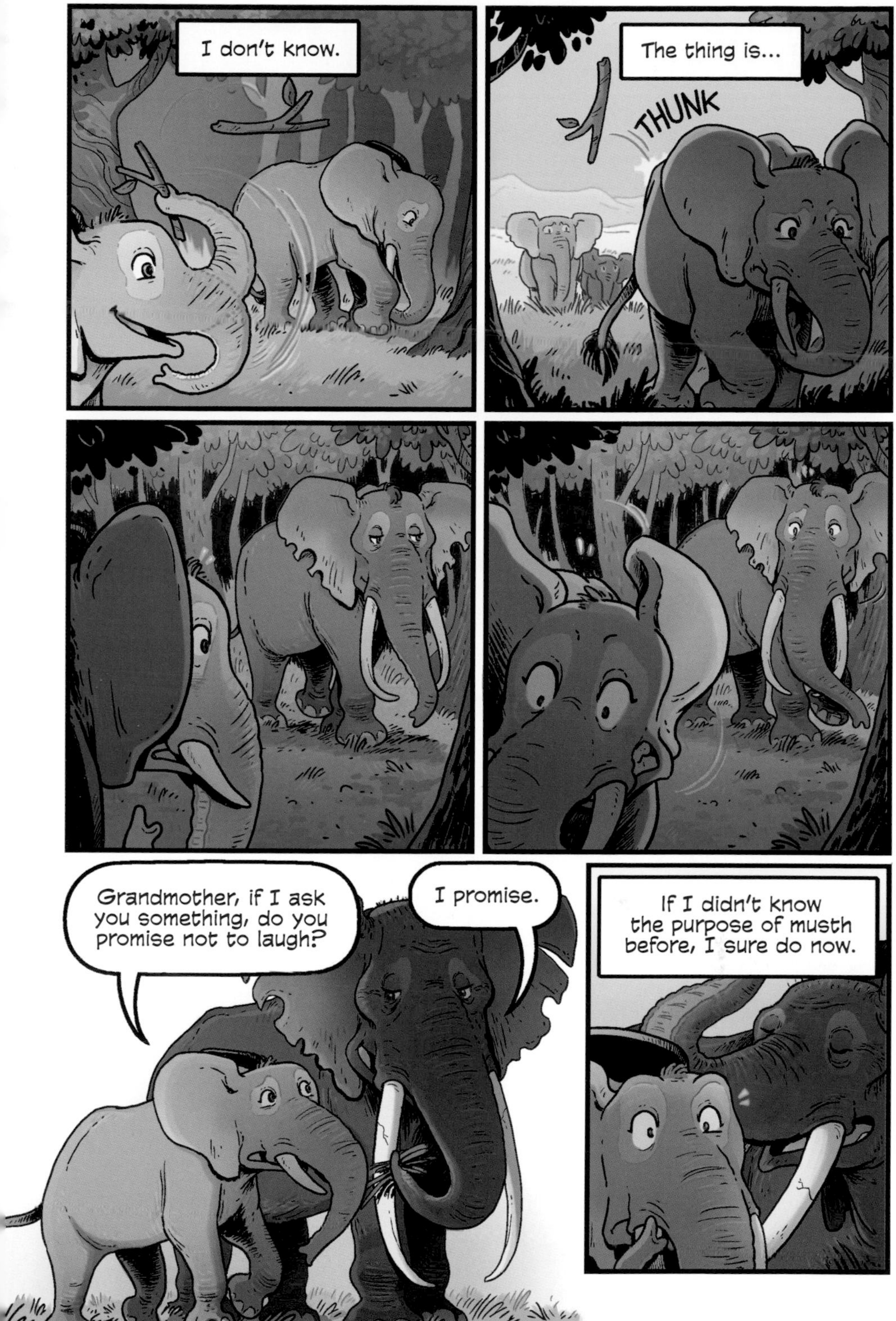

I don't know.
The thing is...
THUNK
Grandmother, if I ask you something, do you promise not to laugh?
I promise.
If I didn't know the purpose of musth before, I sure do now.

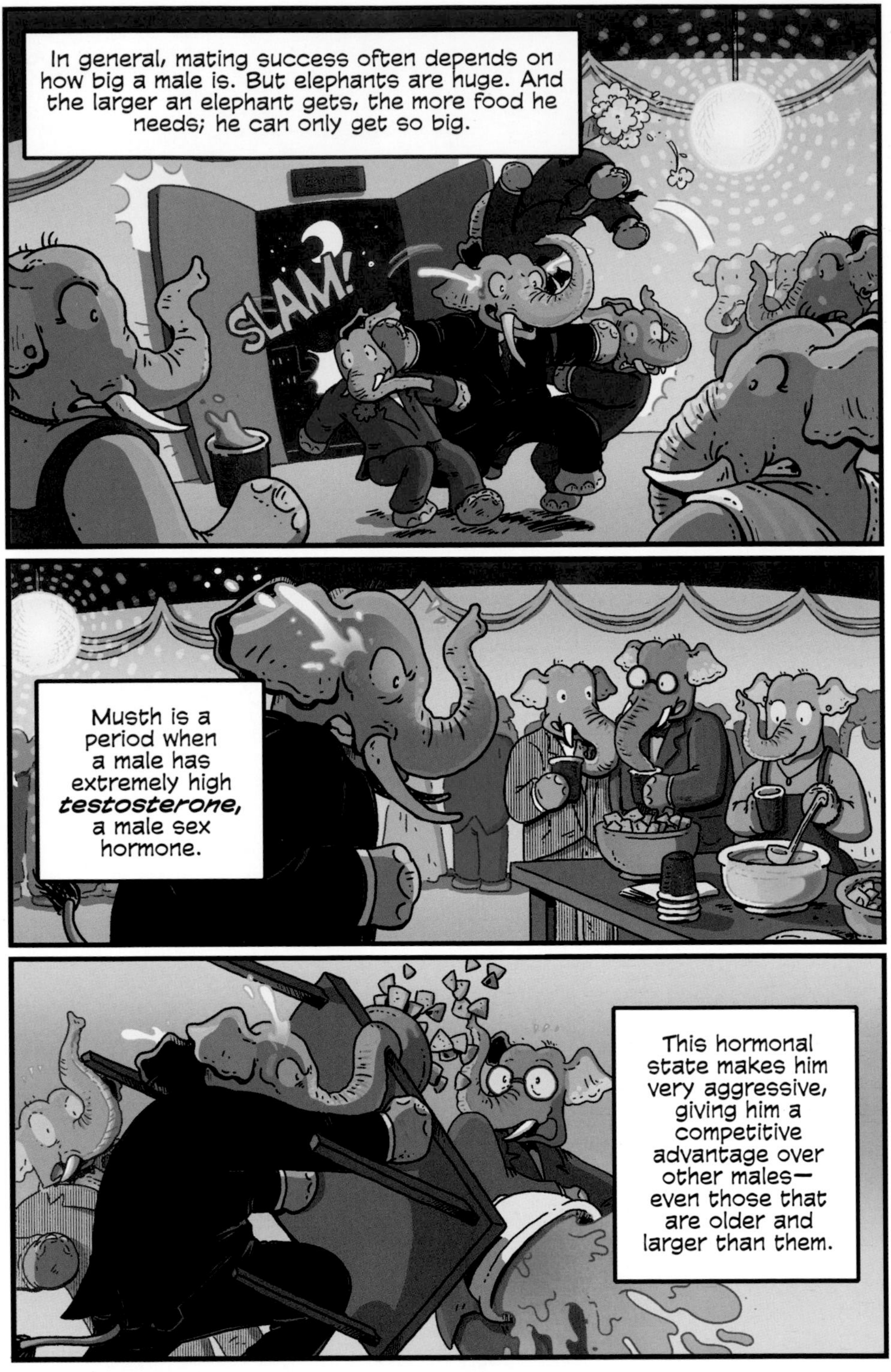
In general, mating success often depends on how big a male is. But elephants are huge. And the larger an elephant gets, the more food he needs; he can only get so big.
SLAM!
Musth is a period when a male has extremely high ***testosterone,*** a male sex hormone.
This hormonal state makes him very aggressive, giving him a competitive advantage over other males—even those that are older and larger than them.

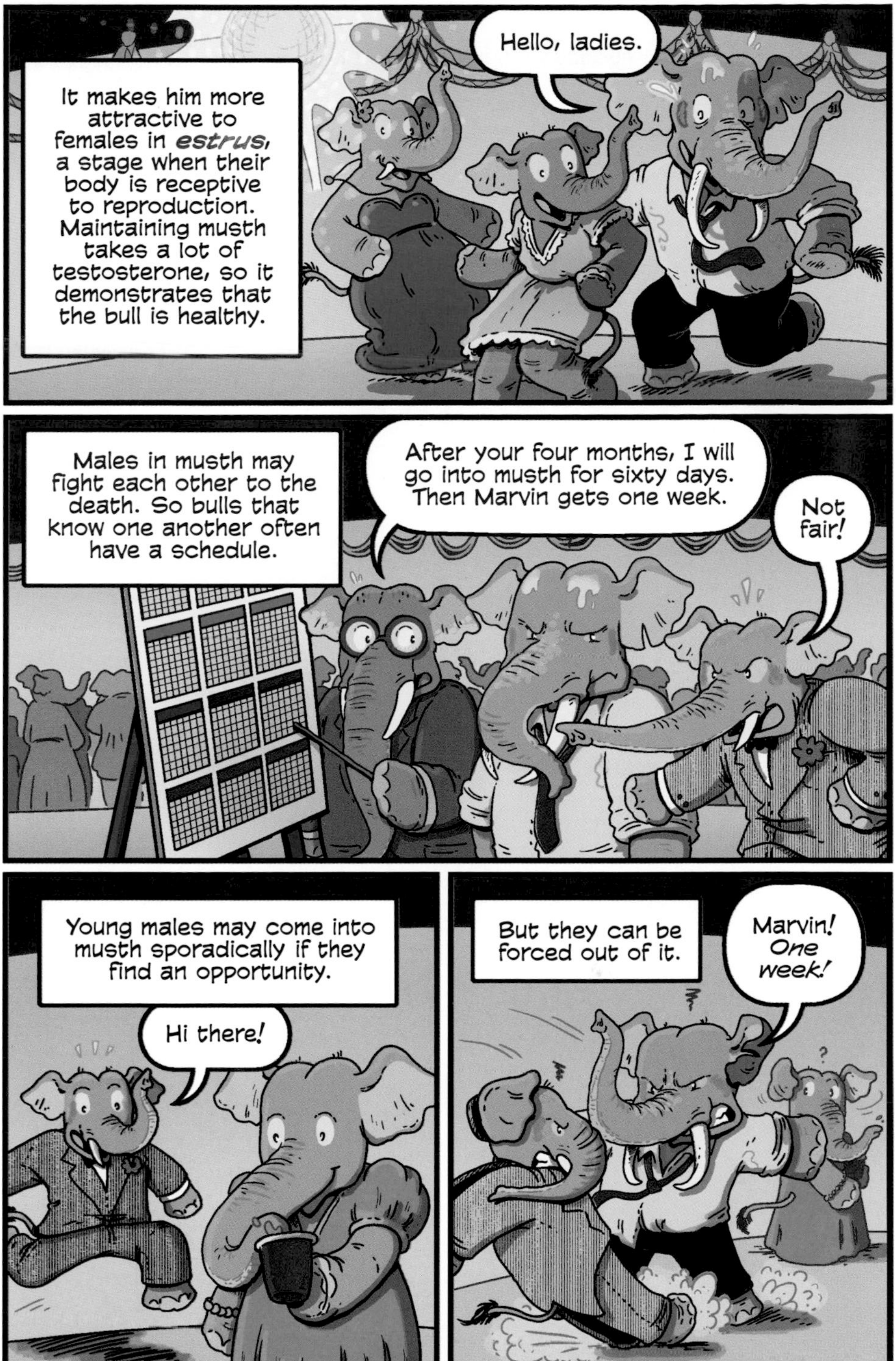

It makes him more attractive to females in *estrus*, a stage when their body is receptive to reproduction. Maintaining musth takes a lot of testosterone, so it demonstrates that the bull is healthy.
Hello, ladies.
Males in musth may fight each other to the death. So bulls that know one another often have a schedule.
After your four months, I will go into musth for sixty days. Then Marvin gets one week.
Not fair!
Young males may come into musth sporadically if they find an opportunity.
Hi there!
But they can be forced out of it.
Marvin! *One week!*

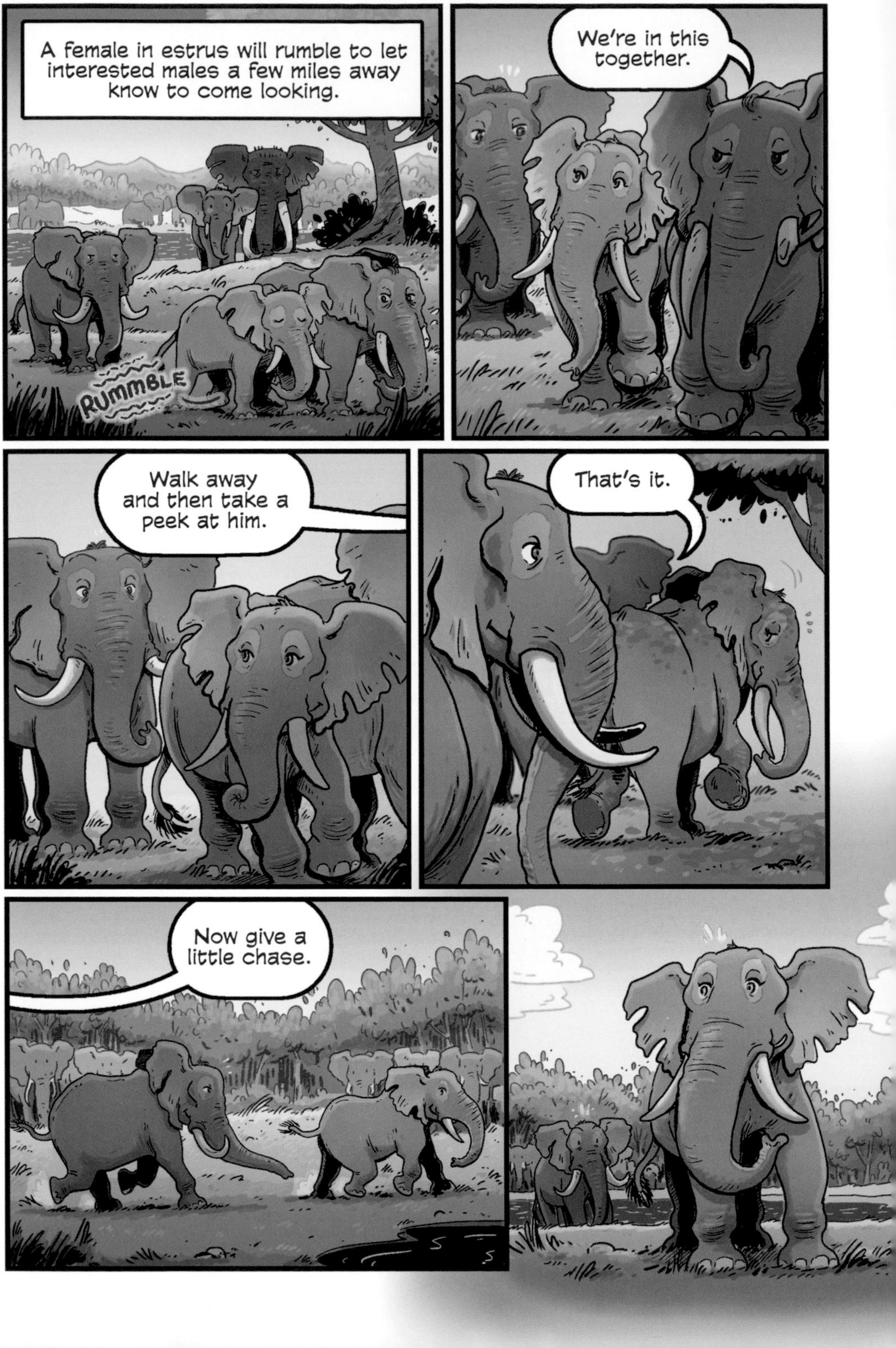
A female in estrus will rumble to let interested males a few miles away know to come looking.
RUMMBLE
We're in this together.
Walk away and then take a peek at him.
That's it.
Now give a little chase.

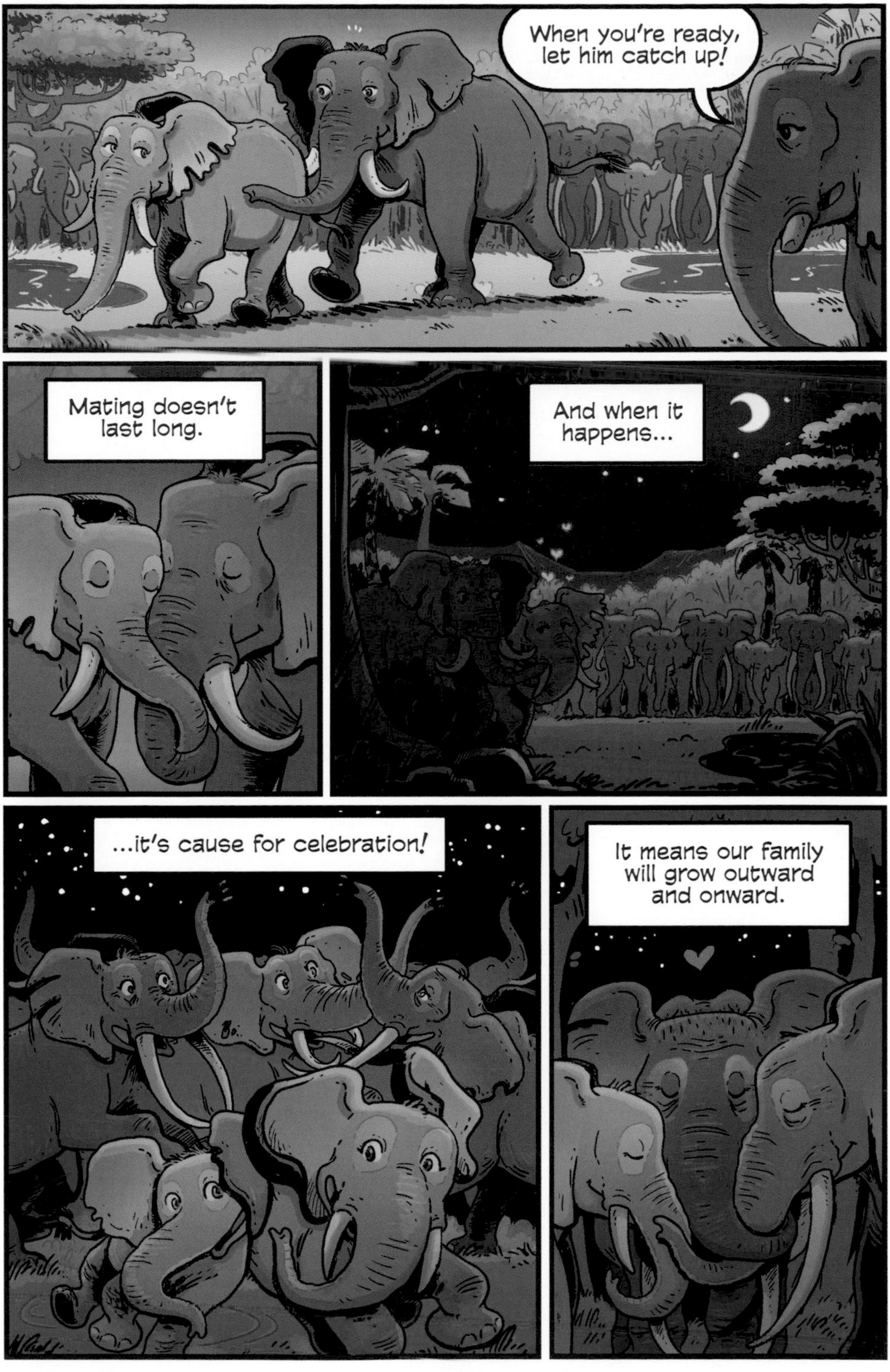
When you're ready, let him catch up!
Mating doesn't last long.
And when it happens...
...it's cause for celebration!
It means our family will grow outward and onward.

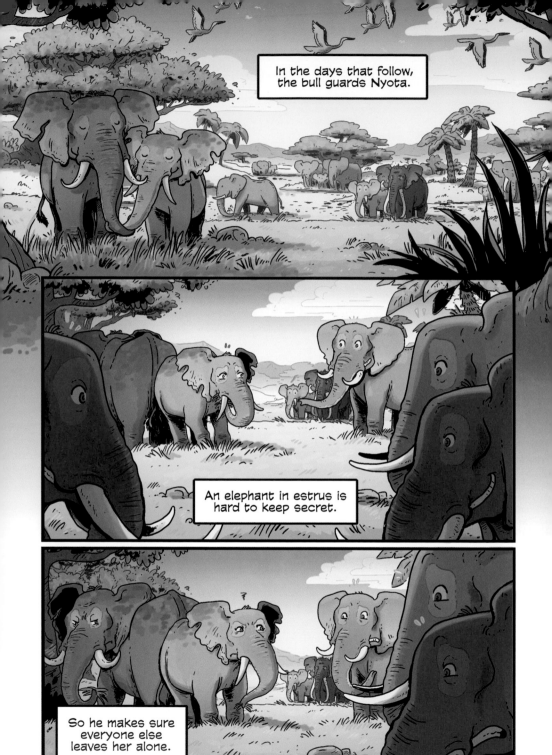

In the days that follow, the bull guards Nyota.

An elephant in estrus is hard to keep secret.

So he makes sure everyone else leaves her alone.

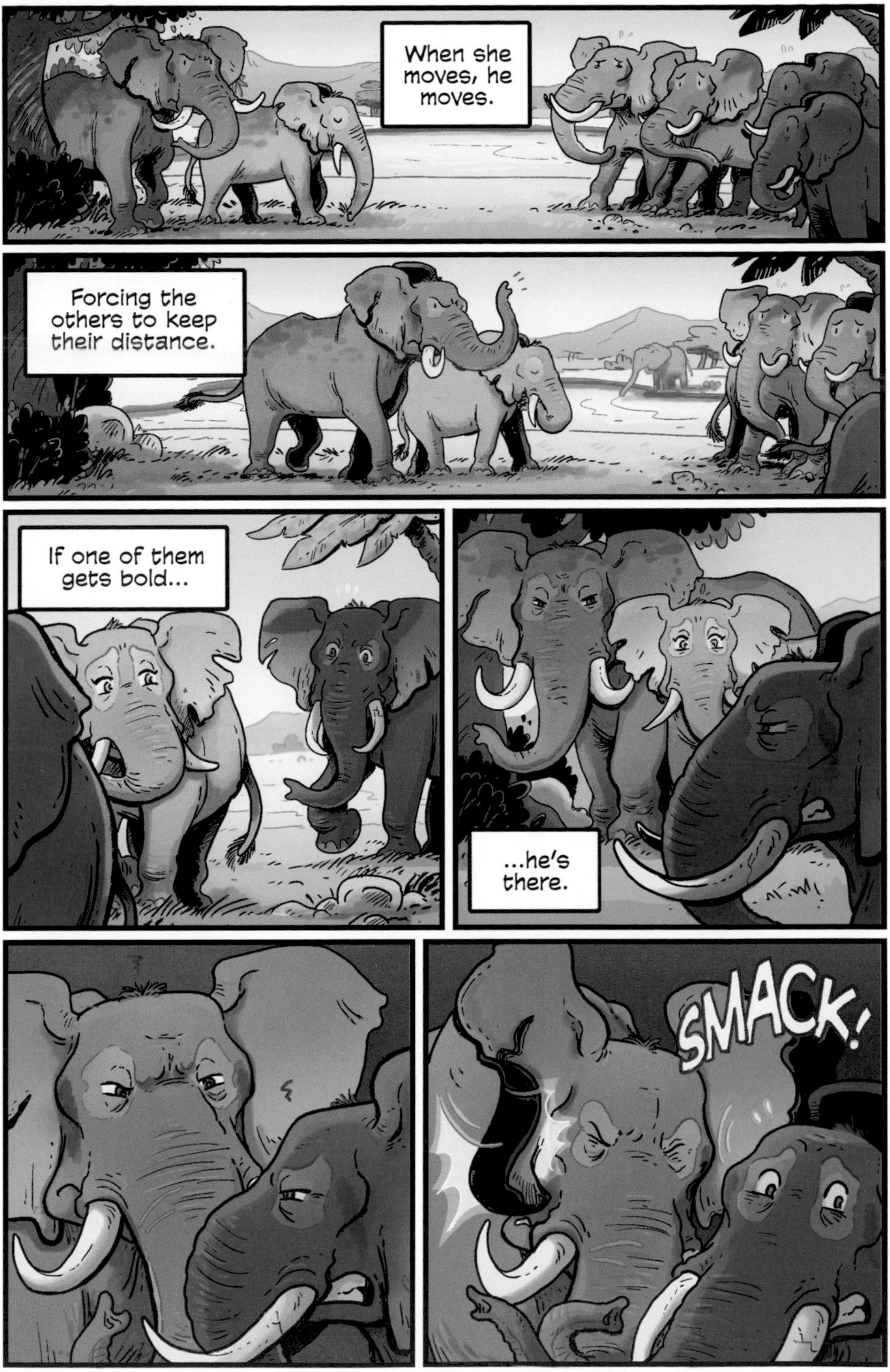
When she moves, he moves.
Forcing the others to keep their distance.
If one of them gets bold...
...he's there.
SMACK!

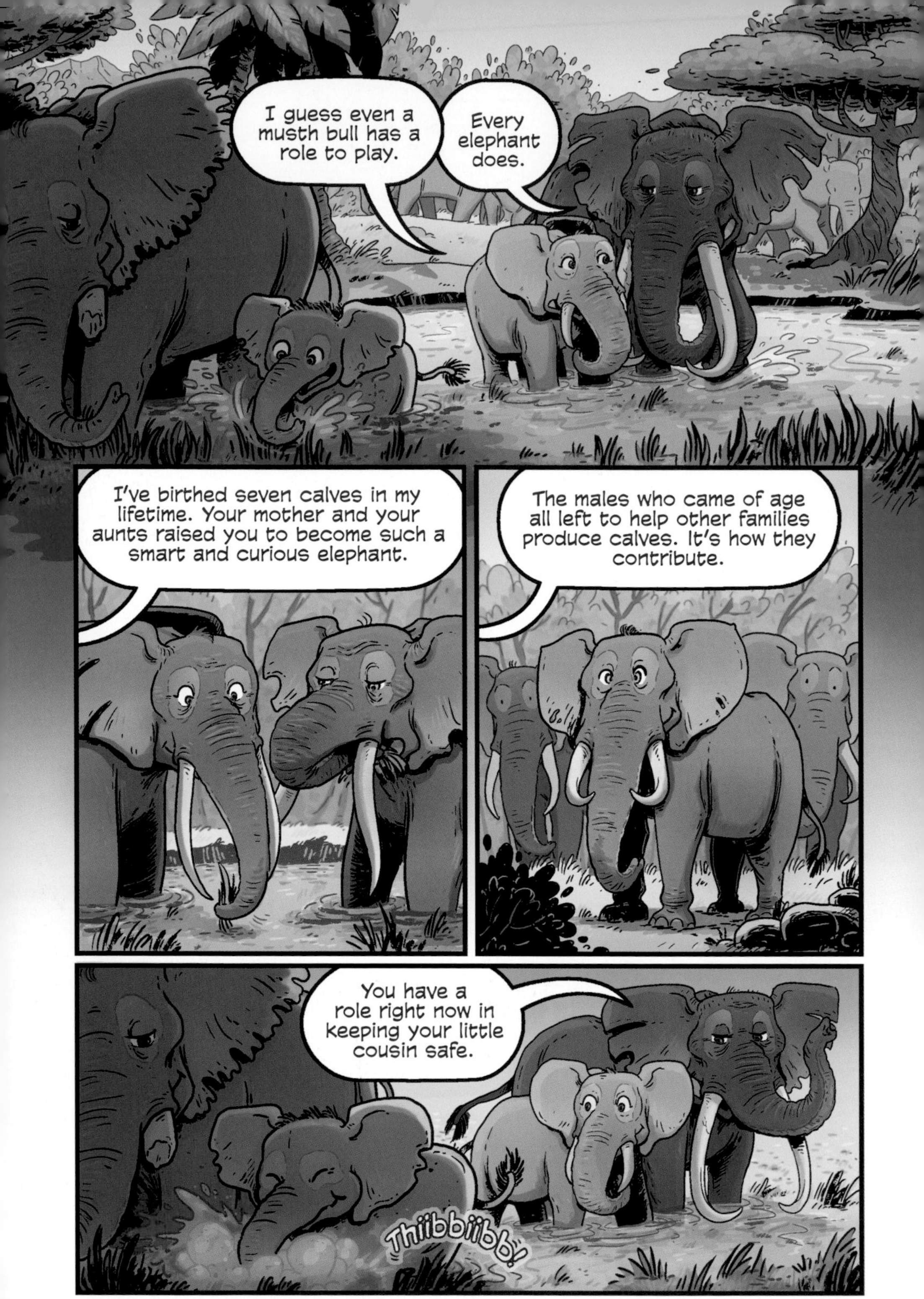
I guess even a musth bull has a role to play.
Every elephant does.
I've birthed seven calves in my lifetime. Your mother and your aunts raised you to become such a smart and curious elephant.
The males who came of age all left to help other families produce calves. It's how they contribute.
You have a role right now in keeping your little cousin safe.
Thiibbiibb!

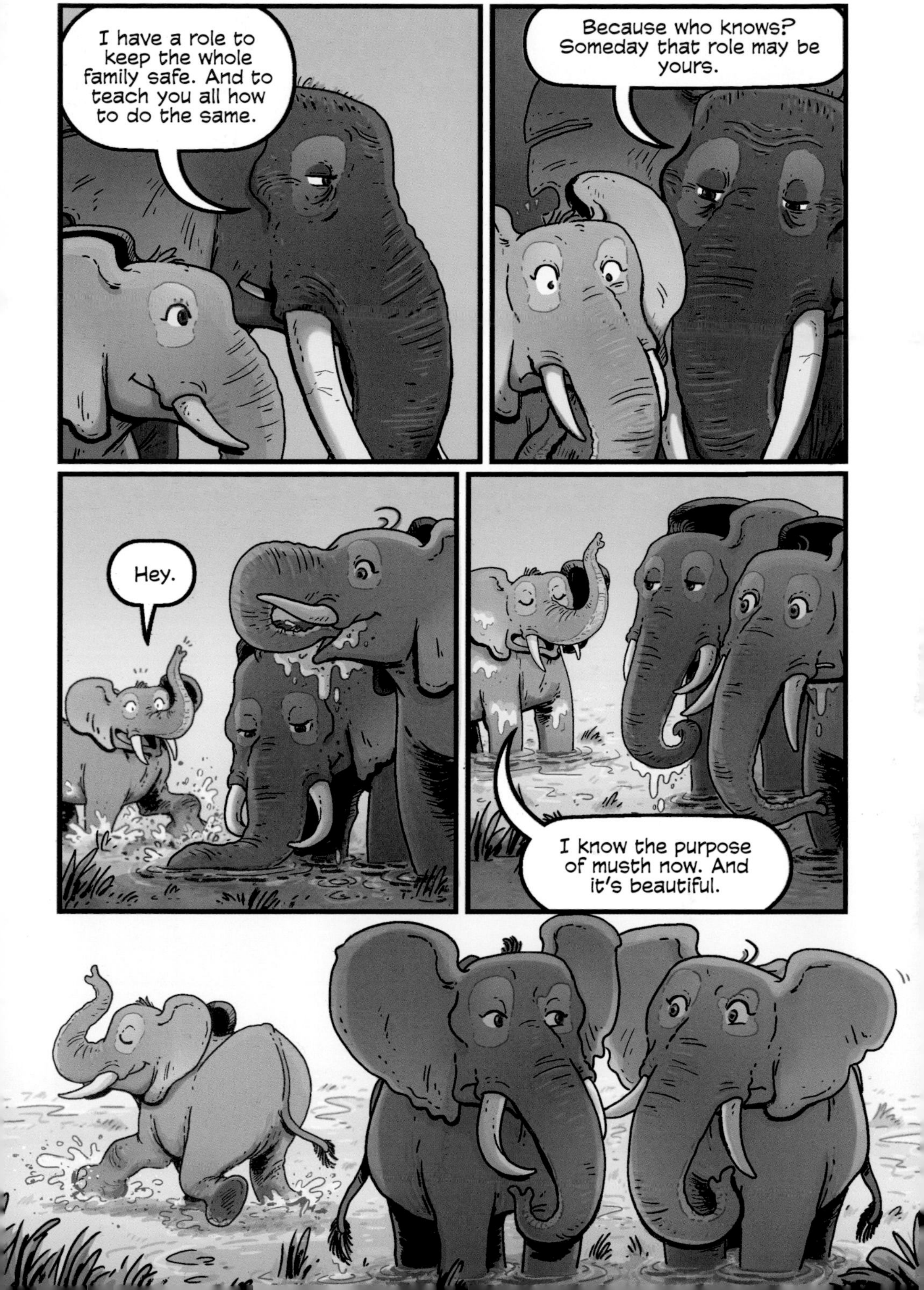
I have a role to keep the whole family safe. And to teach you all how to do the same.
Because who knows? Someday that role may be yours.
Hey.
I know the purpose of musth now. And it's beautiful.

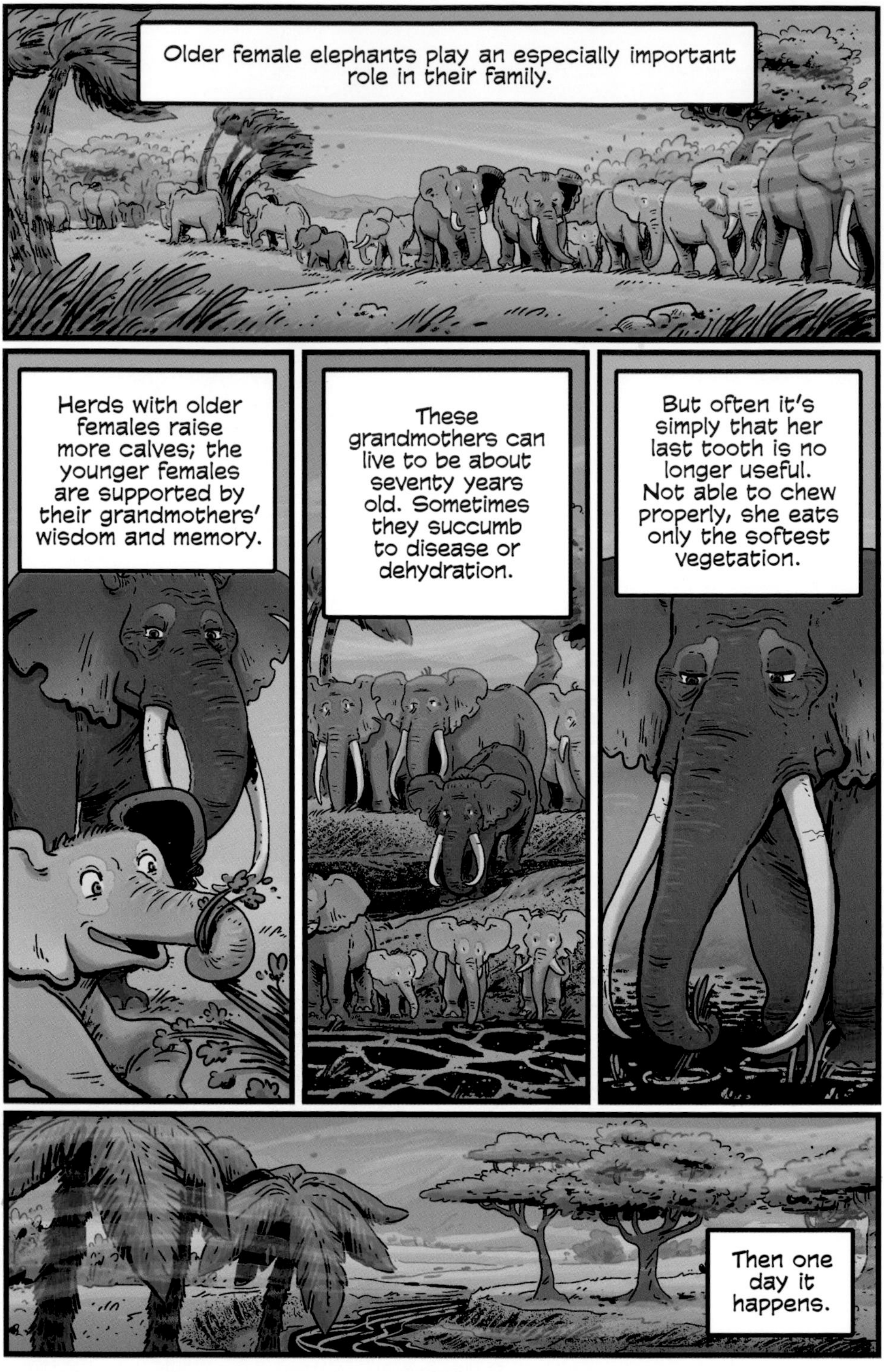
Older female elephants play an especially important role in their family.
Herds with older females raise more calves; the younger females are supported by their grandmothers' wisdom and memory.
These grandmothers can live to be about seventy years old. Sometimes they succumb to disease or dehydration.
But often it's simply that her last tooth is no longer useful. Not able to chew properly, she eats only the softest vegetation.
Then one day it happens.

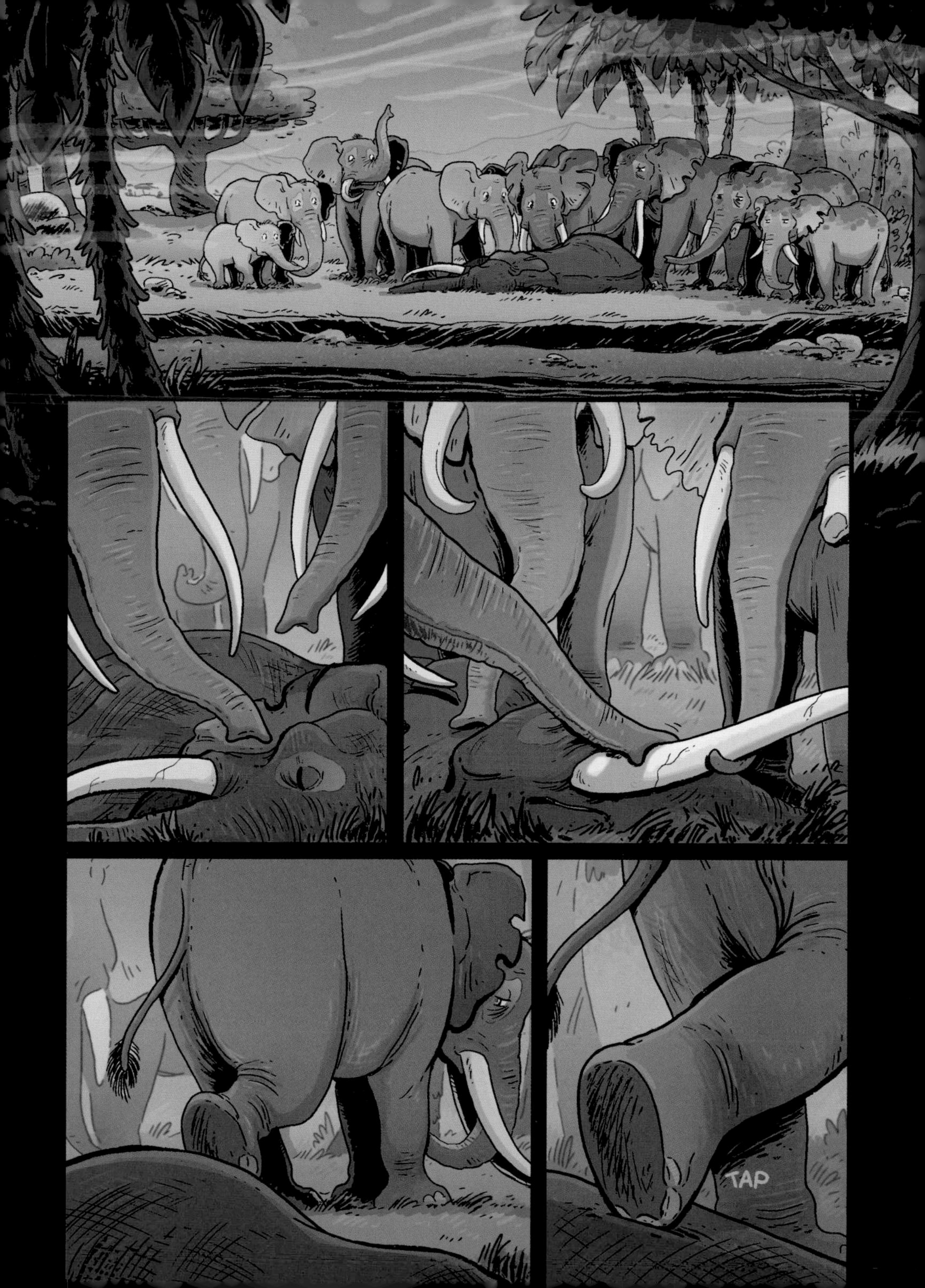
TAP

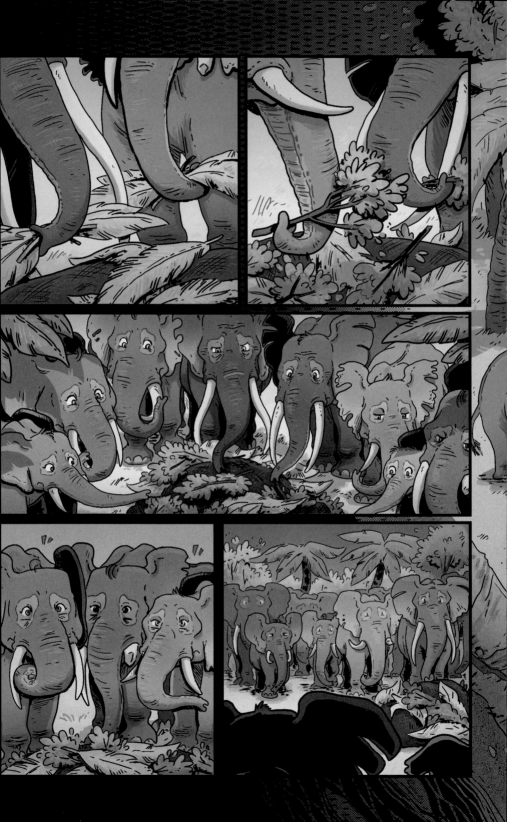

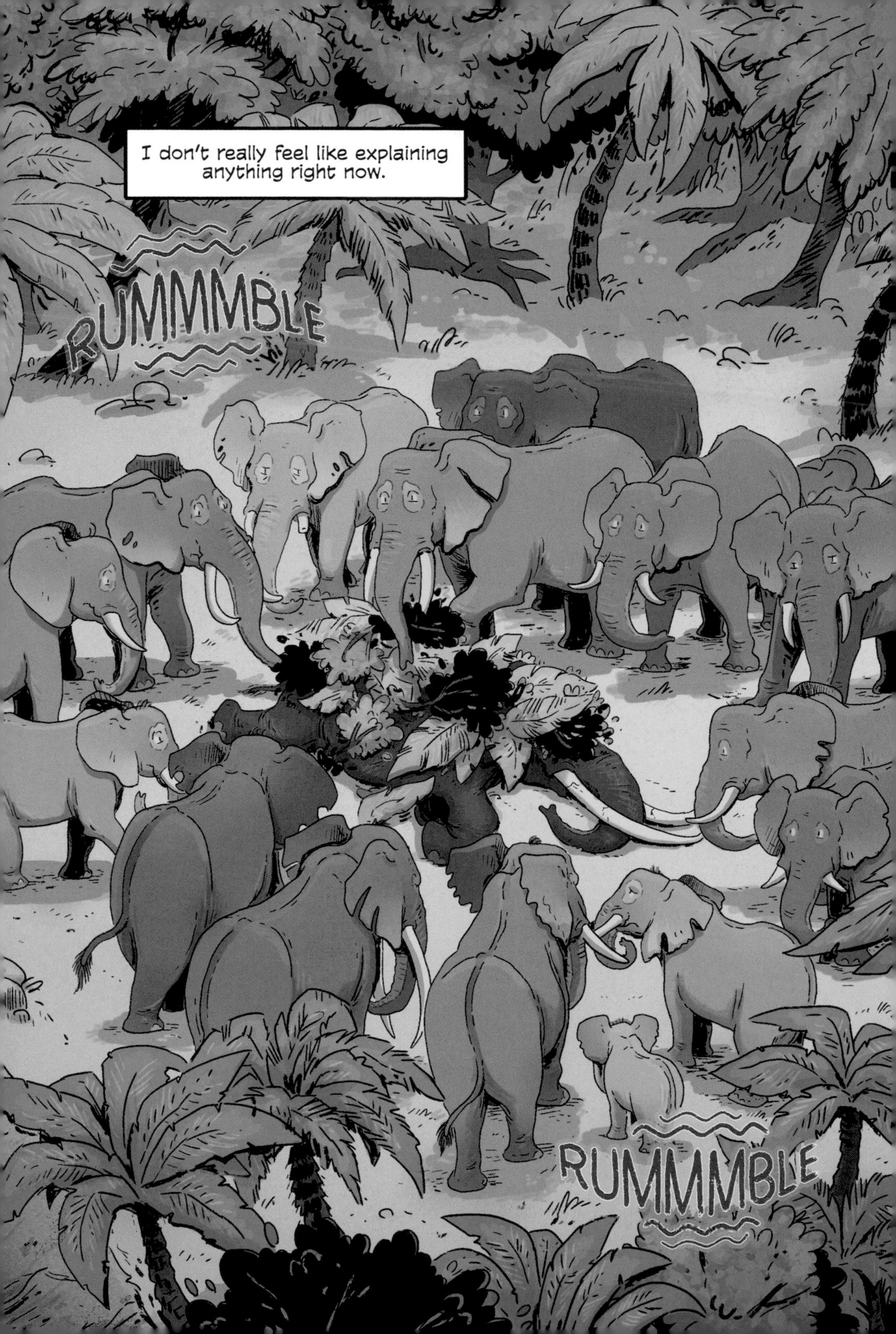

I don't really feel like explaining anything right now.
RUMMMBLE
RUMMMBLE

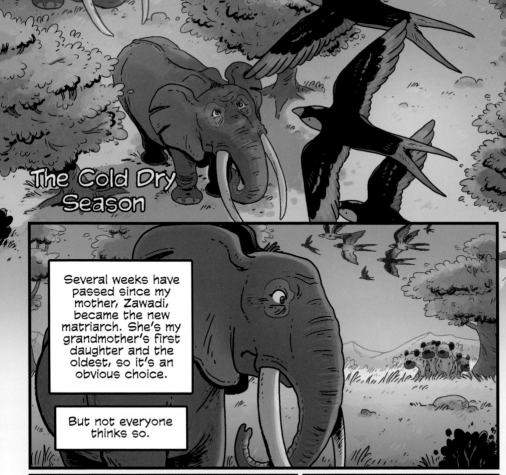

The Cold Dry Season

Several weeks have passed since my mother, Zawadi, became the new matriarch. She's my grandmother's first daughter and the oldest, so it's an obvious choice.

But not everyone thinks so.

It's time to move on.

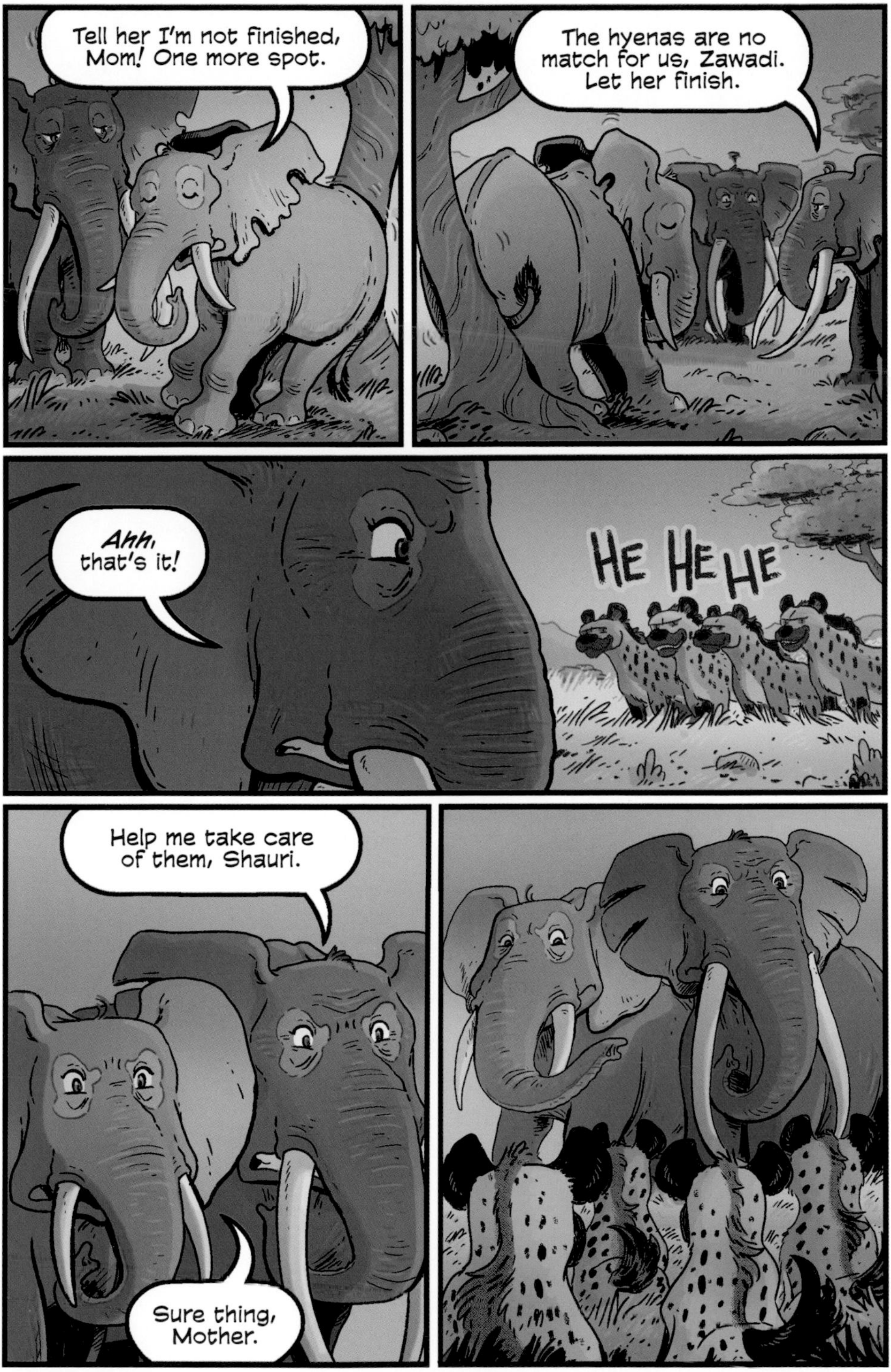
Tell her I'm not finished, Mom! One more spot.
The hyenas are no match for us, Zawadi. Let her finish.
Ahh, that's it!
HE HE HE
Help me take care of them, Shauri.
Sure thing, Mother.

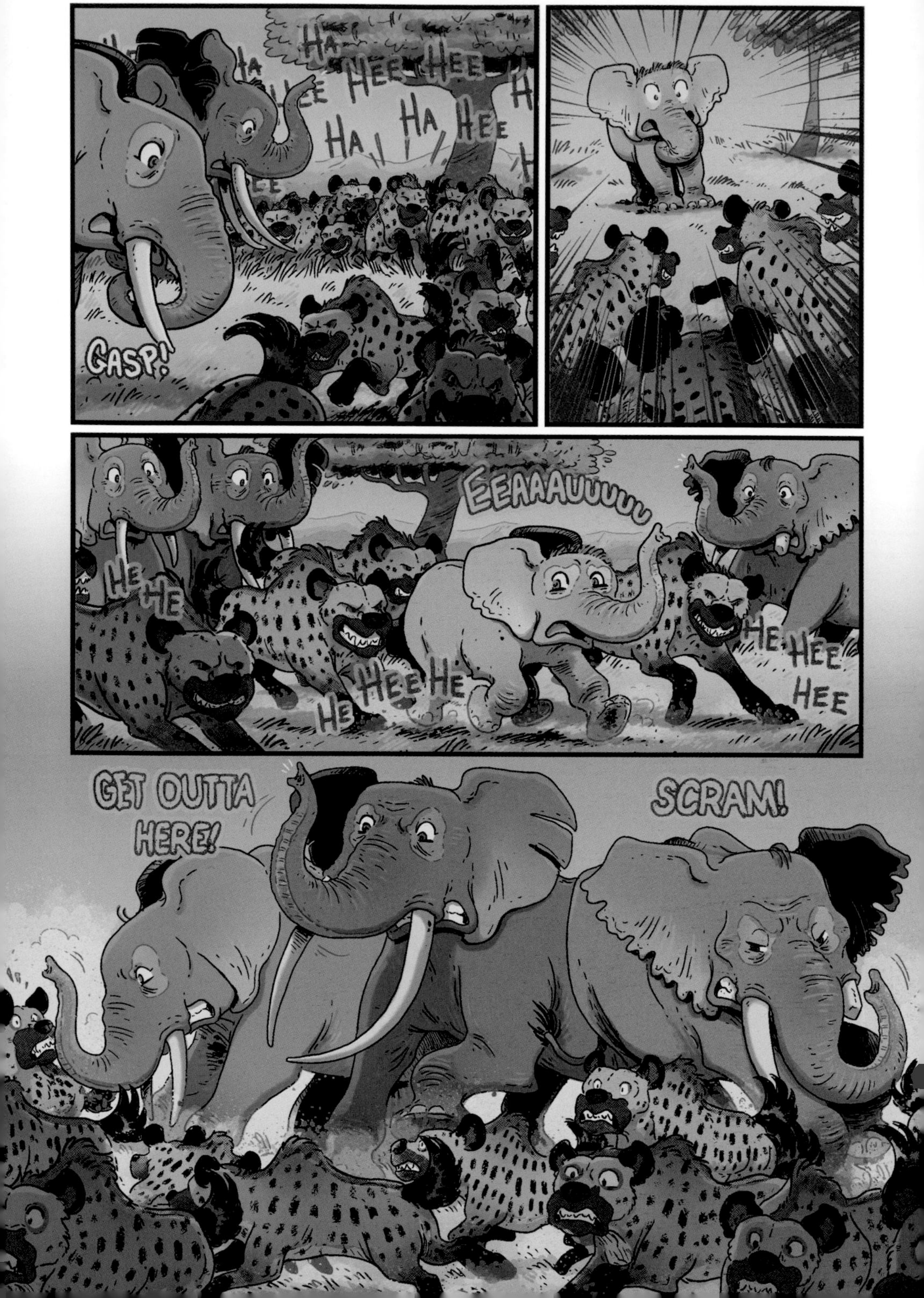

HA
HEE HEE
HA HA HEE
GASP!
EEAAAUUUUU
HE HE
HE HEE HE
HE HEE HEE
GET OUTTA HERE!
SCRAM!

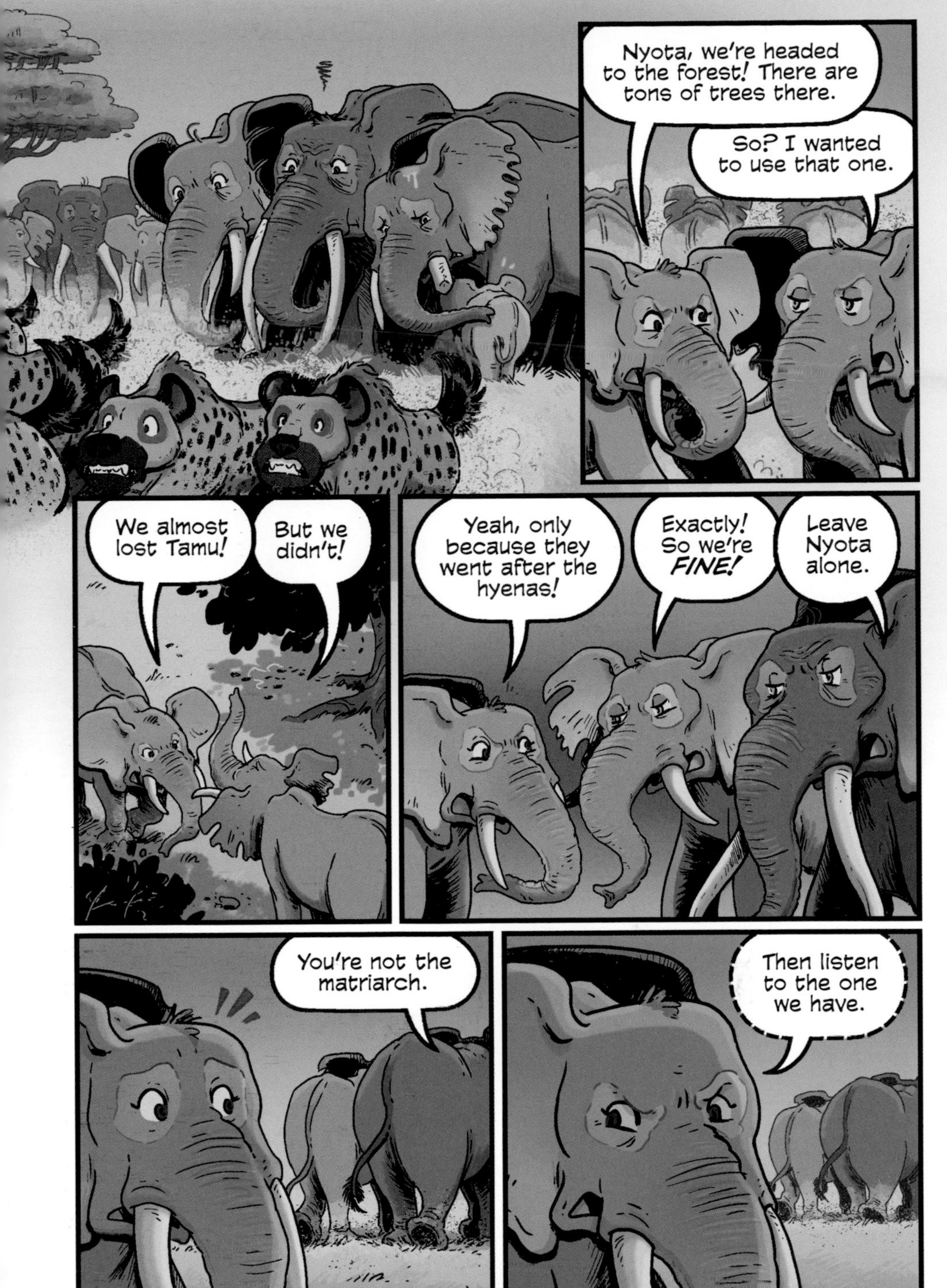
Nyota, we're headed to the forest! There are tons of trees there.
So? I wanted to use that one.
We almost lost Tamu!
But we didn't!
Yeah, only because they went after the hyenas!
Exactly! So we're *FINE!*
Leave Nyota alone.
You're not the matriarch.
Then listen to the one we have.

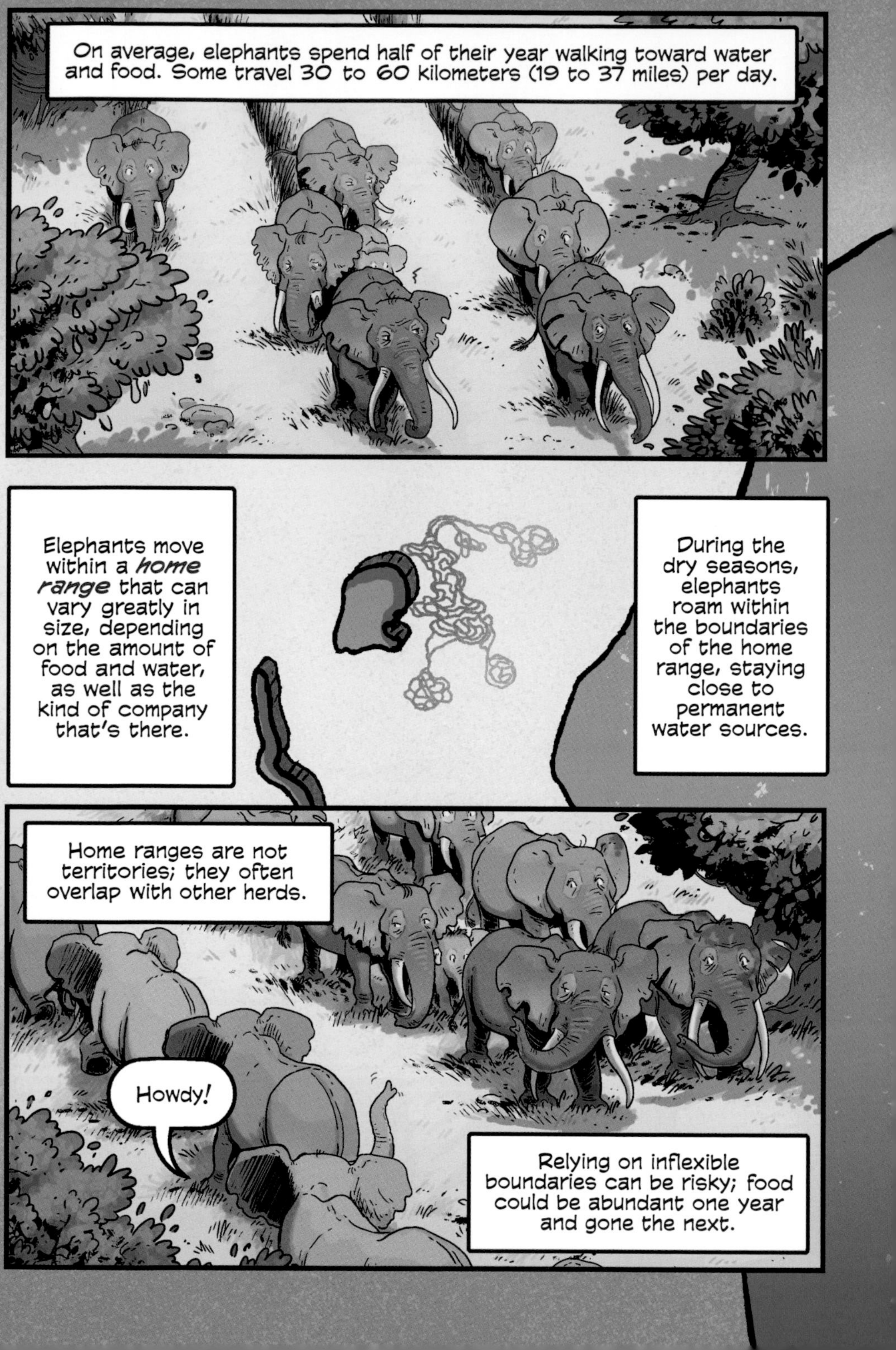
On average, elephants spend half of their year walking toward water and food. Some travel 30 to 60 kilometers (19 to 37 miles) per day.
Elephants move within a *home range* that can vary greatly in size, depending on the amount of food and water, as well as the kind of company that's there.
During the dry seasons, elephants roam within the boundaries of the home range, staying close to permanent water sources.
Home ranges are not territories; they often overlap with other herds.
Howdy!
Relying on inflexible boundaries can be risky; food could be abundant one year and gone the next.

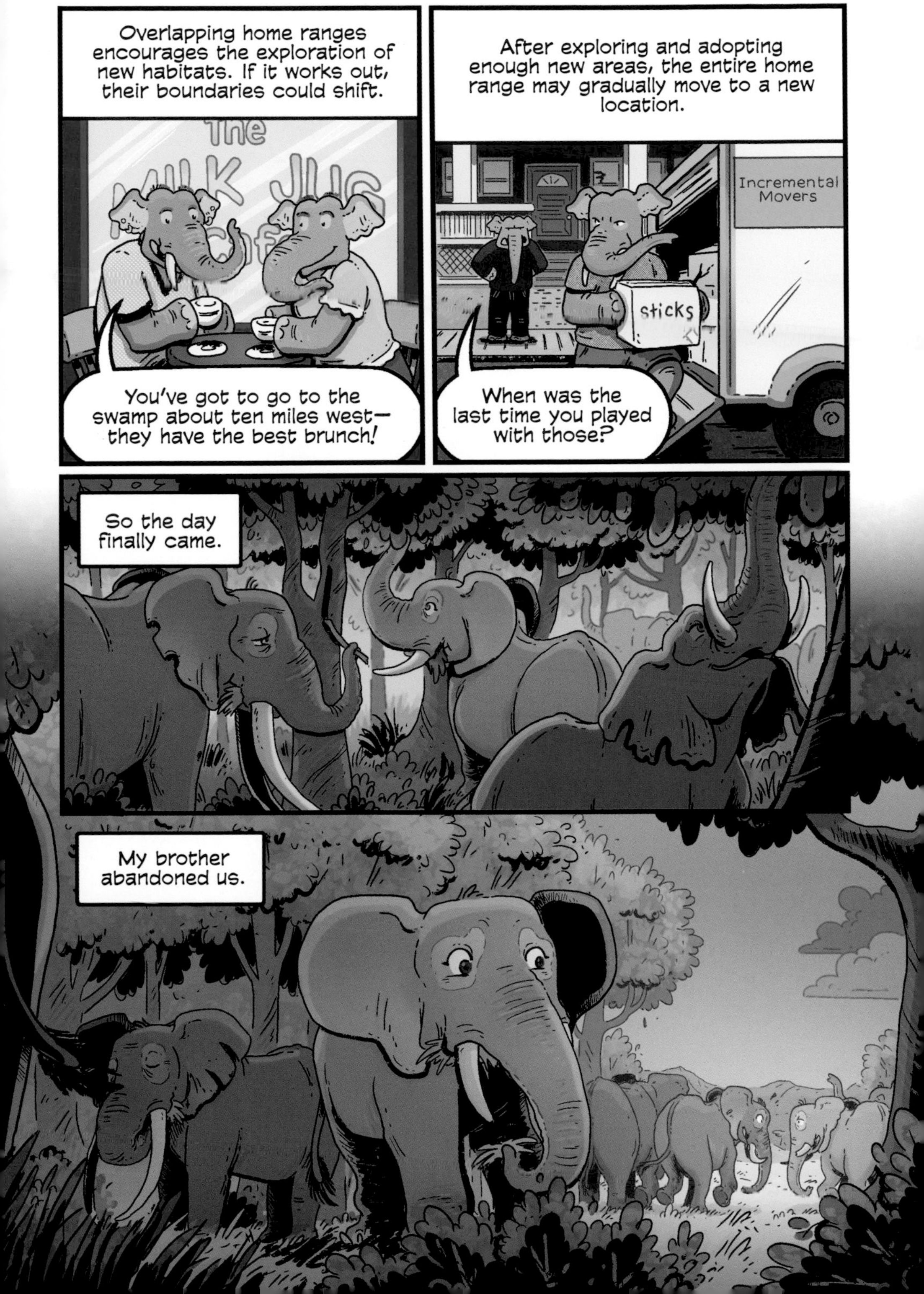

Overlapping home ranges encourages the exploration of new habitats. If it works out, their boundaries could shift.
The MILK JUG Café
You've got to go to the swamp about ten miles west—they have the best brunch!
After exploring and adopting enough new areas, the entire home range may gradually move to a new location.
Incremental Movers
sticks
When was the last time you played with those?
So the day finally came.
My brother abandoned us.

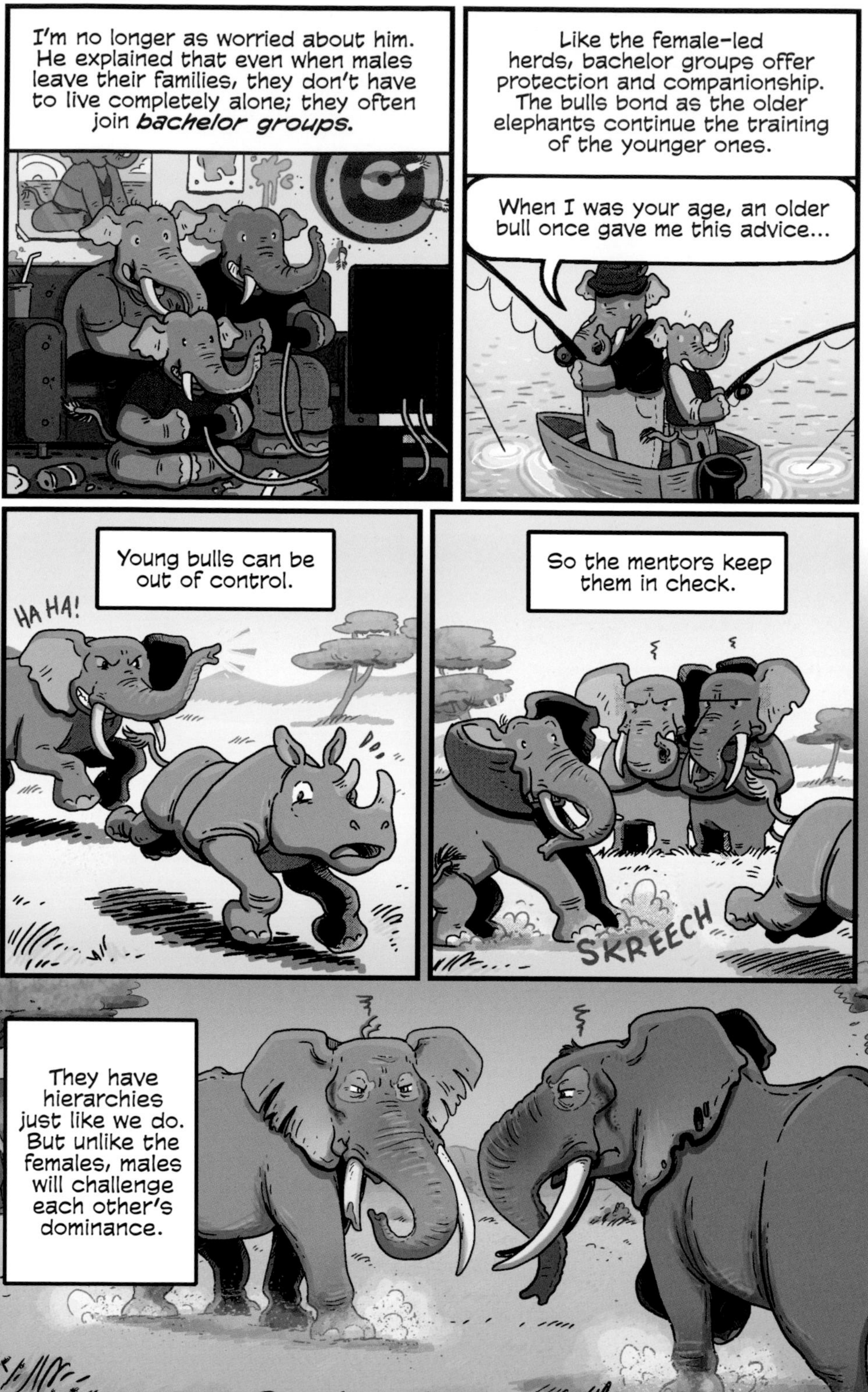
I'm no longer as worried about him. He explained that even when males leave their families, they don't have to live completely alone; they often join *bachelor groups.*
Like the female-led herds, bachelor groups offer protection and companionship. The bulls bond as the older elephants continue the training of the younger ones.
When I was your age, an older bull once gave me this advice...
Young bulls can be out of control.
HA HA!
So the mentors keep them in check.
SKREECH
They have hierarchies just like we do. But unlike the females, males will challenge each other's dominance.

They've learned how to fight from years of play.

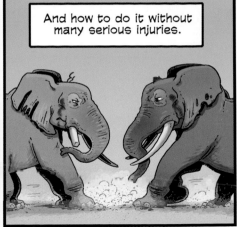

And how to do it without many serious injuries.

SMACK! SMACK!

CHOK!

The goal is to demonstrate what they *could* do.

"Oomph"

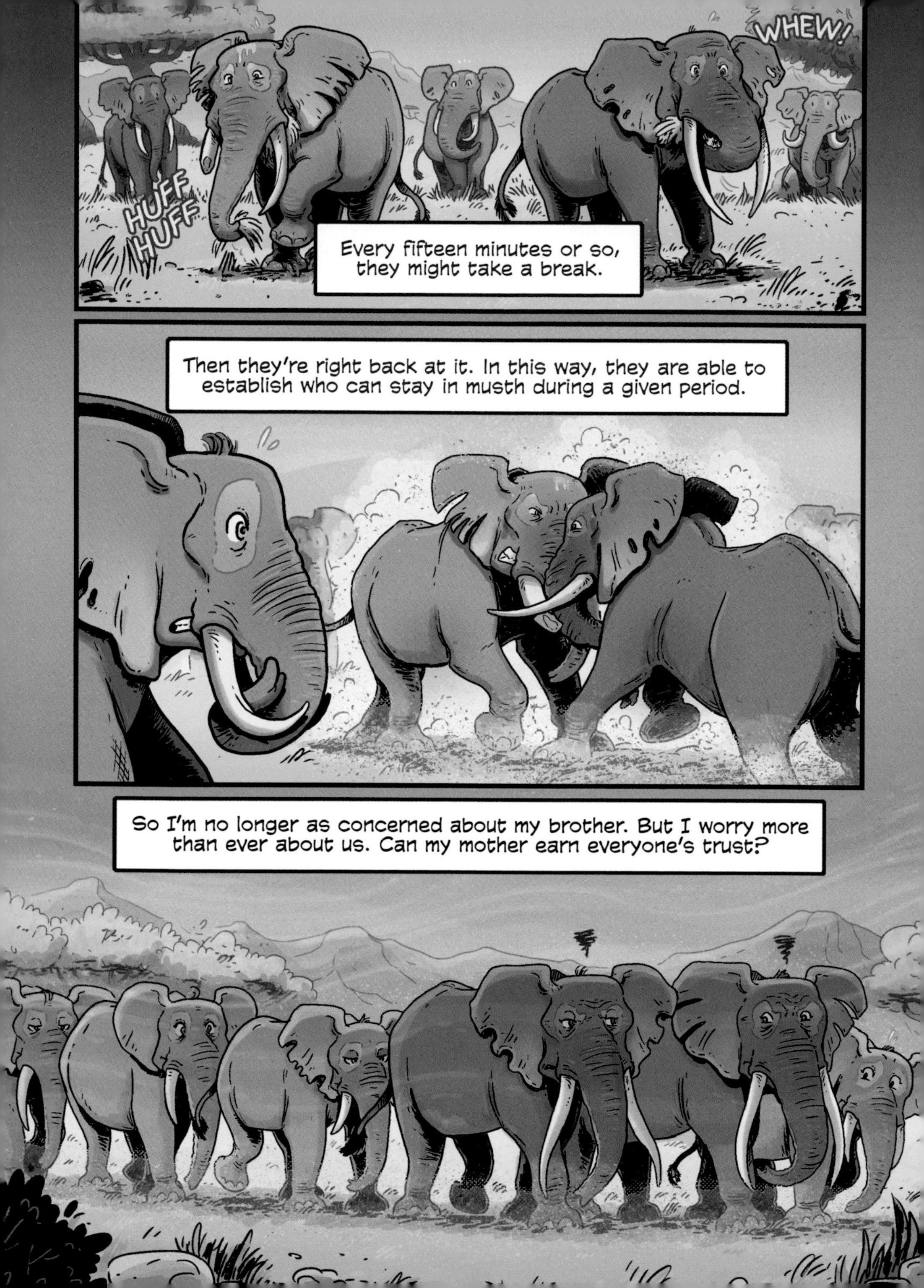
WHEW!
HUFF HUFF
Every fifteen minutes or so, they might take a break.
Then they're right back at it. In this way, they are able to establish who can stay in musth during a given period.
So I'm no longer as concerned about my brother. But I worry more than ever about us. Can my mother earn everyone's trust?

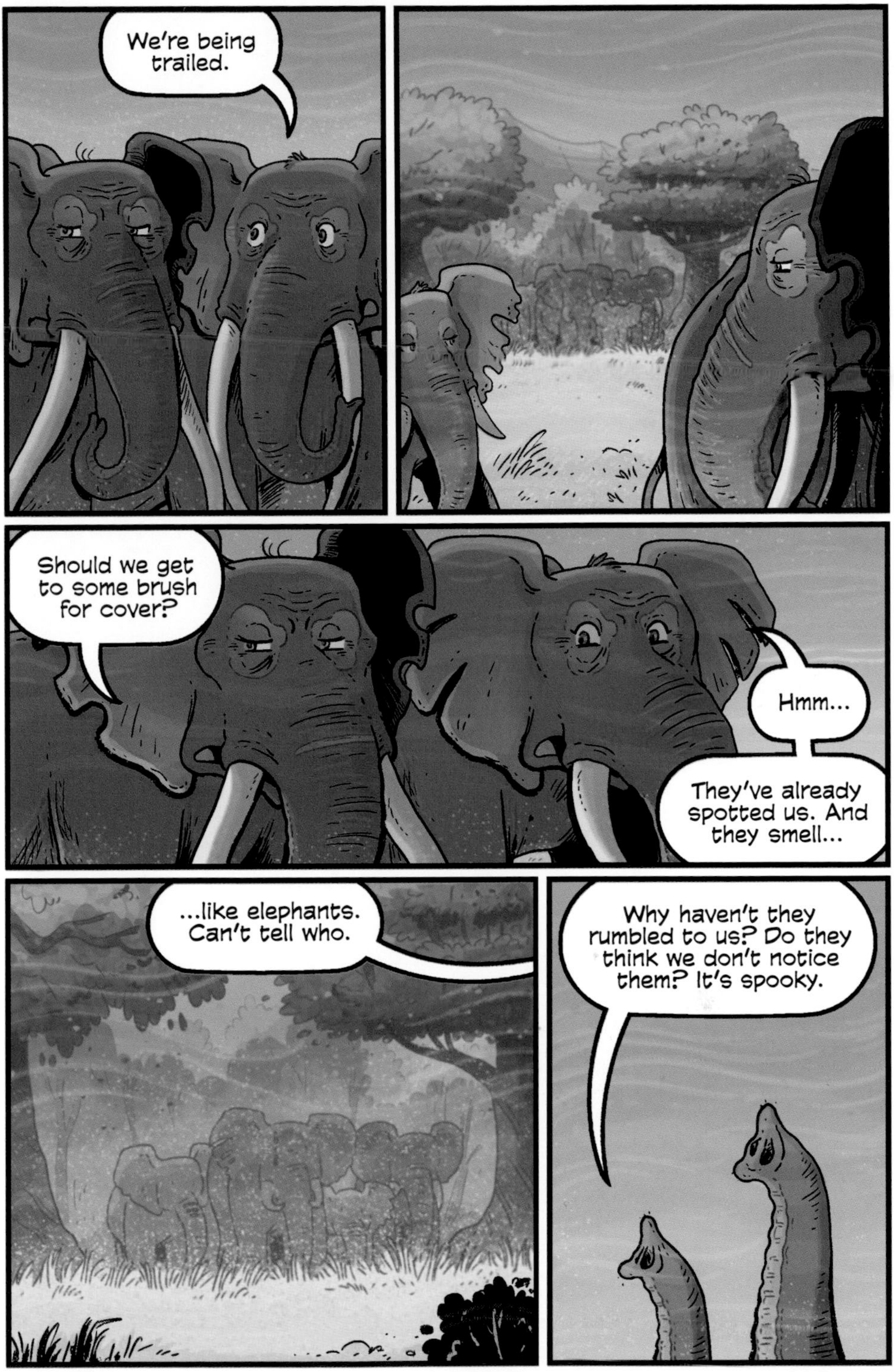
We're being trailed.
Should we get to some brush for cover?
Hmm...
They've already spotted us. And they smell...
...like elephants. Can't tell who.
Why haven't they rumbled to us? Do they think we don't notice them? It's spooky.

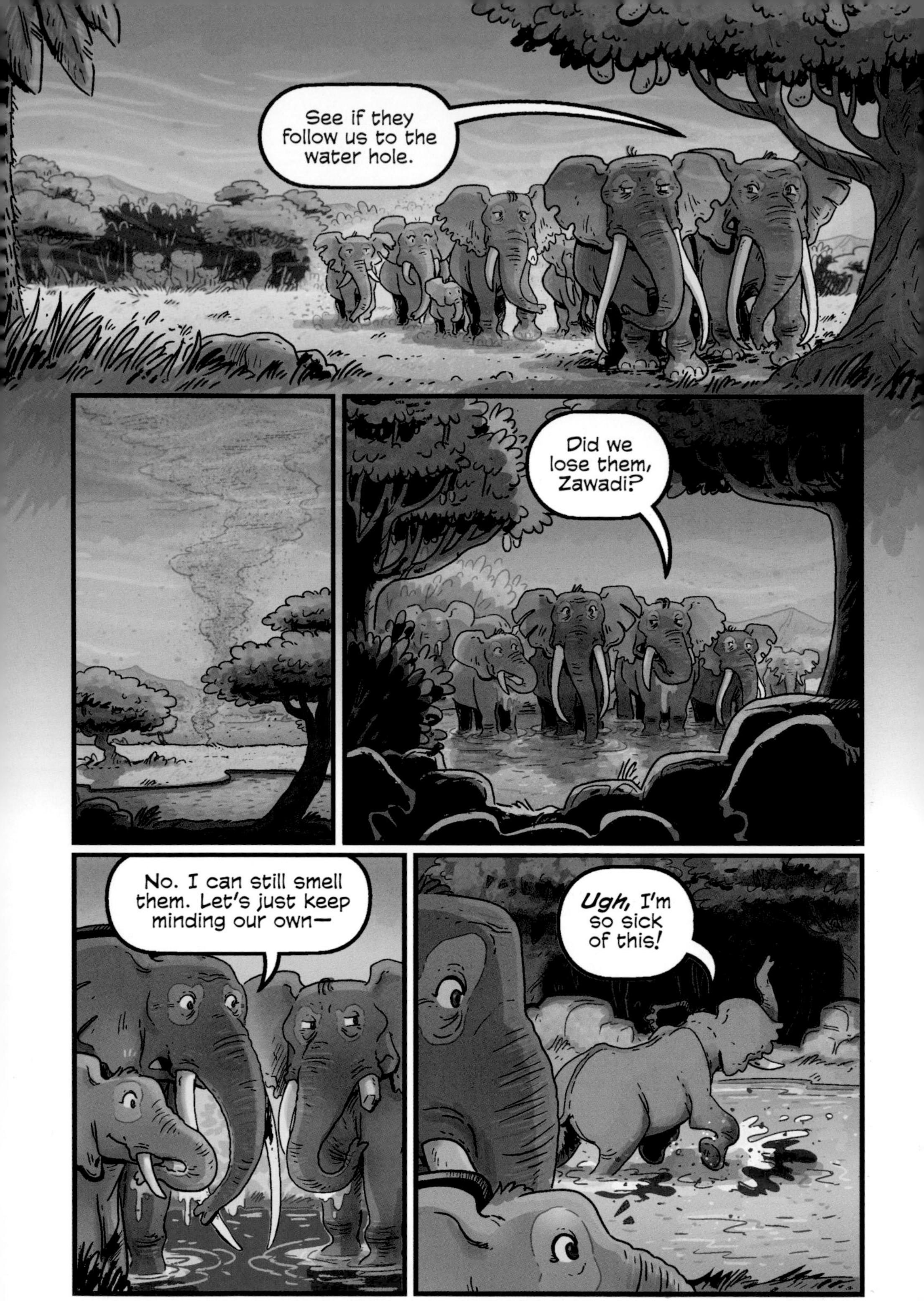
See if they follow us to the water hole.
Did we lose them, Zawadi?
No. I can still smell them. Let's just keep minding our own—
Ugh, I'm so sick of this!

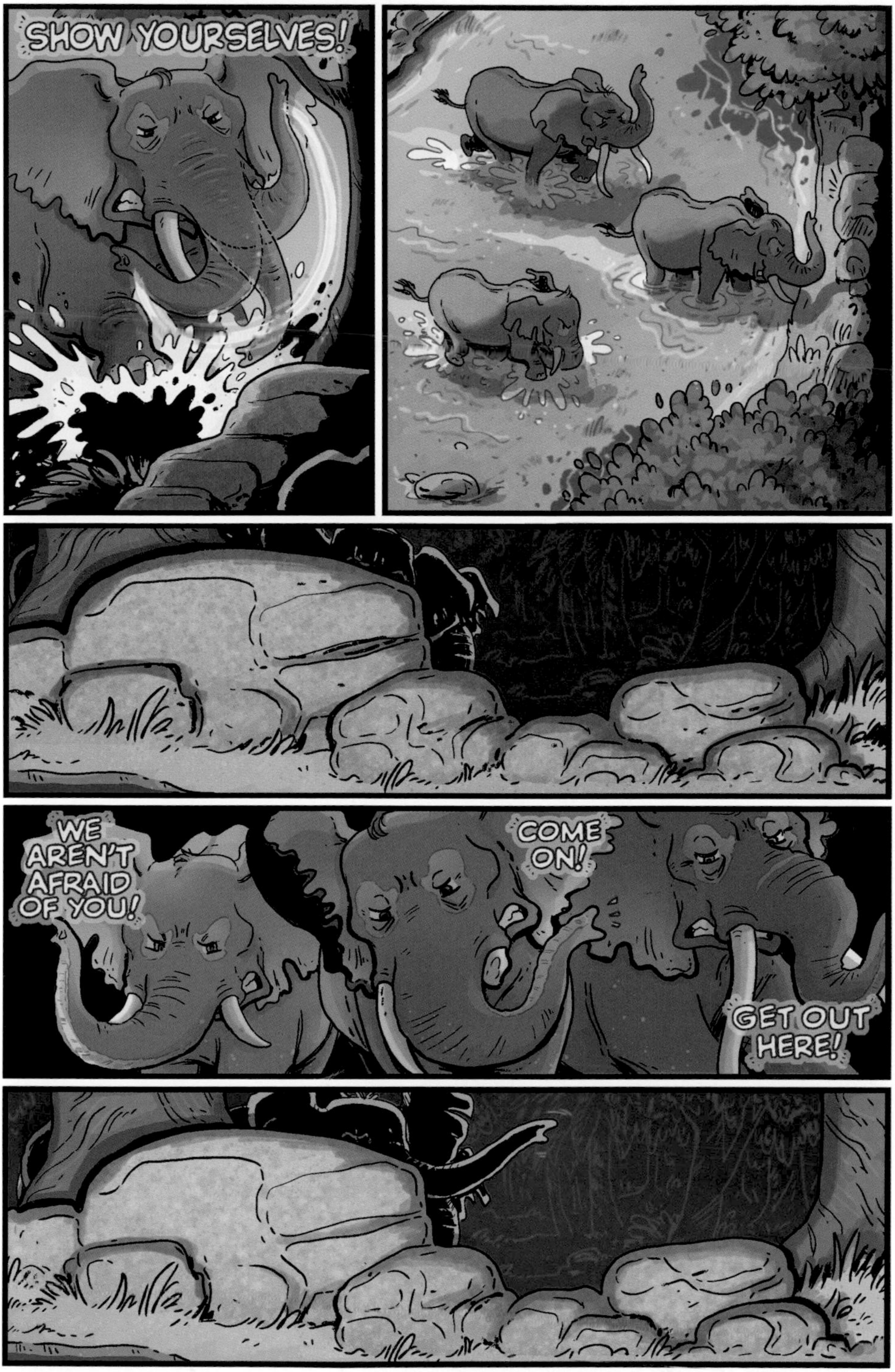
SHOW YOURSELVES!
WE AREN'T AFRAID OF YOU!
COME ON!
GET OUT HERE!

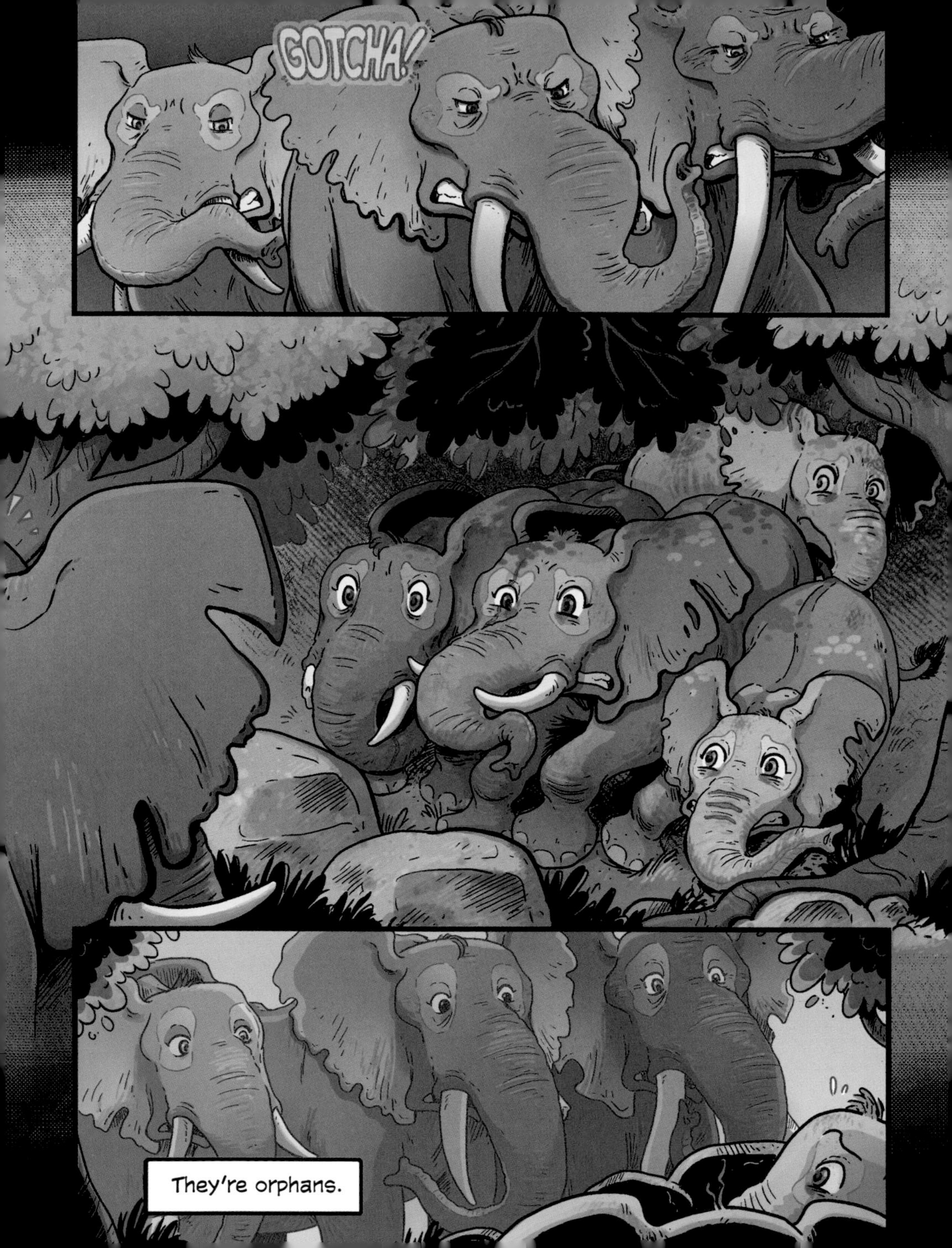
GOTCHA!
They're orphans.

Two of them are about my age. They asked if they could join us.

Where are your mothers? Your aunties?

The adults in our family were all killed by predators.

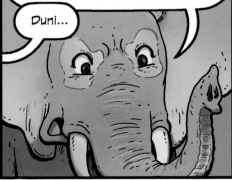

That doesn't make sense. Predators? Lions and hyenas attack the youngest of us—they couldn't kill all the adults.

Duni...

The adults are your defense! Why would they go after—

Duni...

There's another kind of predator. More dangerous than the others.

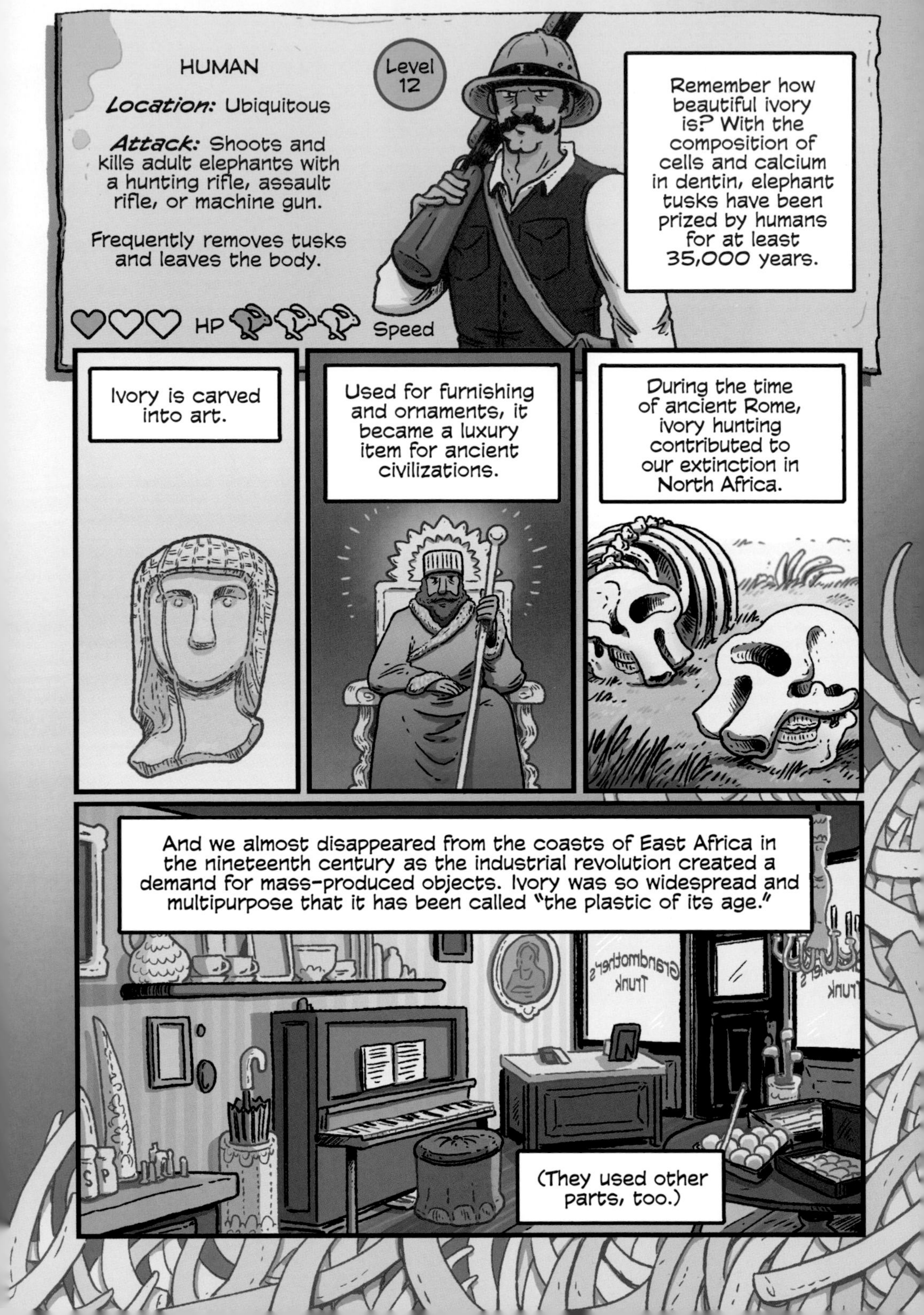
HUMAN
Location: Ubiquitous
Attack: Shoots and kills adult elephants with a hunting rifle, assault rifle, or machine gun.
Frequently removes tusks and leaves the body.
Level 12
HP
Speed
Remember how beautiful ivory is? With the composition of cells and calcium in dentin, elephant tusks have been prized by humans for at least 35,000 years.
Ivory is carved into art.
Used for furnishing and ornaments, it became a luxury item for ancient civilizations.
During the time of ancient Rome, ivory hunting contributed to our extinction in North Africa.
And we almost disappeared from the coasts of East Africa in the nineteenth century as the industrial revolution created a demand for mass-produced objects. Ivory was so widespread and multipurpose that it has been called "the plastic of its age."
Grandmother's Trunk
S P
(They used other parts, too.)

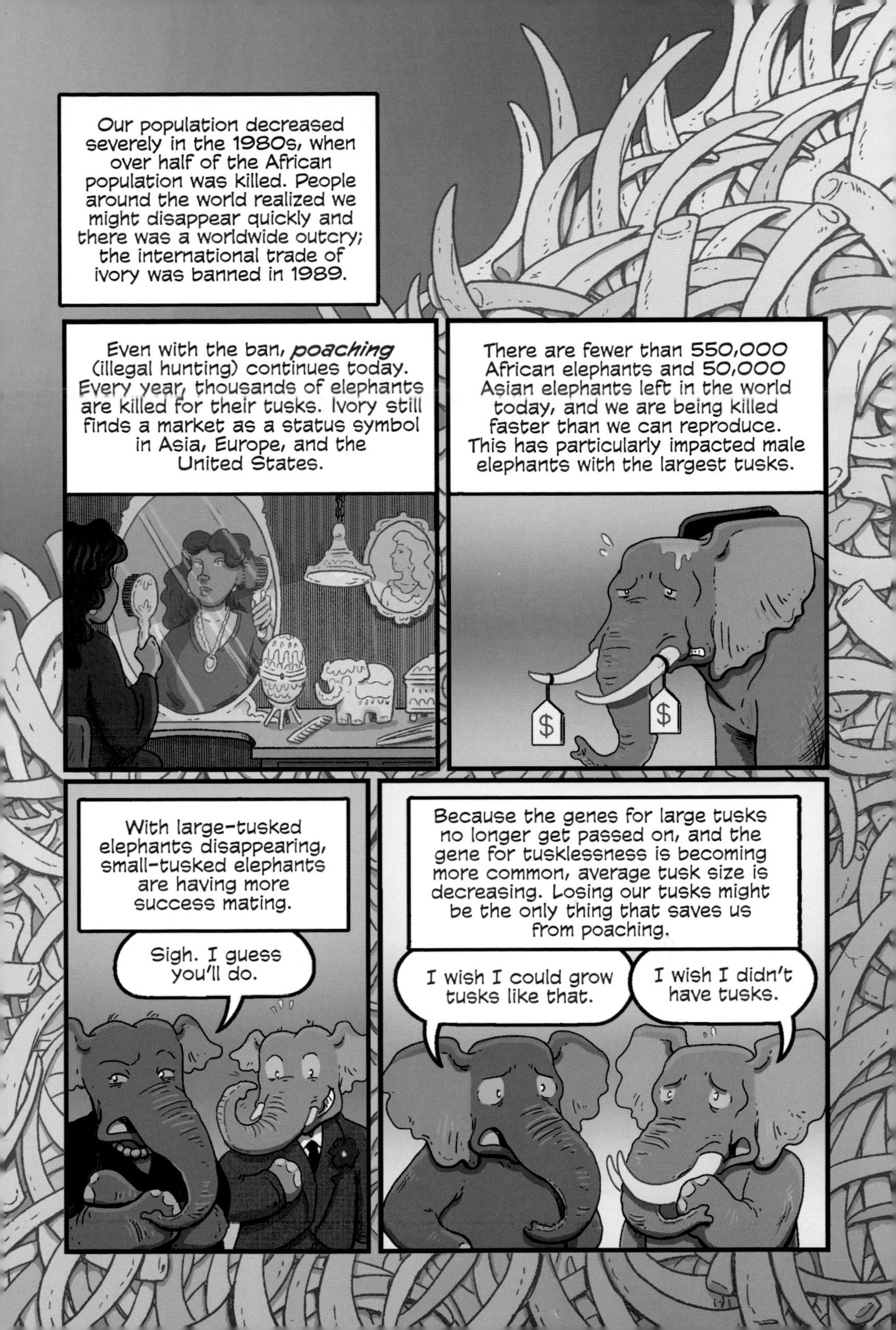

Our population decreased severely in the 1980s, when over half of the African population was killed. People around the world realized we might disappear quickly and there was a worldwide outcry; the international trade of ivory was banned in 1989.
Even with the ban, *poaching* (illegal hunting) continues today. Every year, thousands of elephants are killed for their tusks. Ivory still finds a market as a status symbol in Asia, Europe, and the United States.
There are fewer than 550,000 African elephants and 50,000 Asian elephants left in the world today, and we are being killed faster than we can reproduce. This has particularly impacted male elephants with the largest tusks.
$
$
With large-tusked elephants disappearing, small-tusked elephants are having more success mating.
Sigh. I guess you'll do.
Because the genes for large tusks no longer get passed on, and the gene for tusklessness is becoming more common, average tusk size is decreasing. Losing our tusks might be the only thing that saves us from poaching.
I wish I could grow tusks like that.
I wish I didn't have tusks.

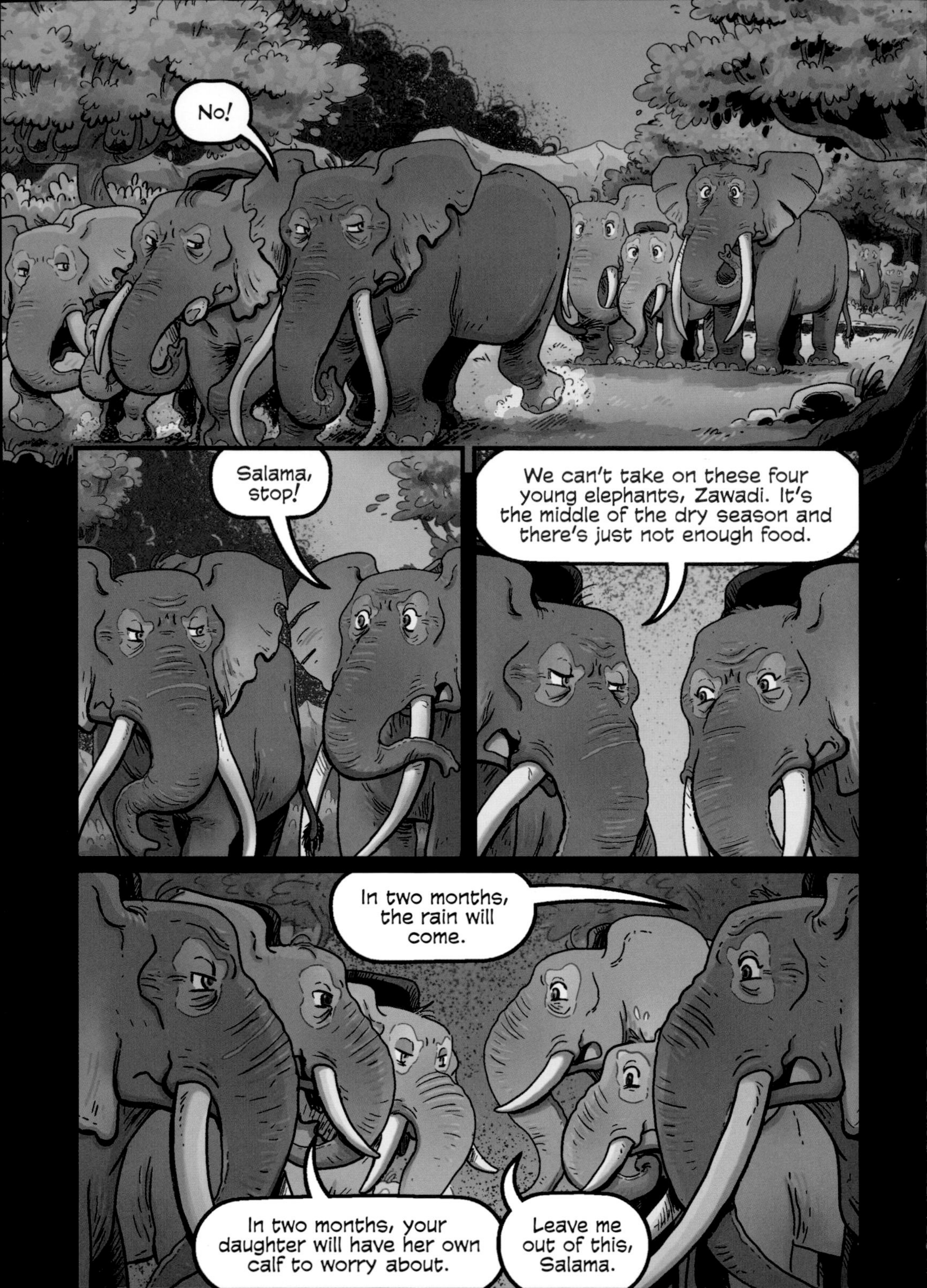
No!
Salama, stop!
We can't take on these four young elephants, Zawadi. It's the middle of the dry season and there's just not enough food.
In two months, the rain will come.
In two months, your daughter will have her own calf to worry about.
Leave me out of this, Salama.

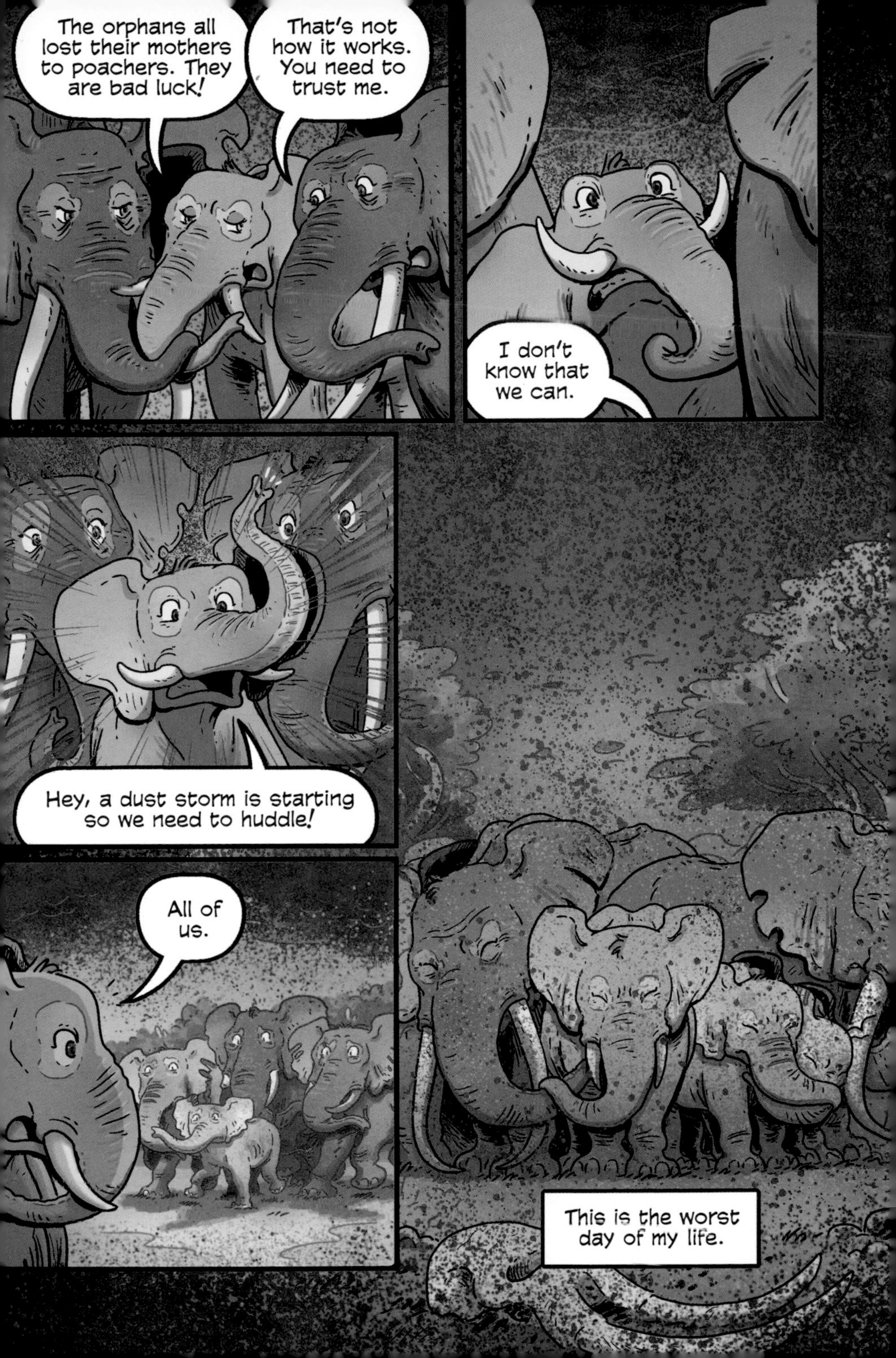
The orphans all lost their mothers to poachers. They are bad luck!
That's not how it works. You need to trust me.
I don't know that we can.
Hey, a dust storm is starting so we need to huddle!
All of us.
This is the worst day of my life.

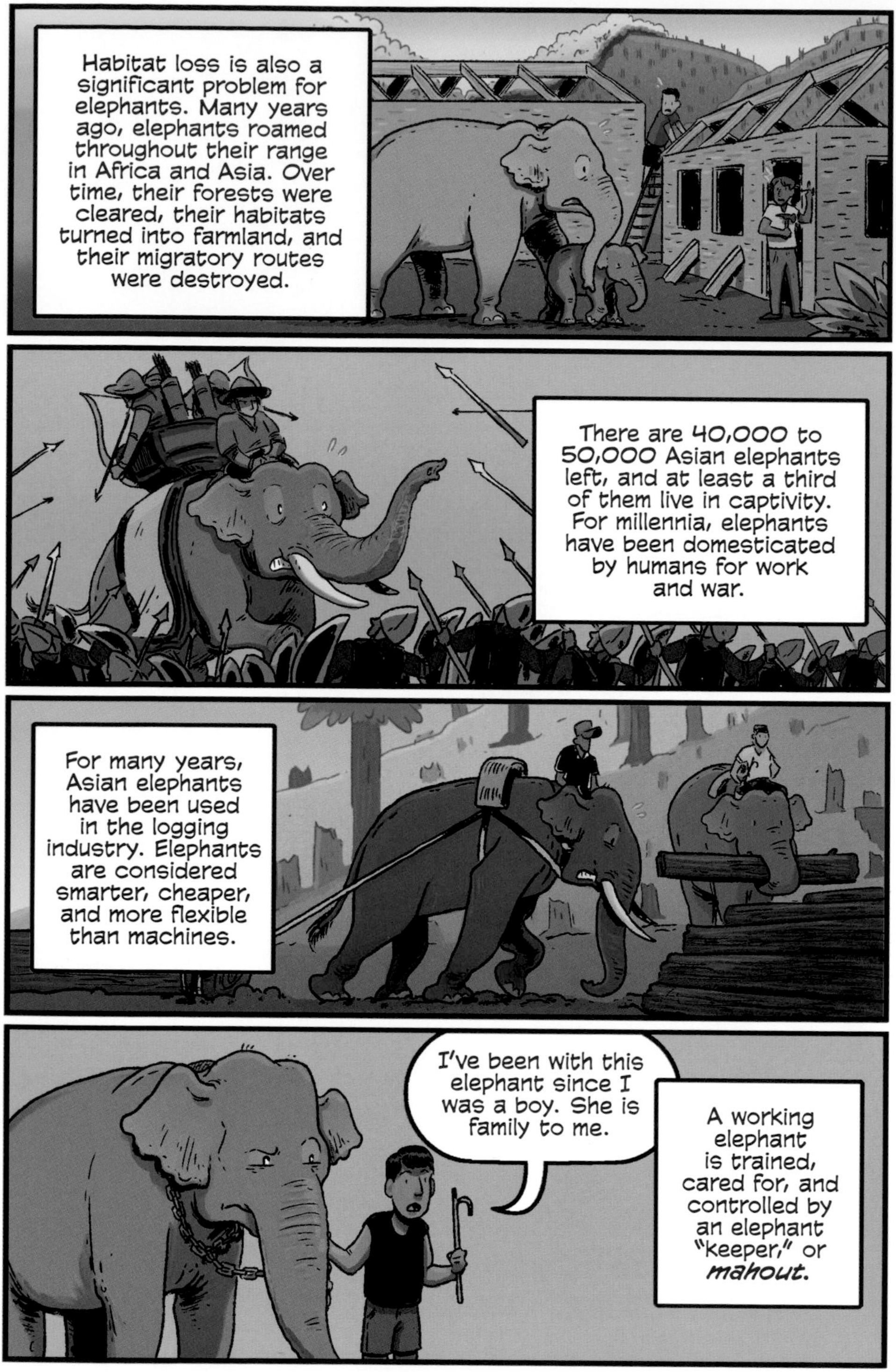
Habitat loss is also a significant problem for elephants. Many years ago, elephants roamed throughout their range in Africa and Asia. Over time, their forests were cleared, their habitats turned into farmland, and their migratory routes were destroyed.
There are 40,000 to 50,000 Asian elephants left, and at least a third of them live in captivity. For millennia, elephants have been domesticated by humans for work and war.
For many years, Asian elephants have been used in the logging industry. Elephants are considered smarter, cheaper, and more flexible than machines.
I've been with this elephant since I was a boy. She is family to me.
A working elephant is trained, cared for, and controlled by an elephant "keeper," or *mahout*.

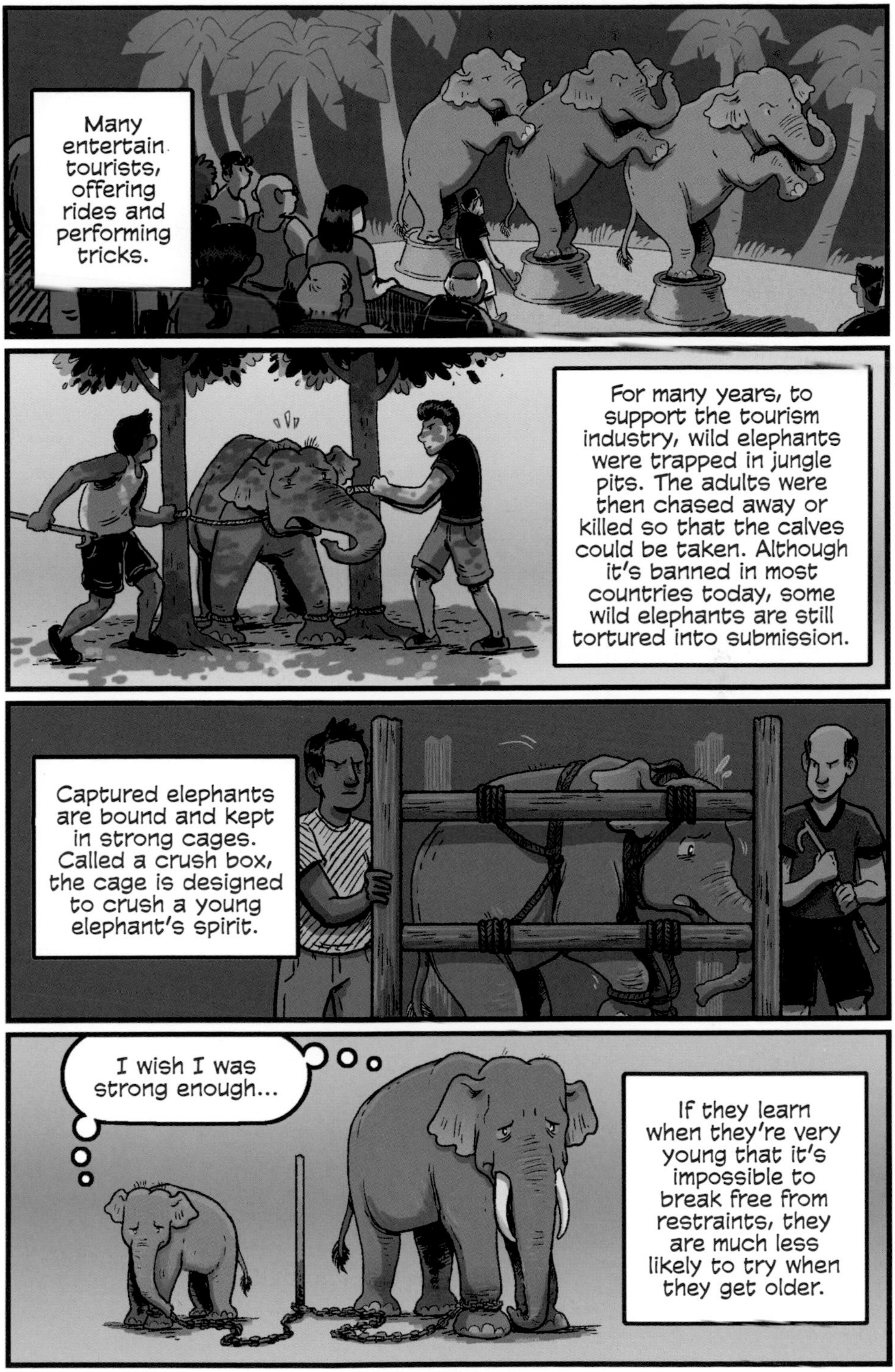
Many entertain tourists, offering rides and performing tricks.
For many years, to support the tourism industry, wild elephants were trapped in jungle pits. The adults were then chased away or killed so that the calves could be taken. Although it's banned in most countries today, some wild elephants are still tortured into submission.
Captured elephants are bound and kept in strong cages. Called a crush box, the cage is designed to crush a young elephant's spirit.
I wish I was strong enough...
If they learn when they're very young that it's impossible to break free from restraints, they are much less likely to try when they get older.

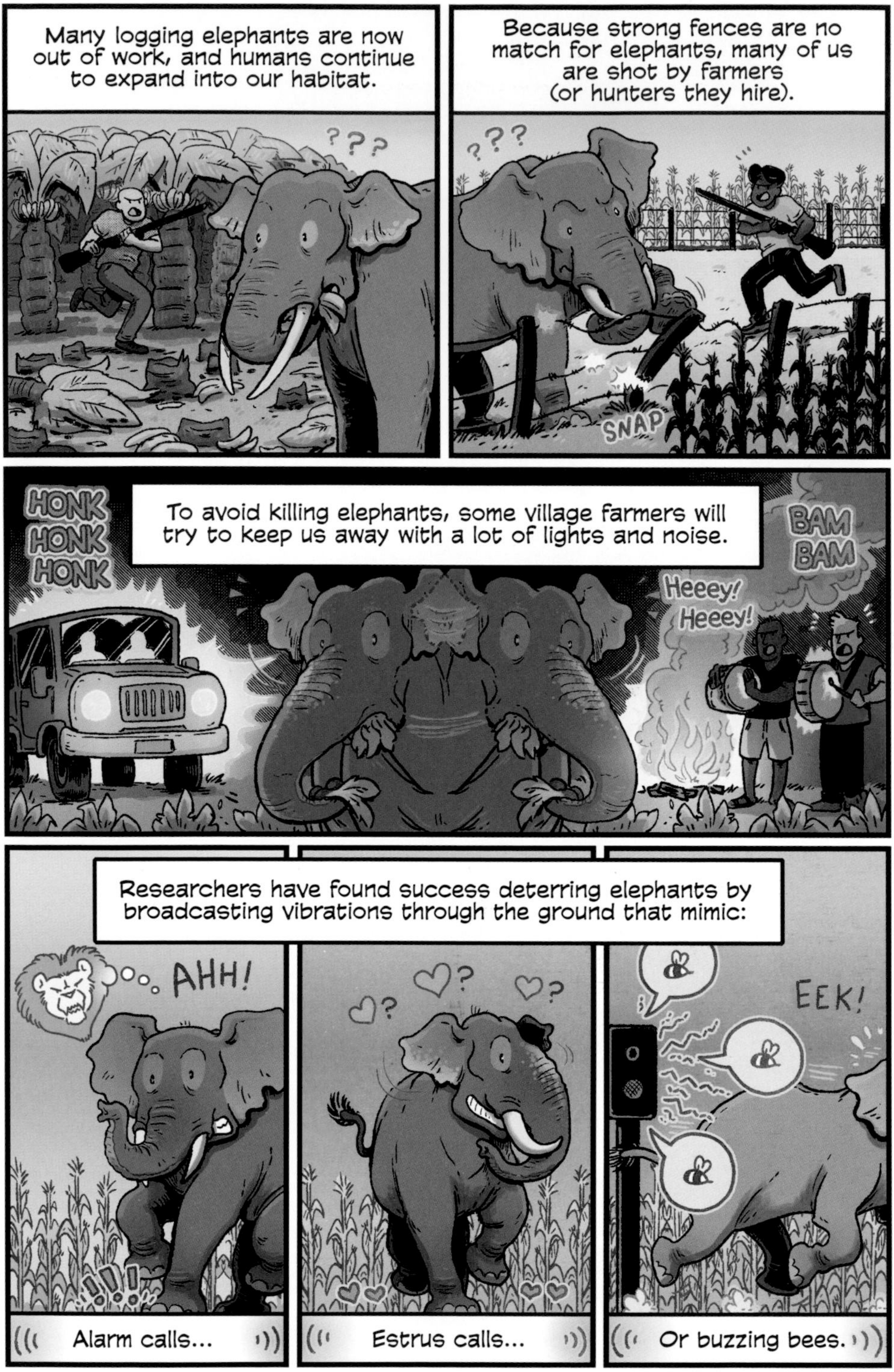
Many logging elephants are now out of work, and humans continue to expand into our habitat.
???
Because strong fences are no match for elephants, many of us are shot by farmers (or hunters they hire).
???
SNAP
To avoid killing elephants, some village farmers will try to keep us away with a lot of lights and noise.
HONK HONK HONK
BAM BAM
Heeey! Heeey!
Researchers have found success deterring elephants by broadcasting vibrations through the ground that mimic:
AHH!
Alarm calls...
Estrus calls...
EEK!
Or buzzing bees.

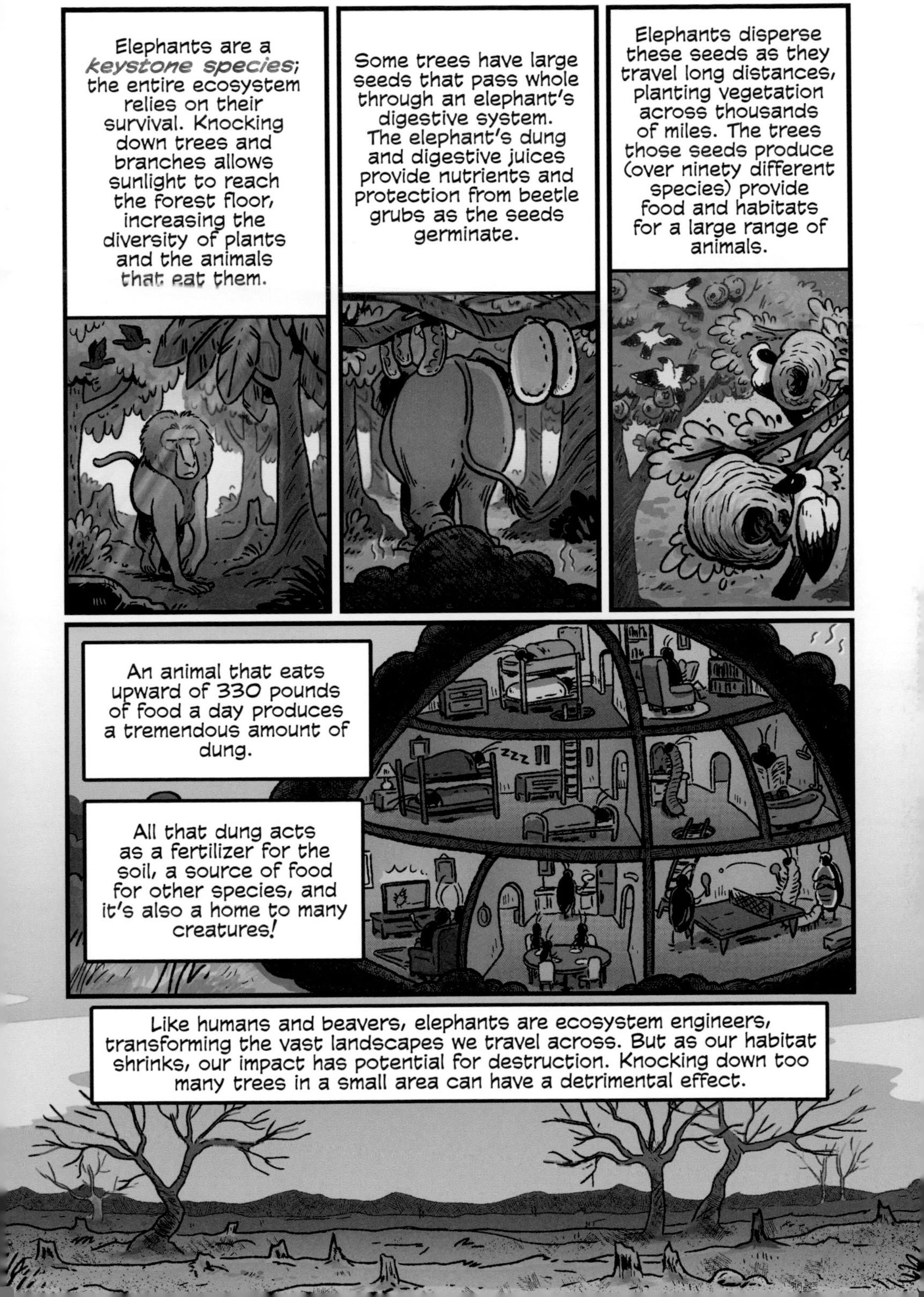
Elephants are a *keystone species*; the entire ecosystem relies on their survival. Knocking down trees and branches allows sunlight to reach the forest floor, increasing the diversity of plants and the animals that eat them.
Some trees have large seeds that pass whole through an elephant's digestive system. The elephant's dung and digestive juices provide nutrients and protection from beetle grubs as the seeds germinate.
Elephants disperse these seeds as they travel long distances, planting vegetation across thousands of miles. The trees those seeds produce (over ninety different species) provide food and habitats for a large range of animals.
An animal that eats upward of 330 pounds of food a day produces a tremendous amount of dung.
All that dung acts as a fertilizer for the soil, a source of food for other species, and it's also a home to many creatures!
ZZZ
Like humans and beavers, elephants are ecosystem engineers, transforming the vast landscapes we travel across. But as our habitat shrinks, our impact has potential for destruction. Knocking down too many trees in a small area can have a detrimental effect.

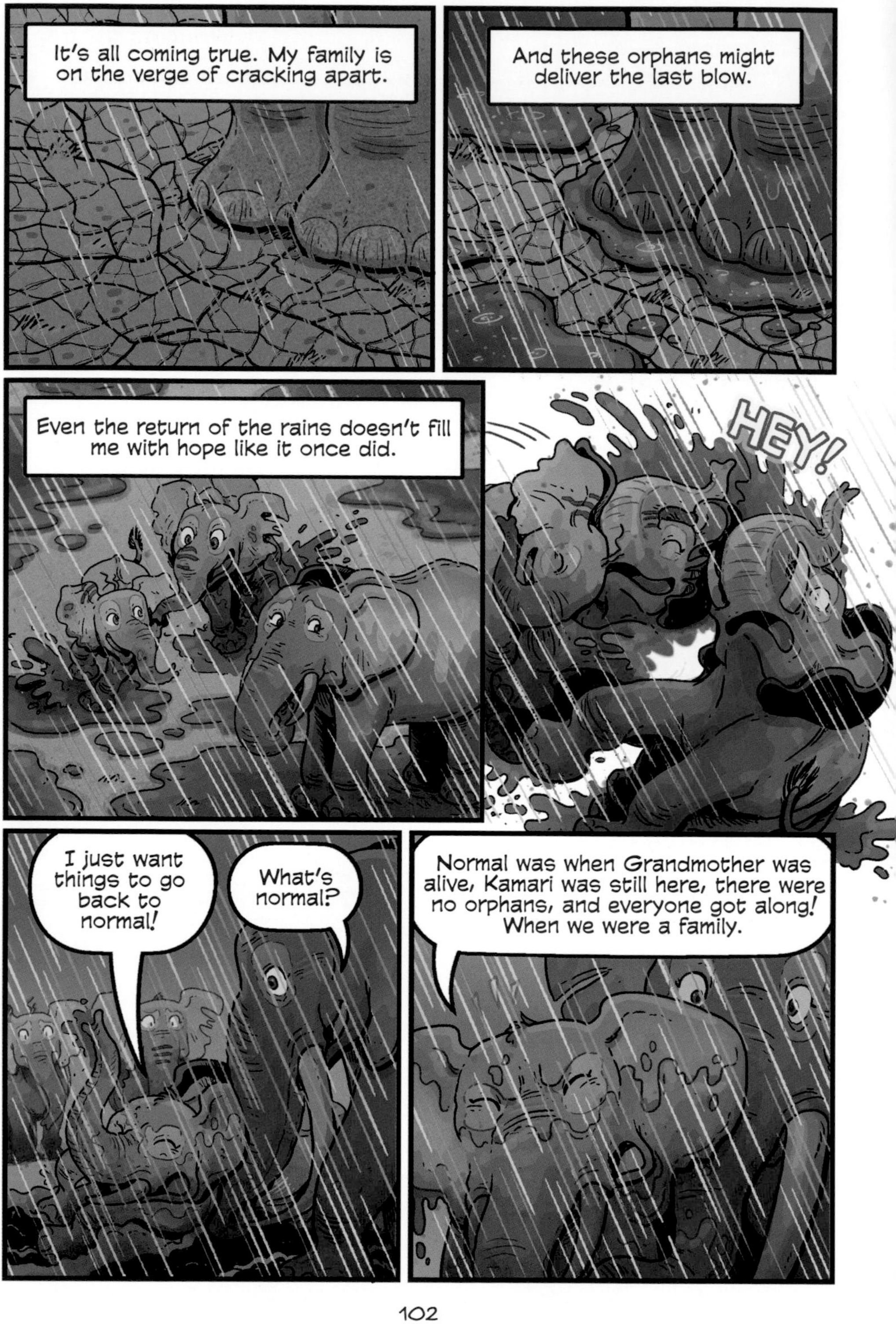
It's all coming true. My family is on the verge of cracking apart.
And these orphans might deliver the last blow.
Even the return of the rains doesn't fill me with hope like it once did.
HEY!
I just want things to go back to normal!
What's normal?
Normal was when Grandmother was alive, Kamari was still here, there were no orphans, and everyone got along! When we were a family.

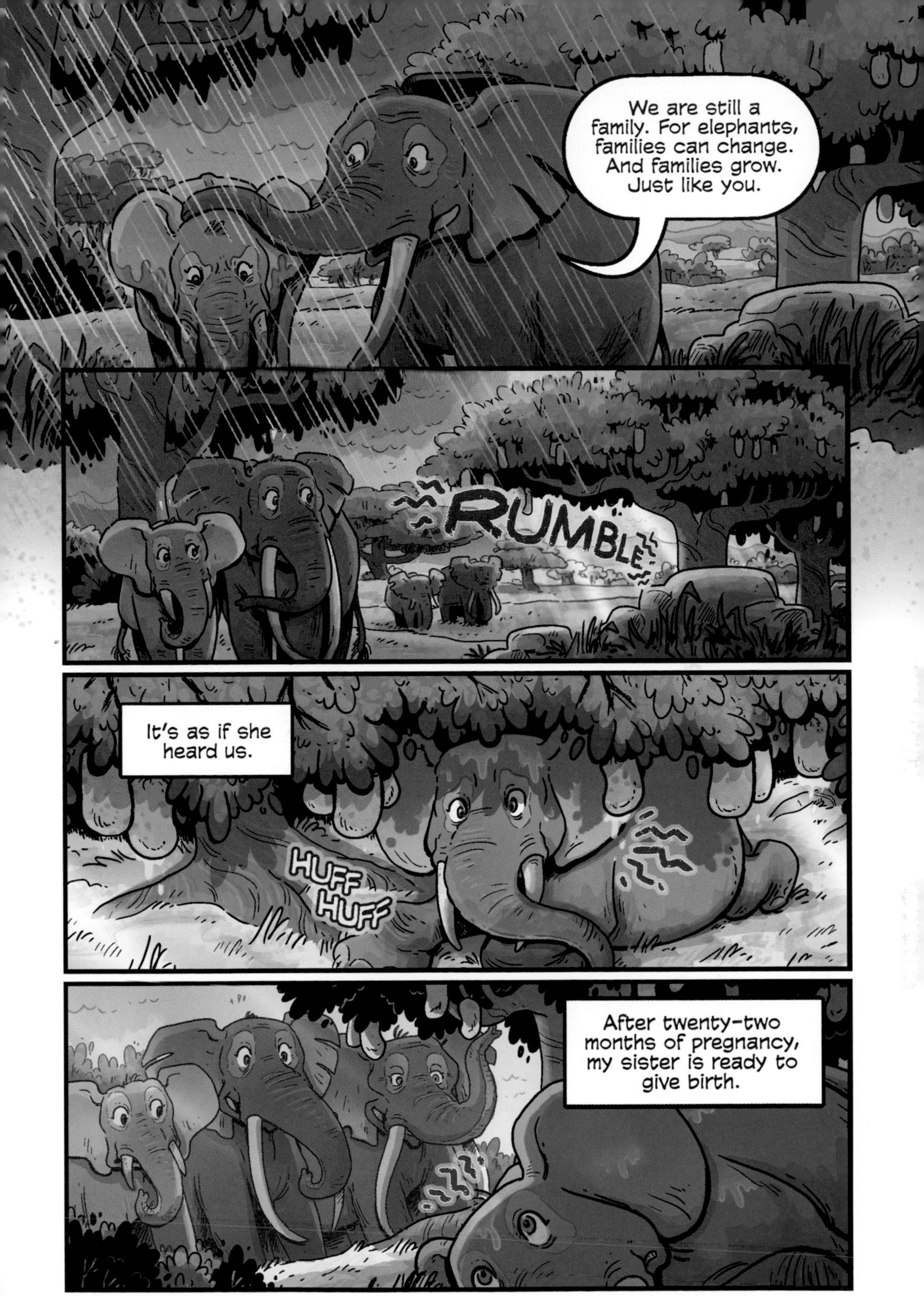
We are still a family. For elephants, families can change. And families grow. Just like you.
RUMBLE
It's as if she heard us.
HUFF HUFF
After twenty-two months of pregnancy, my sister is ready to give birth.

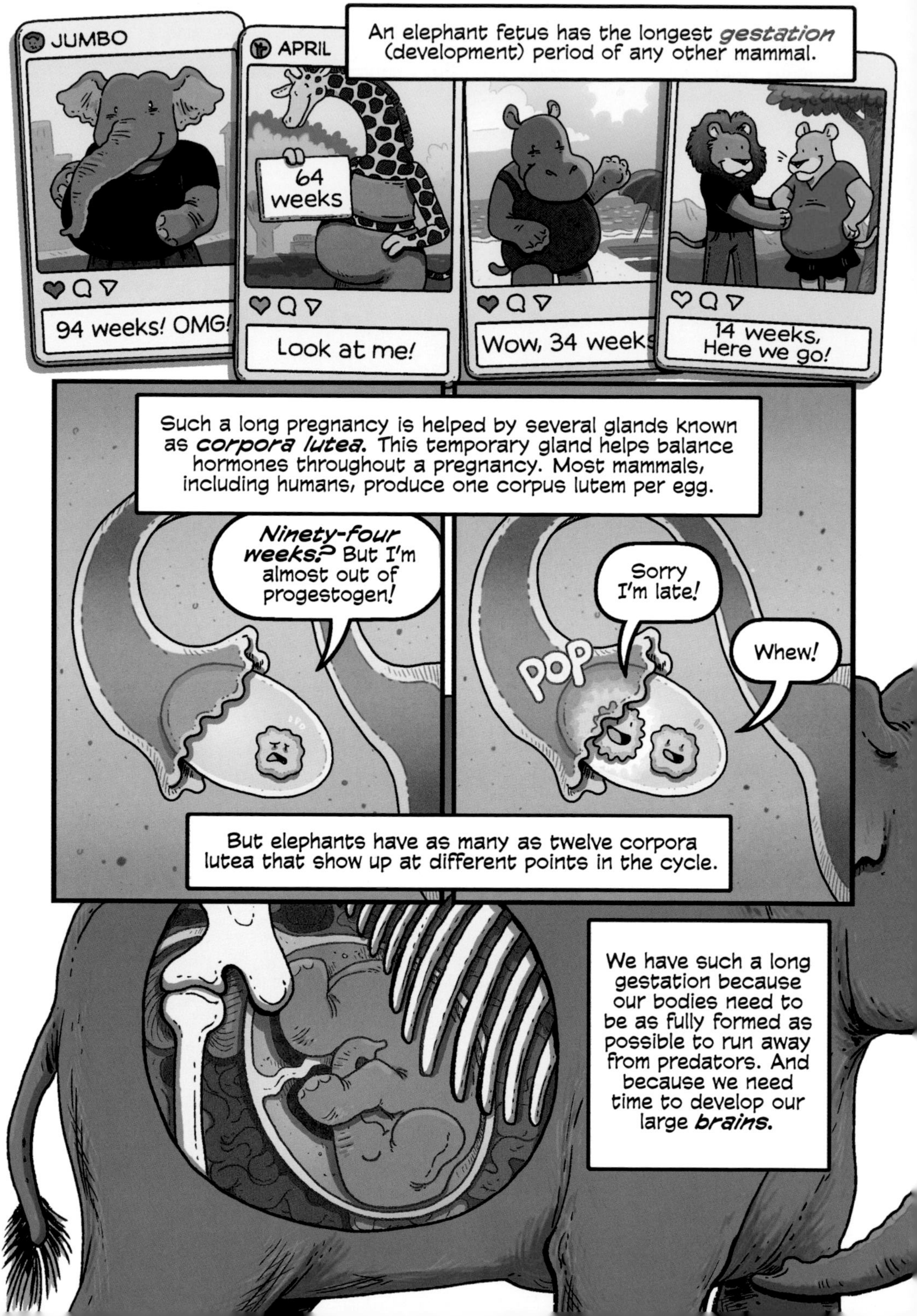
An elephant fetus has the longest *gestation* (development) period of any other mammal.
JUMBO
94 weeks! OMG!
APRIL
64 weeks
Look at me!
Wow, 34 weeks
14 weeks, Here we go!
Such a long pregnancy is helped by several glands known as *corpora lutea.* This temporary gland helps balance hormones throughout a pregnancy. Most mammals, including humans, produce one corpus lutem per egg.
Ninety-four weeks? But I'm almost out of progestogen!
POP
Sorry I'm late!
Whew!
But elephants have as many as twelve corpora lutea that show up at different points in the cycle.
We have such a long gestation because our bodies need to be as fully formed as possible to run away from predators. And because we need time to develop our large *brains.*

Animals that rely on complex communication need large brains. And just like humans, whales, dolphins, and apes, elephants have special brain cells that amplify messages.

ORDINARY NEURON
(Nerve Cell)

SPINDLE NEURON

A big brain means a long way for messages to travel. But high intelligence requires speedy delivery.

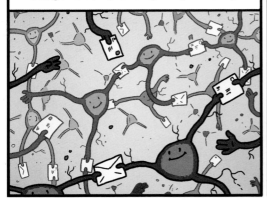

While most neurons have many extensions that send and receive signals, a spindle neuron has only one at each end. Its job is to pass a message along quickly.

Communication and memory are both critical to our survival. Elephants have strong long-term memories, which the matriarchs rely on to identify threats and recall solutions.

Ahh, that reminds me of the drought of '58...

BEEP BOOP

Our working memory is just as powerful, allowing us to track the locations of up to thirty others at a time.

Lucas and Lucia are at the Trunk N' Dunk. Camila's in the bathroom.

Six Trunks

Elena ran off with Tyler and Skyler to...

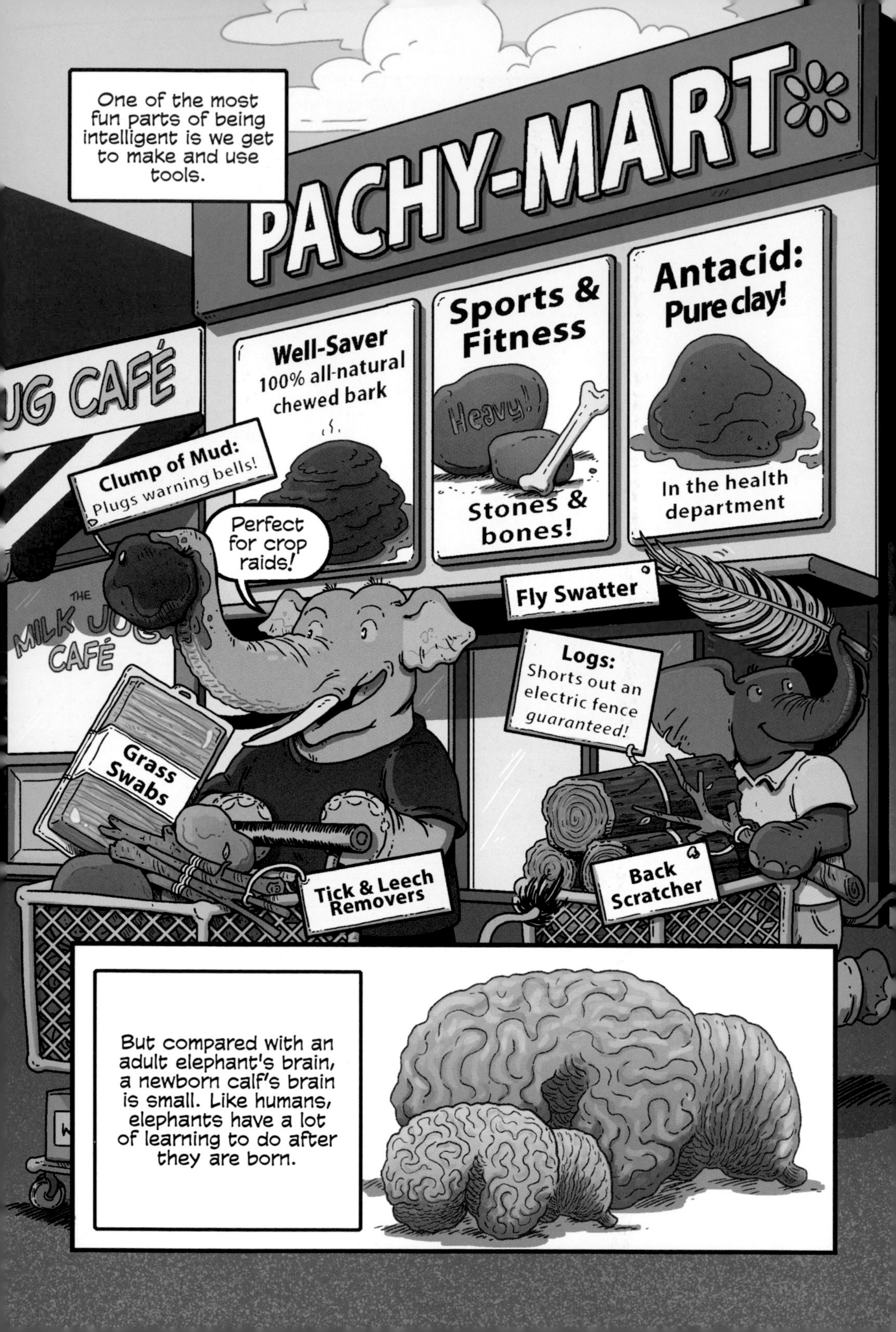

One of the most fun parts of being intelligent is we get to make and use tools.
PACHY-MART
Well-Saver 100% all-natural chewed bark
Sports & Fitness
Heavy!
Stones & bones!
Antacid: Pure clay!
In the health department
Clump of Mud: Plugs warning bells!
Perfect for crop raids!
Fly Swatter
Logs: Shorts out an electric fence guaranteed!
Grass Swabs
Tick & Leech Removers
Back Scratcher
But compared with an adult elephant's brain, a newborn calf's brain is small. Like humans, elephants have a lot of learning to do after they are born.

AROOOOO! WEEEEUUUU!

RUMBLE RUMBLE

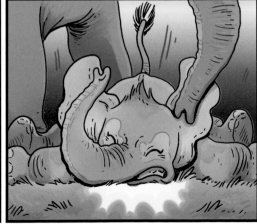

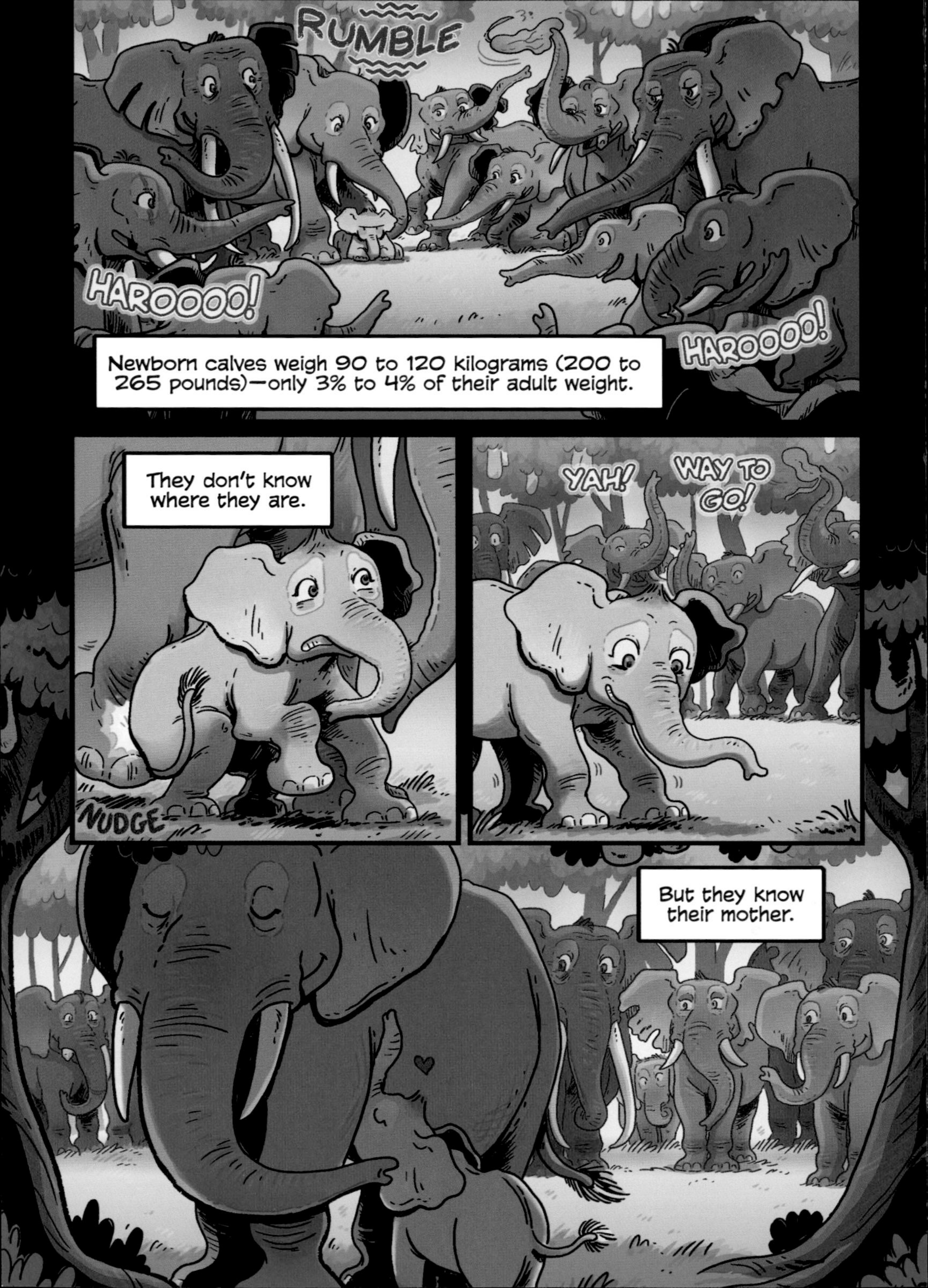
RUMBLE
HAROOOO!
HAROOOO!
Newborn calves weigh 90 to 120 kilograms (200 to 265 pounds)—only 3% to 4% of their adult weight.
They don't know where they are.
NUDGE
YAH!
WAY TO GO!
But they know their mother.

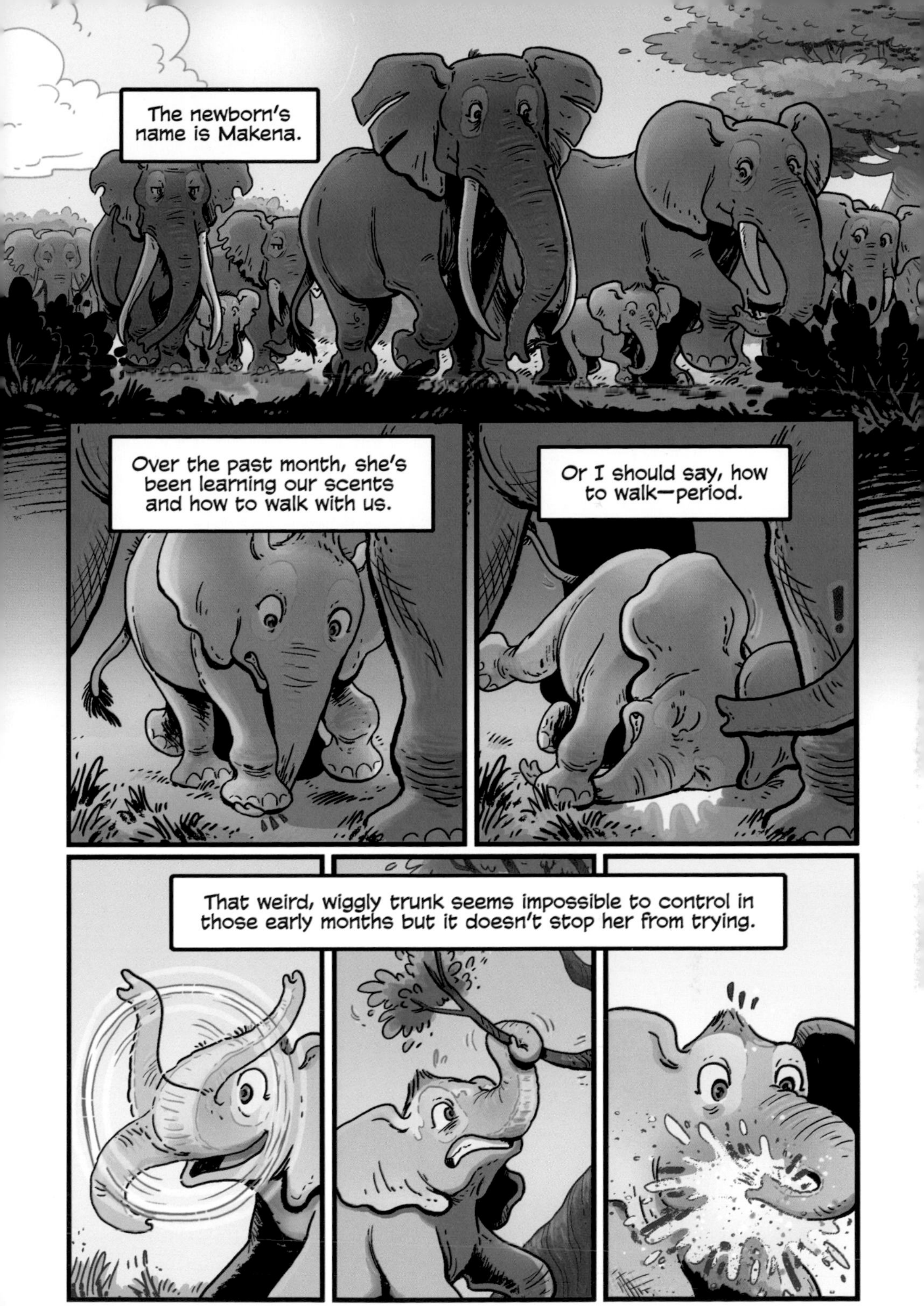
The newborn's name is Makena.
Over the past month, she's been learning our scents and how to walk with us.
Or I should say, how to walk—period.
!
That weird, wiggly trunk seems impossible to control in those early months but it doesn't stop her from trying.

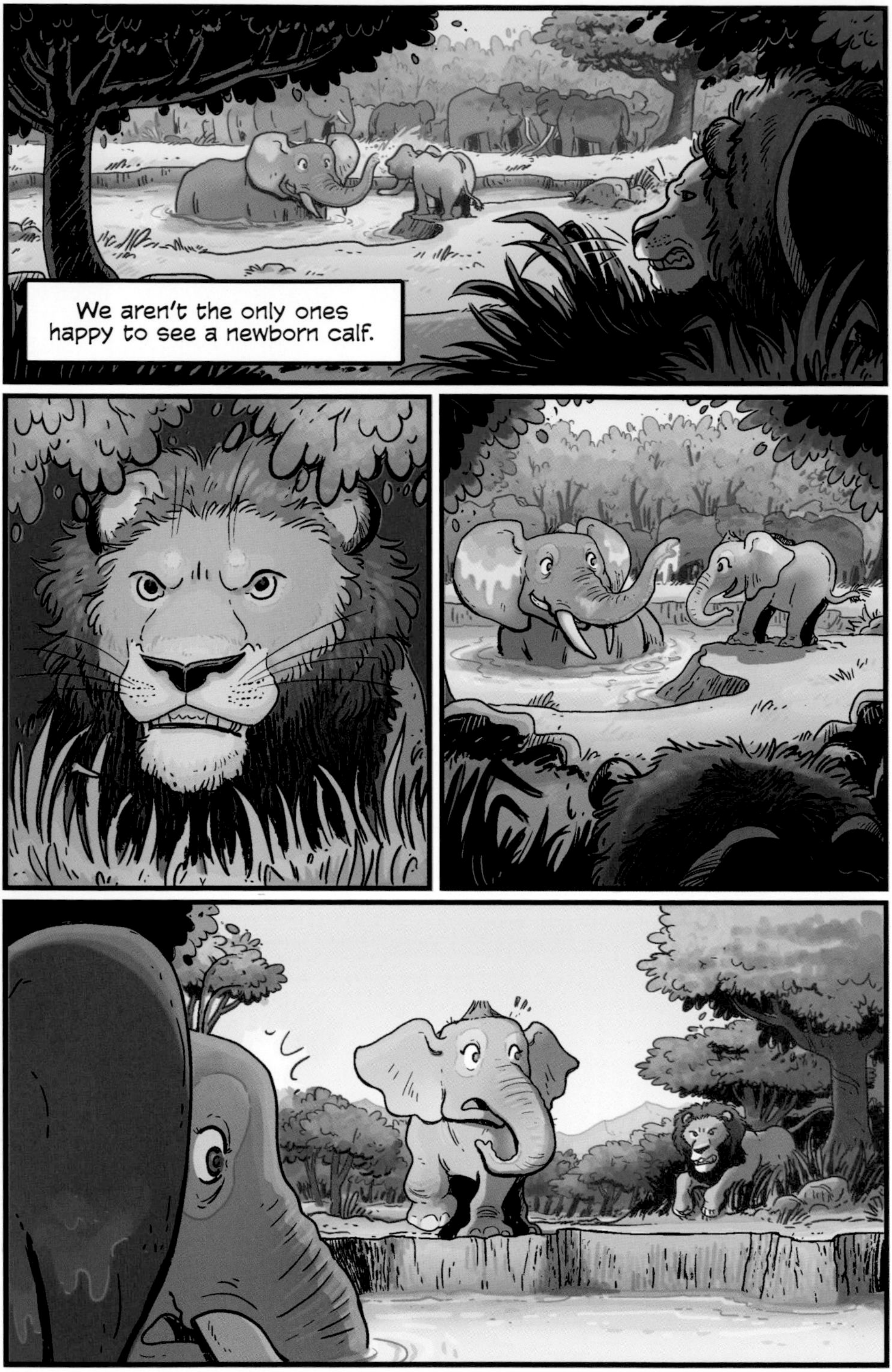
We aren't the only ones happy to see a newborn calf.

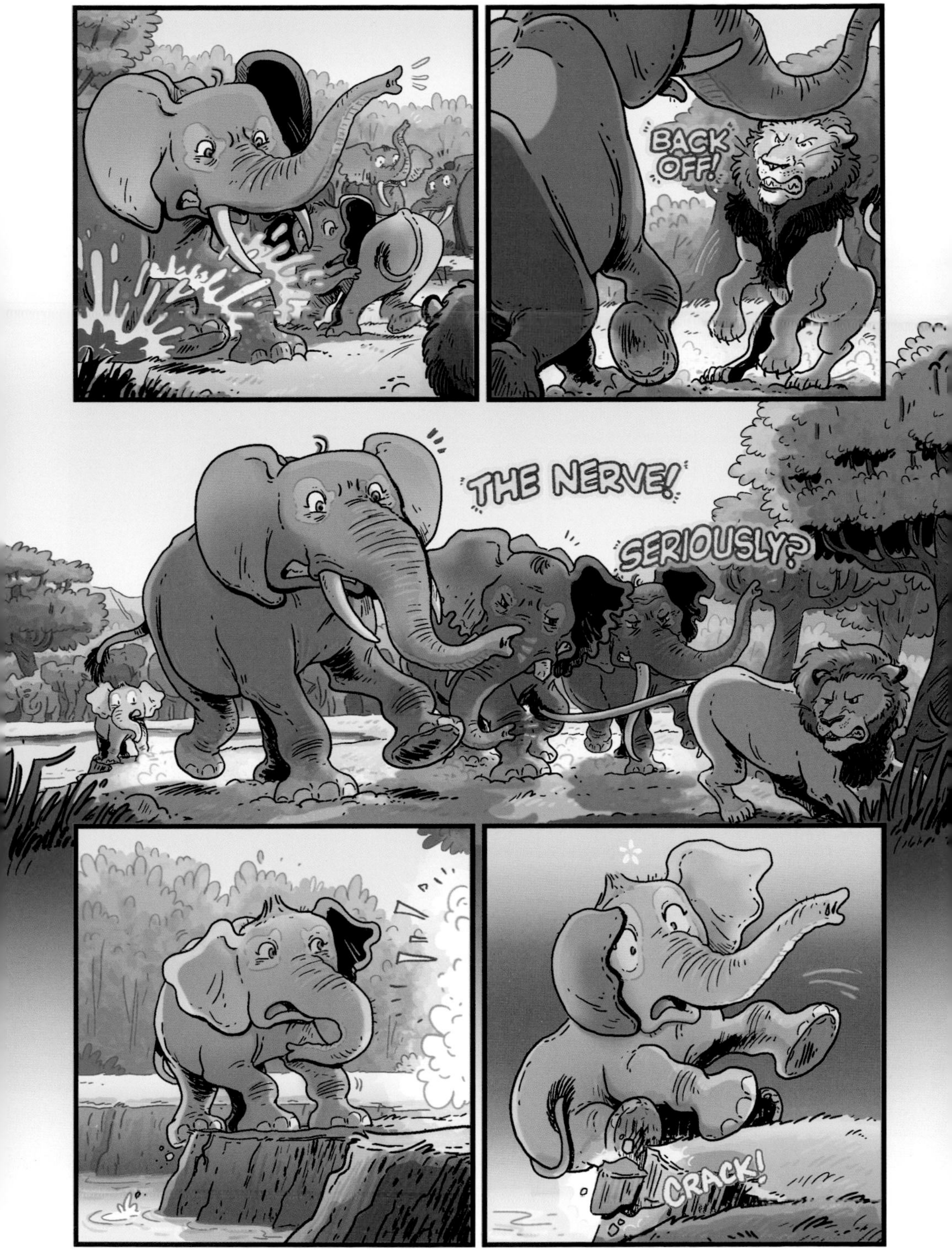
BACK OFF!
THE NERVE!
SERIOUSLY?
CRACK!

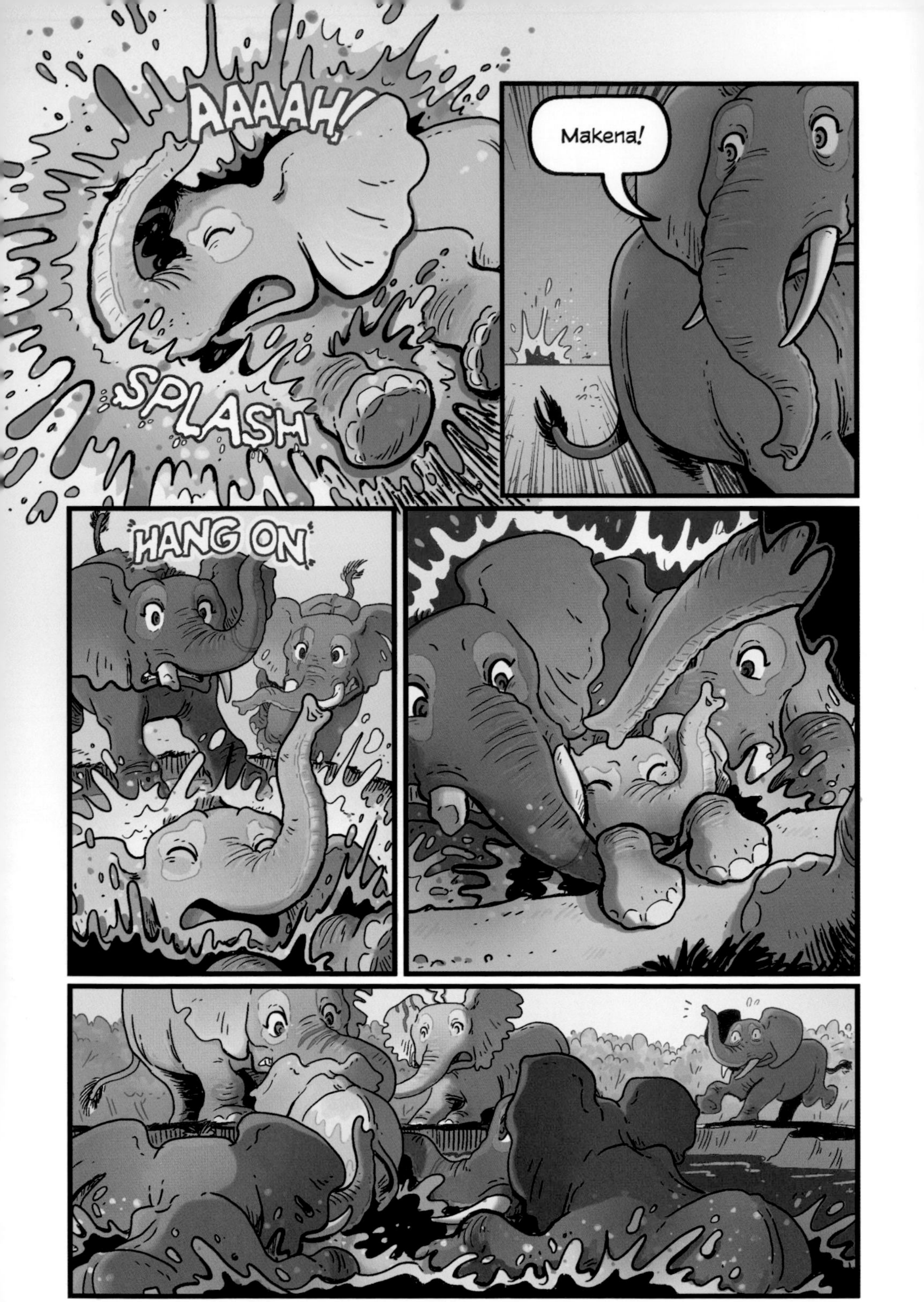
AAAAH!
SPLASH
Makena!
HANG ON

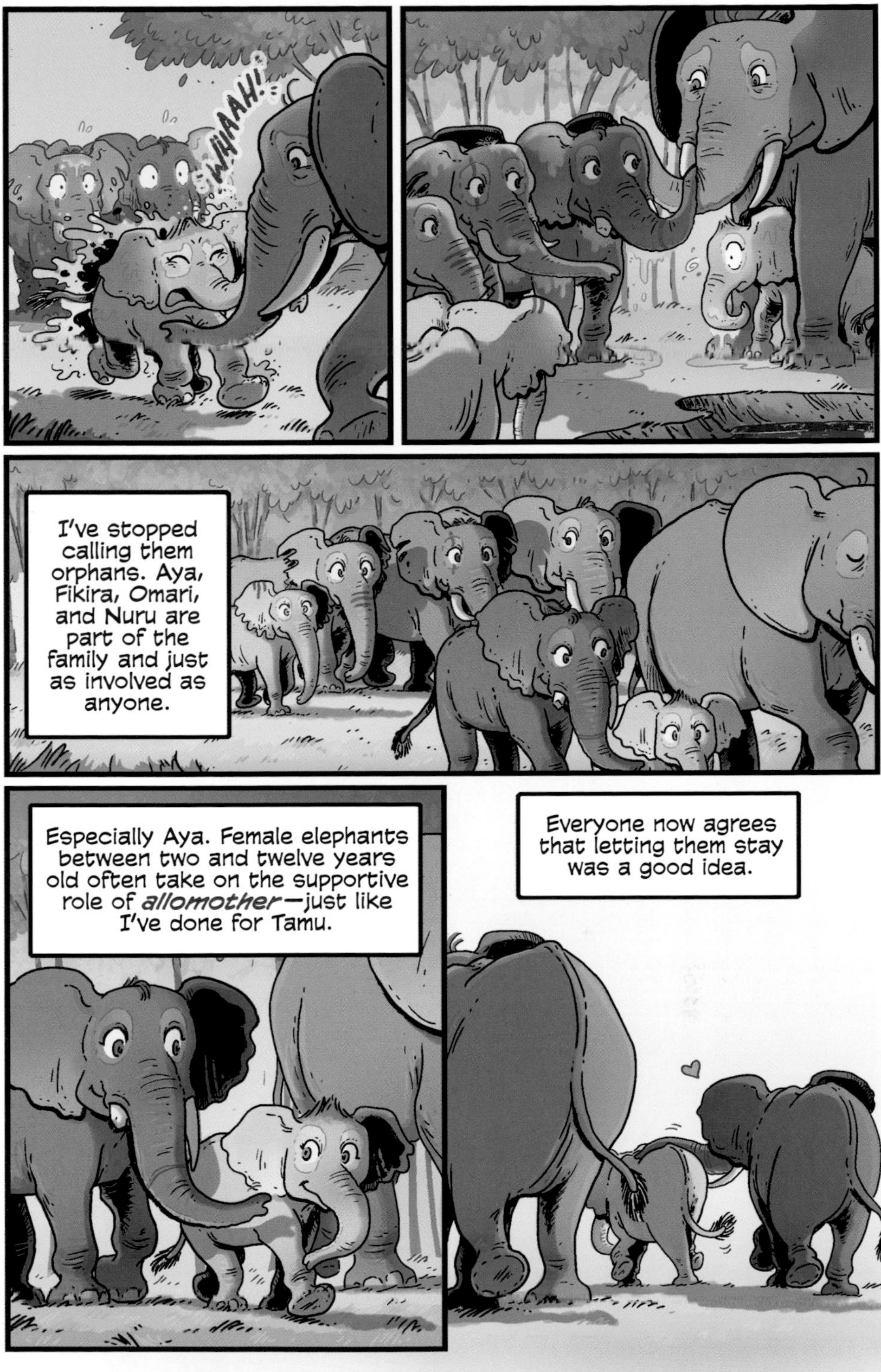
WHAAAH!
I've stopped calling them orphans. Aya, Fikira, Omari, and Nuru are part of the family and just as involved as anyone.
Especially Aya. Female elephants between two and twelve years old often take on the supportive role of *allomother*—just like I've done for Tamu.
Everyone now agrees that letting them stay was a good idea.

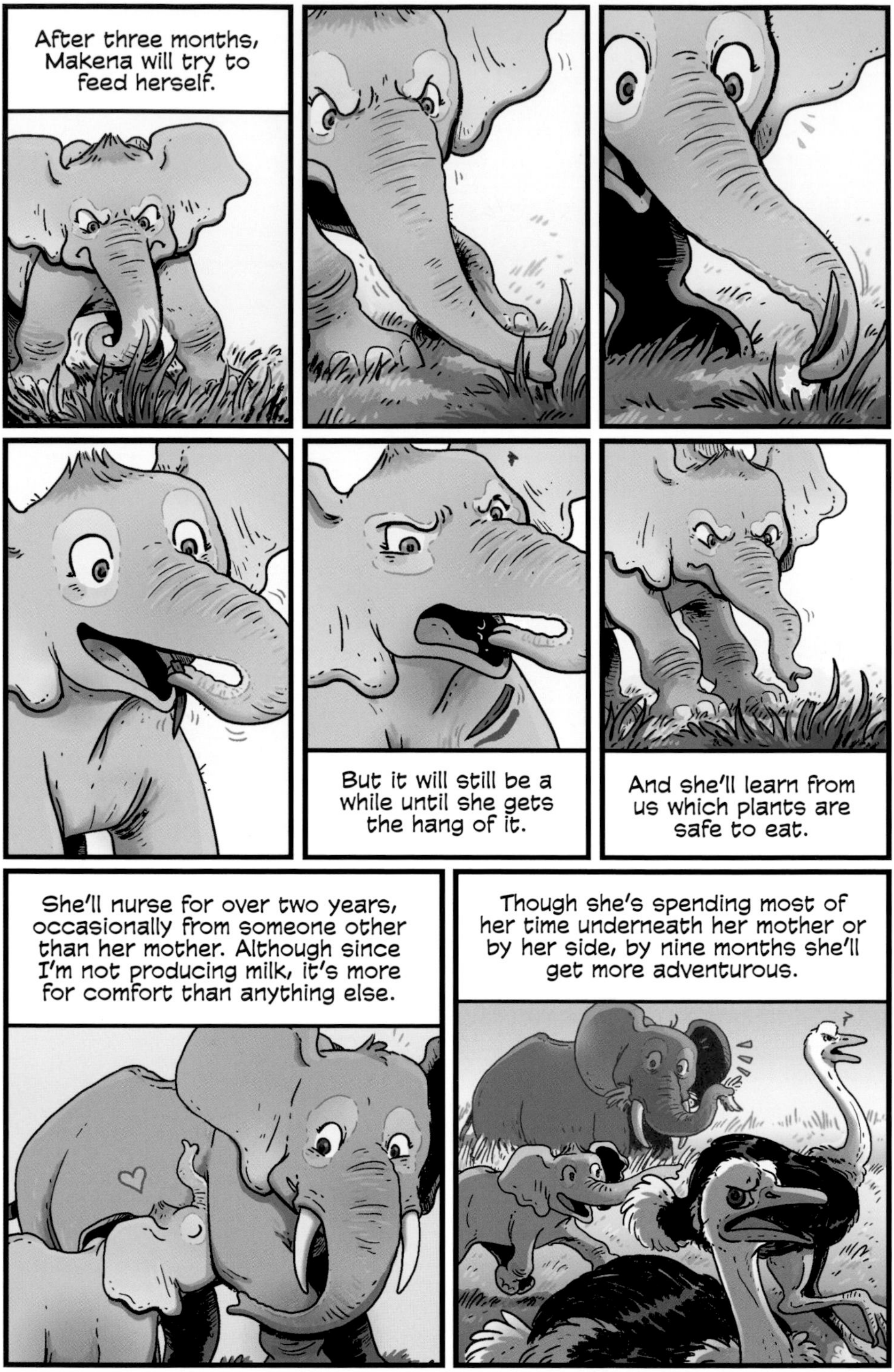
After three months, Makena will try to feed herself.
But it will still be a while until she gets the hang of it.
And she'll learn from us which plants are safe to eat.
She'll nurse for over two years, occasionally from someone other than her mother. Although since I'm not producing milk, it's more for comfort than anything else.
Though she's spending most of her time underneath her mother or by her side, by nine months she'll get more adventurous.

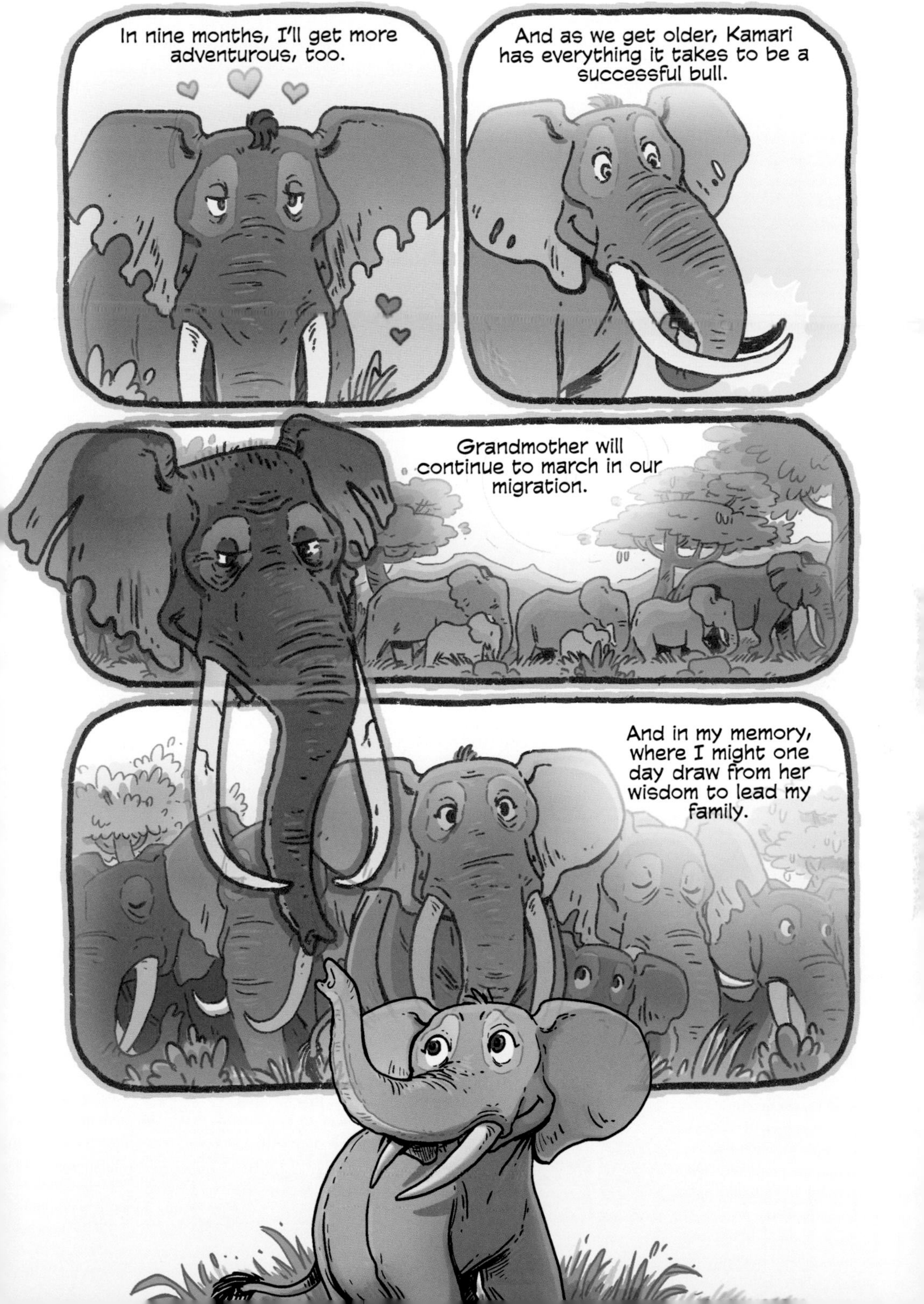
In nine months, I'll get more adventurous, too.
And as we get older, Kamari has everything it takes to be a successful bull.
Grandmother will continue to march in our migration.
And in my memory, where I might one day draw from her wisdom to lead my family.

Like our home range, an elephant family follows a cycle...

...while also changing, growing, and moving.

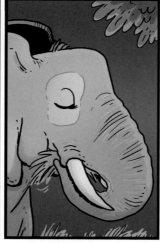

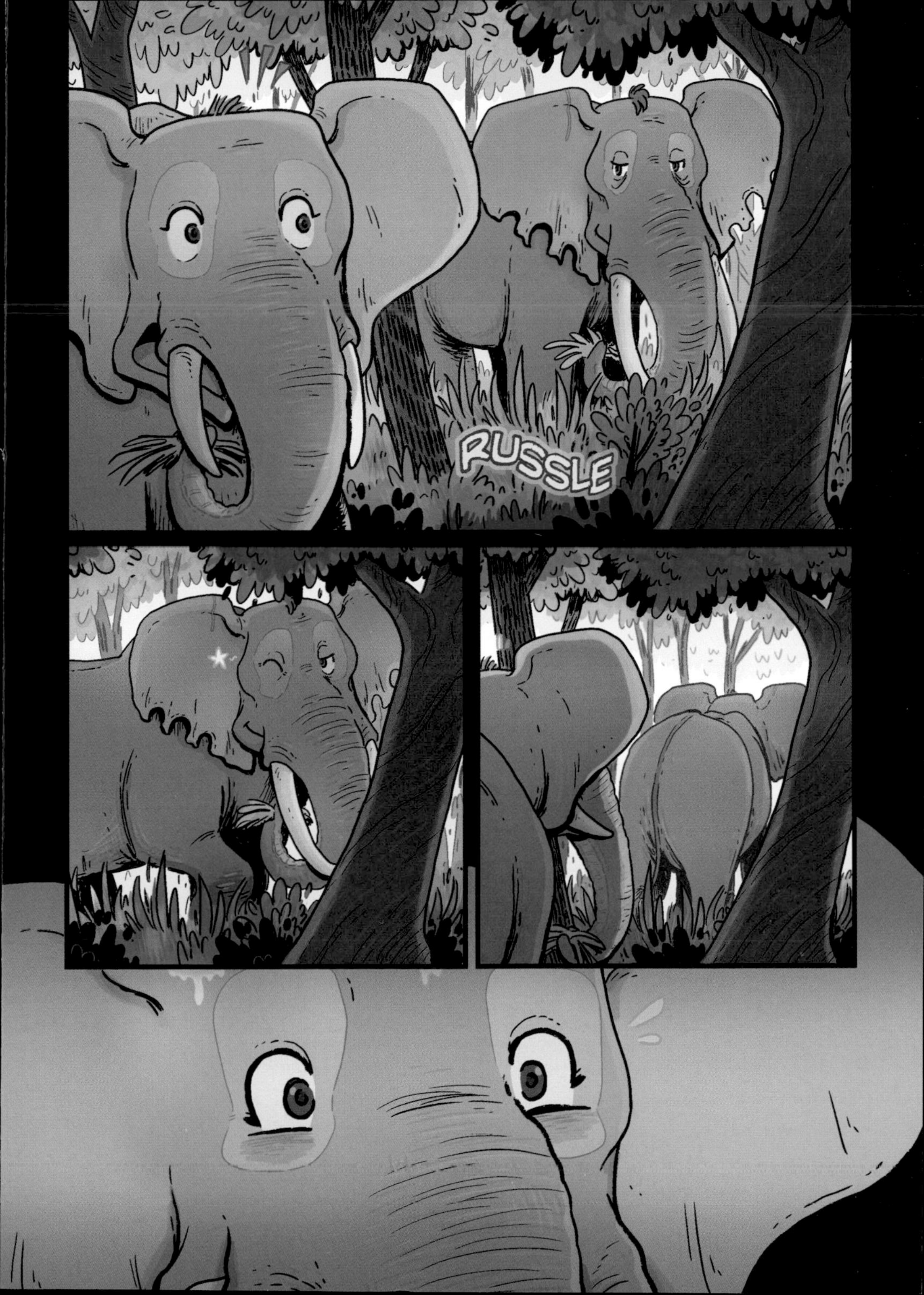
RUSSLE

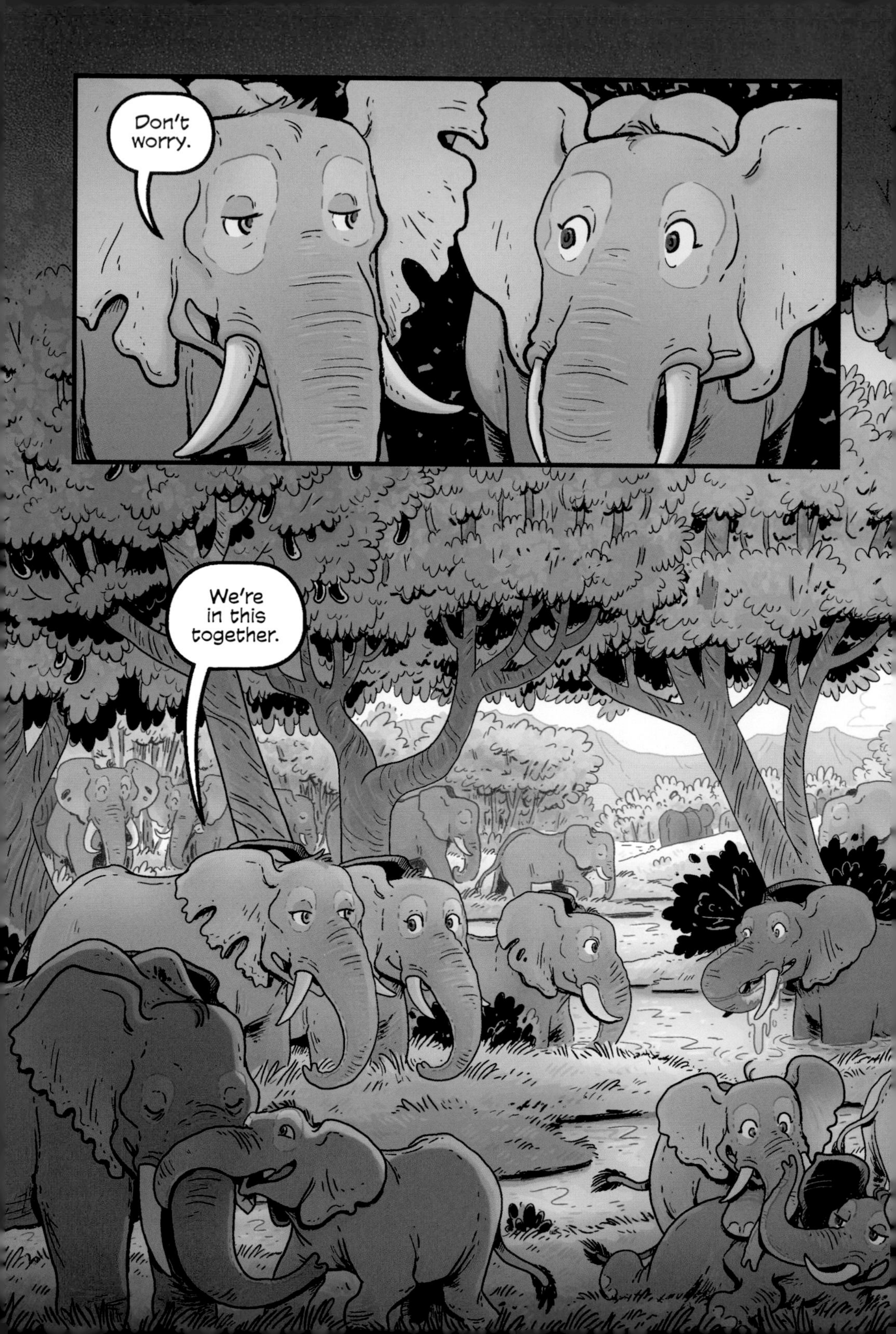
Don't worry.
We're in this together.

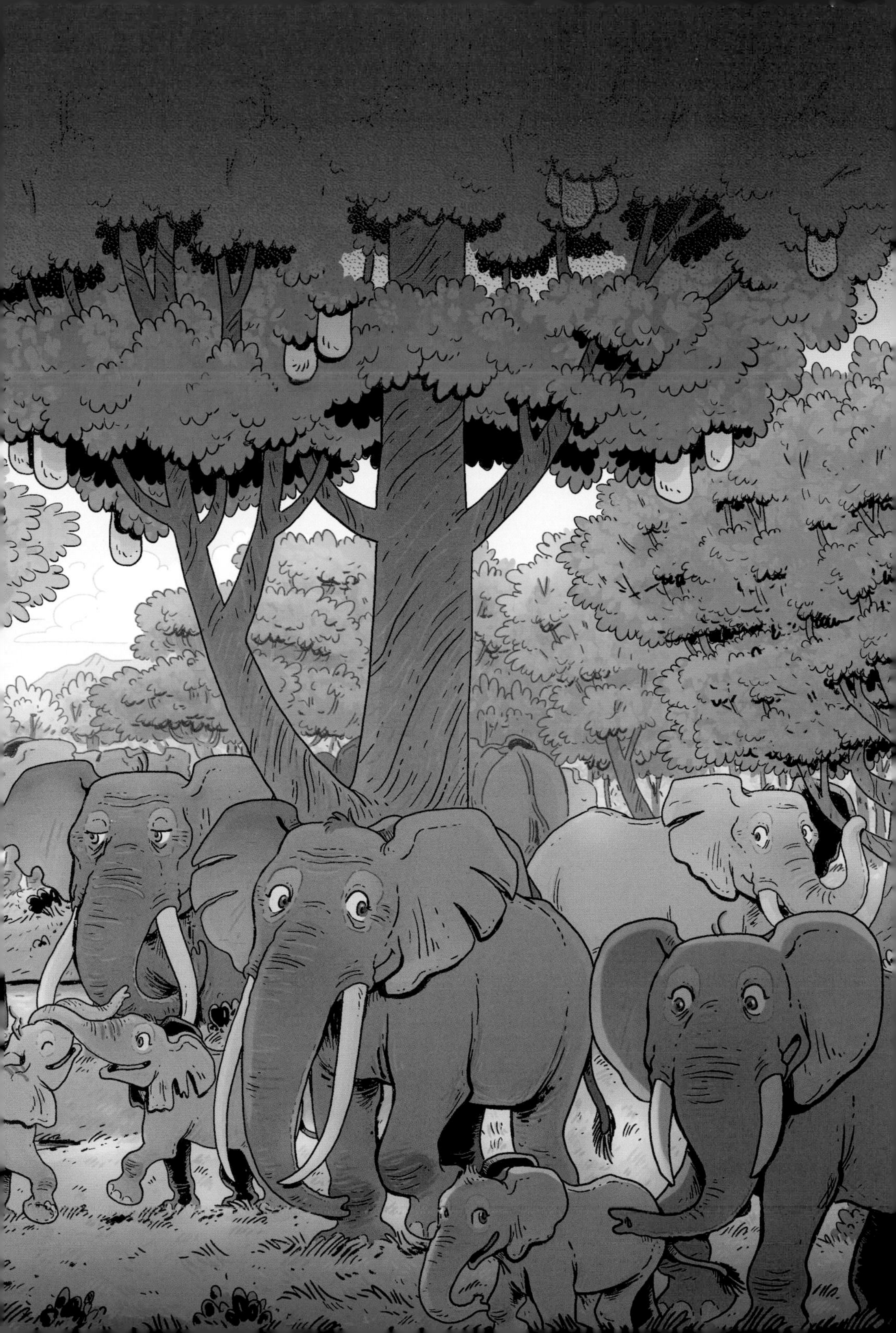

—GLOSSARY—

Allomother
A female who assists in caring for another's offspring. In elephants, allomothers (or "aunties") are usually between two and twelve years old.

Audio frequency
The number of cycles a sound vibration completes in one second. Also known as pitch.

Bond group
A cooperative social group of two to five extended elephant families.

Clan
Highest level of elephant society consisting of families who share the same land area.

Dentin
Sensitive tissue that forms teeth and tusks.

Estrus
The recurring period of time for a female mammal when her body is most receptive to reproduction.

Fission–fusion society
Social structure characterized by regular changes in the size and makeup of the group as animals come together and split apart.

Gestation
In mammals (and some non-mammals), the period of time between conception and birth.

Herbivore
An animal that eats mainly plants.

Home range
A large area where an animal ranges. For some animals, like elephants, boundaries shift depending upon food availability and other conditions.

Keystone species
A species on which the survival of many other species in an ecosystem depends.

Matriarch
The female leader of a family.

Musth
A period of heightened aggression that an adult male elephant experiences when he is ready to mate.

Poaching
Illegally hunting or capturing a wild animal.

Prehensile
Able to grasp and hold, like with a hand or trunk.

Seismic communication
Transmitting and responding to messages sent as vibrations through a substance like earth.

Temporin
Strong-smelling substance secreted from the temporal gland beneath the skin. Elephants secrete temporin in periods of excitement and particularly during musth.

Vibrissae
Stiff hairs on a mammal's face (such as whiskers), inside the nostrils, or surrounding the tip of a trunk, which are used as sense organs.

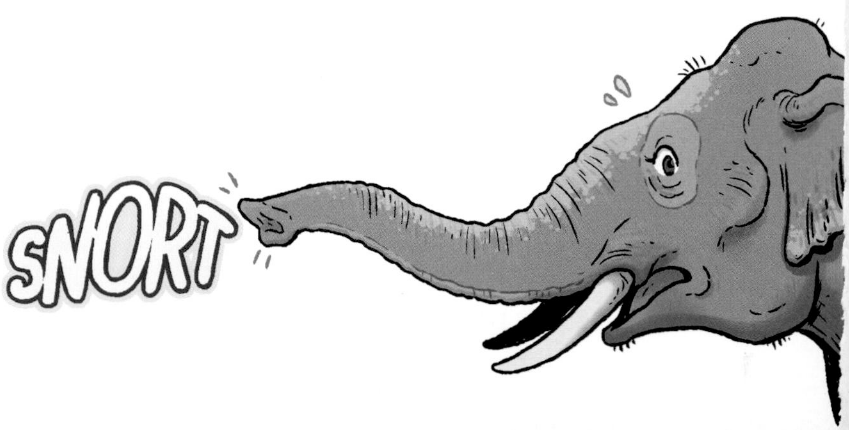
SNORT